More praise for *Italian Ways*

"Relaxed, humorous, meandering [and] charming." —Brigitte Frase,
Minneapolis Star Tribune

"Revealing. . . . With his novelist's gift he sets out life on the long train
ride from Verona to Palermo." —Richard Eder, *Boston Globe*

"Parks [treats] his subject with the sort of bemused affection that
allows for warmth and yet keeps sentimentality at arm's length. . . . He
gives us a country that is as frustrating as it is endlessly fascinating."
—Marjorie Kehe, *Christian Science Monitor*

"The stories [Parks tells] yield considerable satisfaction and riches,
wonderful scenes and quotes, and shrewd larger insights extrapolated
from seemingly small moments." —Alexander Stille,
New York Review of Books

"[Parks is] a perfect guide—an outsider, but one with a deep famil-
iarity and respect (plus a dash of exasperated skepticism)—to the
country's celebrated eccentricities. Parks has a charming voice and a
novelist's eye." —Chloë Schama, *Smithsonian*

"It is Parks's mixture of love and irritation, summary judgment and
self-deprecation, acute observation and strong point of view, that
makes this the wonderful book that it is." —Katherine A. Powers,
Barnes & Noble Review

"Fascinating [and] droll. . . . Parks [is] perhaps the most faithful foreign inamorato Italy has ever had." —Andrea Lee, newyorker.com

"Unmistakably an expression of love for his adopted country and its people. . . . Lovely and clever."   —Mark O'Connell, The Millions

"Incisive [and] hilarious."   —Alexander Aciman, *Daily Beast*

"This is not a 'railway book' in any conventional sense. It is sharp-eyed and sharp-tongued about the absurdities of 'Italian ways.' "
—John Lloyd, *Financial Times*

"Delightful [and] hilarious. . . . Combining wonderfully evocative prose with a wry analysis, Parks provides local color while continually seeking hidden social meaning. . . . The result is a fascinating portrait of a society that seems rooted in place no matter how fast it goes."
—*Publishers Weekly*, starred review

"Funny. . . . Enchanting travels with the good-natured Parks."
—*Kirkus Reviews*

"A search for the Italian character, which [Parks] evokes in dozens of gorgeously written scenes. . . . *Bravo*."   —David Shields,
author of *How Literature Saved My Life*

"Tim Parks has reinvented the narrative of the train journey with an epic voyage into the essence of Italy itself. With a novelist's keen eye he mines absurdity and deep meaning from small, overlooked moments and gestures."   —Tom Vanderbilt, author of *Traffic*

"This is the best book I've ever read about Italy. Never have I encountered a more insightful and hilarious insider/outsider portrait of the country at the center of Western civilization."   —Sean Wilsey,
best-selling author of *Oh the Glory of It All*

ITALIAN WAYS

Also by TIM PARKS

FICTION

The Server
Dreams of Rivers and Seas
Cleaver
Rapids
Judge Savage
Destiny
Talking About It
Europa
Mimi's Ghost
Shear
Goodness
Cara Massimina
Family Planning
Home Thoughts
Loving Roger
Tongues of Flame

NONFICTION

Teach Us to Sit Still: A Skeptic's
Search for Health and Healing

The Fighter: Essays

Medici Money: Banking, Metaphysics
and Art in Fifteenth-Century Florence

A Season with Verona: Travels
Around Italy in Search of Illusion,
National Character and Goals

Hell and Back: Reflections on Writers
and Writing from Dante to Rushdie

Adultery and Other Diversions

Translating Style: English Modernists
and Their Italian Translations

An Italian Education: The Further
Adventures of an Expatriate in Verona

Italian Neighbors

ITALIAN WAYS

ON AND OFF THE RAILS FROM
MILAN TO PALERMO

TIM PARKS

W. W. NORTON & COMPANY

NEW YORK / LONDON

A portion of this book appeared in different form in *Granta*.
Maps by David Atkinson, Hand Made Maps Ltd.

For information about permission to reproduce selections from this book,
write to Permissions, W. W. Norton & Company, Inc.,
500 Fifth Avenue, New York, NY 10110

For information about special discounts for bulk purchases, please contact
W. W. Norton Special Sales at specialsales@wwnorton.com or 800-233-4830

Manufacturing by Courier Westford
Book design by Barbara Bachman
Production manager: Louise Mattarelliano

Library of Congress Cataloging-in-Publication Data

Parks, Tim.
Italian ways : on and off the rails from Milan to Palermo / Tim Parks. — First edition.
pages cm
ISBN 978-0-393-23932-4 (hardcover)
1. Railroad travel—Italy. 2. Italy—Description and travel. 3. Italy—Social life and customs. 4.
Parks, Tim—Travel—Italy. I. Title.
DG430.2.P37 2013
385'.220945—dc23
2013011386

ISBN 978-0-393-34882-8 pbk.

W. W. Norton & Company, Inc.
500 Fifth Avenue, New York, N.Y. 10110
www.wwnorton.com

W. W. Norton & Company Ltd.
Castle House, 75/76 Wells Street, London W1T 3QT

1 2 3 4 5 6 7 8 9 0

For all those who love to read on trains.

CONTENTS

PREFACE   XIII

PART ONE / THE TRAIN OF THE LIVING DEAD

CHAPTER 1   **Verona–Milano**   *3*
CHAPTER 2   **Milano–Verona**   *42*

PART TWO / FIRST CLASS, HIGH SPEED

CHAPTER 3   **Verona–Milano**   *81*
CHAPTER 4   **Milano–Firenze**   *117*

PART THREE / TO THE END OF THE LAND

CHAPTER 5   **Milano–Roma–Palermo**   *147*
CHAPTER 6   **Crotone–Taranto–Lecce**   *194*
CHAPTER 7   **Lecce–Otranto**   *232*

EPILOGUE   255

ACKNOWLEDGMENTS   263

LIST OF MAPS

———

Fig 1.   Italy   xii

Fig 2.   Northern Italy   2

Fig 3.   Central Italy   80

Fig 4.   Southern Italy   146

PREFACE

––––––

A TRAIN IS A TRAIN IS A TRAIN, ISN'T IT? PARALLEL LINES across the landscape, wheels raised on steel, the power and momentum of the heavy locomotive leading its snake of carriages through a maze of switches, into and out of the tunnels, the passenger sitting a few feet above the ground, protected from the elements, hurtled from one town to the next while he reads a book or chats to friends or simply dozes, entirely freed from any responsibility for speed and steering, from any necessary engagement with the world he's passing through. Surely this is the train experience everywhere.

Yet only in India have I been able to stand at an open door as the carriage rattles and sways through the sandy plains of Rajasthan. The elegant melancholy of the central station in Buenos Aires, designed in a French style by British architects, its steel arches shipped from distant Liverpool, has much to tell about Argentina past and present. Certainly the history and zeitgeist of Thatcher's and then Blair's England could very largely be deduced from the present confusion of the country's overpriced, clumsily privatized, manifestly unhappy railways. In America the lack of investment in train travel speaks eloquently of a country always ready to appear righteous but pathologically averse to surrendering car and plane for a more eco-friendly, community-conscious form of mobility.

The train arrived in Italy in 1839 with four and a half miles of line under the shadow of Vesuvius from Naples to Portici, followed in 1840 by nine miles from Milan to Monza. Borrowing from the English, the Italians coined the word *ferrovie*, literally "ironways." Unlike the English they had little iron for rails, almost no coal to drive the trains, and only a fraction of the demand for freight and passenger transport that the English industrial revolution had generated. It was hard to fill the trains and harder still to run them at a profit. But where business wasn't good there was politics. The Risorgimento process that aimed to unite the peninsula's separate, often foreign-run states into a single nation was in full swing; all sides in the struggle understood that rapid communication would encourage and later consolidate unification. There were also military considerations. What better way to move a large body of men quickly than in trucks on rails?

So railway building was almost always politically motivated, which again made the commercial side of the operation more difficult. After unification, debates over the routes of strategic lines offered a new battleground for an ancient *campanilismo*, that eternal rivalry that has every Italian town convinced its neighbors are conspiring against it. Amid all the idealism and quarreling, by the end of the nineteenth century the railway unions had become the biggest and most militant in the country and hence would play an important role in the struggle between socialism and Fascism; after the Second World War they became central to the government's policy of keeping the electorate happy by creating nonexistent jobs and awarding generous salaries and pensions. More than one person has claimed that the whole history of Italy as a nation-state could be reconstructed through an account of the country's railways.

But this is not a history book, nor exactly a travel book, though there is travel and history in it. Nor did I plan it and set to work on it in quite the same way I did with my other books on Italy. A few words of explanation are in order for the passenger who has just purchased his ticket and climbed on board *Italian Ways*.

My first sight of Italy came through the windows of a train. It was dawn on a summer morning in 1974. I had been dozing through France and woke near Ventimiglia to see the light graying on the Côte d'Azur as we flew over viaducts and through tunnels. It wasn't the first time I had seen palm trees, but one of the first. I was nineteen and traveling alone on an InterRail pass. Having met two likely Lancashire girls who had it in their heads to see the Byzantine mosaics in Ravenna, I tagged along with them, not appreciating that such a cross-country trip ran absolutely against the grain of Italy's topography and traffic flow; only a masochist would attempt to get from Ventimiglia to Ravenna by rail.

A few days later, on the platform at Firenze Santa Maria Novella, I bought a flask of Chianti with two German boys, the kind of wine they sell in bellied bottles with straw aprons, and after no more than a couple of swigs passed out, to wake up in my vomit three hours later in the corridor of an evening Espresso to Rome. Those were the days, fortunately long over, when cheap wine might be cut with almost anything. I spent that night in a sleeping bag on a patch of grass outside Roma Termini with thirty or forty other travelers, and while I slept, my shoulder bag, which was looped around my neck, was razored away; when I woke I had lost my shoes, guidebook, and passport but not my wallet, which was in my underpants. That morning my bare feet burned on the scorching tar as I began the first of many bureaucratic odysseys in this country that years later would become my home. Of the language I knew not a word. These were rites of passage; I had been delivered into my Italian future by train.

I have now lived in Italy for thirty-two years. There are plateaus, then sudden deepenings; all at once a corner is turned and you understand the country and your experience of it in a new way. You could think of it as a jigsaw puzzle in four dimensions; the ordinary three, plus time: you will never fill in all the pieces, if only because the days keep rolling by, yet the picture does seem more complete and above all denser and more convincing with every year. You're never quite a native, but you're no longer a stranger. So just as my knowledge of Italian literature has slowly extended from the novels of Natalia Ginzburg and Alberto Moravia, which I read to learn the language, underlining every word, back through the masterpieces of Svevo and Verga, Manzoni and Leopardi, then farther and farther into the past until I was finally ready for Dante and Boccaccio, likewise my knowledge of *le ferrovie italiane* has extended and deepened and intensified. It's not a question anymore of liking or hating them; these ironways are family.

At first train travel was just a chore. In 1992 I gave up language teaching at the University of Verona for a career track job at a university in Milan. With small children we didn't want to move to the big city, so I was condemned to commuting two or three times a week. I had no idea then that Italian railways were hitting an all-time low and even less knowledge of the reasons why that was so. I just suffered and of course laughed, since laughter is preferable to tears, and more sustainable. But often I enjoyed too: for to move on rails through a beautiful landscape is always a pleasure, and strangely conducive to reading, which is a major part of my life. Plus there was this: the deeper you get into a country, the more every new piece of information, every event and discovery, arrives as a fascinating confirmation, or challenge: how can I reconcile this bizarre thing that has happened with what I already know about the place? What might have seemed trivial or merely irritating the first year you were here now enriches and shifts the picture.

I began to take notes. I began to think that if someone wanted to understand Italy they might start by understanding how the train ticketing system works, or by listening to the platform announcements at Venezia Santa Lucia and Roma Termini, the strange emphasis given to certain names, the completely impractical order in which information is presented. In 2005 the magazine *Granta* asked me to write a travel piece and, cheating a little, because this was not strictly travel writing, I had a chance to use my jottings. Out of character, I wrote four times as much as they wanted, 120 pages, far too much for a magazine piece, not really enough for a book; but then I hadn't been thinking of a book; I was just having fun, so much more fun than I'd expected, writing about the railways, the Italian way of running their railways. *Granta* published a fragment.

Seven years later, Italian trains have changed enormously, Italy has changed, as have Europe and the world. Not to mention the author. Last year I came back to the book that wasn't quite a book. Were these pages simply out of date? Or could the difference between the way things were then and the way they are now be used to show something that has always fascinated me: how national character manifests itself most clearly when the things you thought couldn't change finally do. If you look at the way high-speed trains are being introduced into Italy while the regional services languish, if you look at the way the mobile phone is used in the business class compartments of a Milano–Roma Frecciarossa, if you look at how ticketing has been computerized and watch the way the frightening old on-board inspectors deal with it, if you travel the south coast of Calabria and Puglia and see how European Community money has been spent or misspent on the deserted railways, again and again, for good or ill, there it is, undeniably, the Italian way of doing things.

That is what I have tried to capture in this book.

Part One

THE TRAIN OF THE
LIVING DEAD

2005

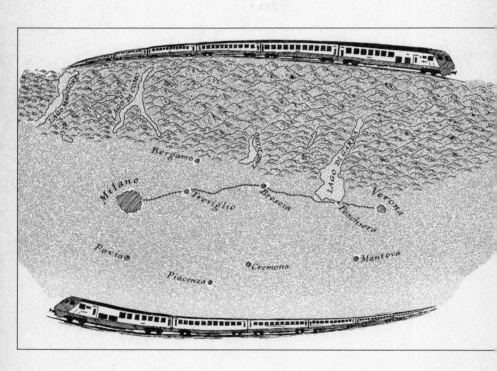

Chapter 1

VERONA–MILANO

ITALIANS COMMUTE. EVERY SEPTEMBER I RECEIVE A LETTER FROM the administration of the university where I teach, in Milan, reminding me that since I am not resident in the city, I have to apply for a *nullaosta* for the forthcoming year. This piece of paper, signed by the rector himself, will say that *nulla ostacola* . . . nothing prevents me from working in Milan while living a hundred miles away, in Verona.

What on earth could prevent me?

Only Trenitalia, the railways.

As so often in Italy, there is no official form to fill in; you have to make up the request yourself. This can cause anxiety when Italian is not your mother tongue and you are aware that there may be special formulas and terms of address. A university lecturer does not wish to seem inept.

"What if I just ignore it?" I once asked a colleague. "It's only a formality."

That was many years ago, in the nineties. I was innocent then. It was explained to me that in Italy a formality is a sort of dormant volcano. It might seem harmless for years, then suddenly blow your life away. So, one day, if I misbehaved in class, or supported the wrong candidate in some hotly disputed faculty election, the rector might decide that Trenitalia really wasn't reliable enough for me to be resident in Verona and work at the university in Milan. In the same way, in Italy, after years of neglect, certain laws on accounting or political-party fund-raising might quite suddenly be vigorously enforced for reasons that have little to do with someone's having broken the law. Never say *only* a formality.

Rather discouragingly, the colleague who enlightened me with this dormant volcano analogy later suggested that I might want to apply for an available lectureship in Lecce. Disturbed, I pointed out that if Milan was a hundred miles from Verona, Lecce was six hundred. At that point surely the nullaosta would not be a formality at all. "There's an overnight train, Verona–Lecce," I was told. "No problem. You could go twice a week. Or stay the week and come home at weekends."

It was a serious proposition. Hundreds of thousands of Italians do this. In Milan I have colleagues who are resident in Rome, in Palermo, in Florence. I have students who return to Naples or Udine every weekend. Thousands upon thousands of miles are traveled. Italians like to live where they live—where they were born, that is—with Mamma and Papà. Then they commute. Even when it offers no work, your hometown is always the best town; a thick web of family ties and bureaucracy anchors you there. Trenitalia connects these city-states. It makes the nation possible and allows it to remain fragmented, allows people to live double lives. Not for nothing is the holding company called Le Ferrovie dello Stato. State railways. *Nulla ostacola*.

TO BE PRESENT AT a nine-o'clock lesson or thesis commission in Milan, I have to get the 6:40 Interregionale from Verona Porta Nuova to Genova Piazza Principe. It's the train of the living dead. But at least, leaving home at six, many of the city's traffic lights are still only flashing yellow. You can move. You can even stop moving and park.

Verona's main station was rebuilt, like the roads around it and the nearby stadium, for soccer's 1990 World Cup. The cup took place before the roads were finished, at which point urgency if not interest was lost. The big teams of the time didn't come to Verona. I vaguely recall Belgium beating Uruguay. I can't remember the names of the other teams. Did anybody go and watch? In all my later years as a season-ticket holder at the stadium no one has mentioned these games. But the hastily conceived road system will be with us for decades to come, an underpass on a tight bend that has claimed a dozen lives, and likewise the attractive stone floor inside Verona Porta Nuova Station. It's made of small dark metamorphic slabs that mix a highly polished, almost mirror finish with mottling patches of rough gritty brown. Very stylish. When the Tangentopoli, or Bribesville, crackdown on political corruption began in the early nineties, it was suggested that much of the building for the World Cup in Verona had involved the mayor and his cronies giving contracts to friends and relatives. No one paid more than a brief visit to jail. No one really thought that this was an especially bad thing to have done.

Alas, even at 6:15 in the morning there's an impossibly long line at the ticket windows. The serious commuter has to have a season ticket. But what kind of season ticket? In England now there are different tickets for different trains run by different companies. There is the confusion and clamor of free enterprise, and, in an attempt to balance supply and demand, there are differently priced tickets for peak and off-peak travel. This is annoying, but comprehensible and all very Anglo-Saxon. In Italy the complications are of a different nature. Truly to get a grip on them would be to understand Italian politics and social policy since the Second World War.

First and foremost, train tickets must be cheap, and be seen to be so. People's desire to live in one city while working in another, coupled with the fact that Italian salaries are among the lowest in the European Community, require this. A student has to be able to afford to travel home *every* weekend or every other. The friends you make at primary school are your friends for life. You can't be without them. Who will

do your laundry, if not your dear mother? There are few Laundromats
in Italy. So to travel from Verona to Milan—148 kilometers, my ticket
tells me, or about 92 miles—costs only €6.82, peak or off-peak, weekend or weekday.* About $8.00 at the time of writing. It's cheap.

At the same time, the railways have traditionally been used as an
organization to absorb excess labor and keep unemployment down.
"What a lot of officials!" wrote D. H. Lawrence on the station in Messina, Sicily, in 1920. "You know them by their caps. Elegant tubby
little officials in kid-and-patent boots and gold-laced caps, tall long
nosed ones in more gold-laced caps, like angels in and out of the gates
of heaven they thread in and out of the various doors."

Having shed a hundred thousand staff in the past twenty years,
Trenitalia is no longer so dramatically overmanned but still employs
far more personnel per mile traveled than France, Germany, or Britain. Ten thousand of the ninety-nine thousand rail workers are considered unnecessary. And the officials still have smart caps with gold
bands, and shiny buttons on their dark jackets.

Returning from Venice one evening to the tiny station of Verona
Porta Vescovo, I discovered that the doors would not open. On the
Interregionale there is a red handle you pull upward when the train
stops. The door should slide open. One passenger after another
yanked and tugged. Imprecation, blasphemy. Since there were platforms on both sides of the train, they yanked and tugged on both
sides. Just as the train began to move off, a door jerked open and a
handful of passengers spilled out.

At which point, still congratulating ourselves on our close shave,
we were yelled at by a man with a wonderfully peaked cap, a cap far
larger and rounder and above all redder than seemed necessary. It
was the cap of the *capostazione*, the stationmaster. Someone explained
why we had gotten off when the train was already in motion, which

---

* All the information in this first part of the book refers to 2005. Prepare for surprises in the
second part, where everything changes so that much can remain the same.

of course is strictly forbidden. *"Non esiste!"* the important man protested. It wasn't possible that the doors wouldn't open. We must have done something wrong. Various passengers corroborated the story. "Non esiste!" he insisted. It can't be. Perhaps to work for Trenitalia sometimes requires living in denial.

For example, it's clear that if ticket prices are to be low (less than half the prices on Deutschebahn, less than a third of British railway companies) and manning high, the train service will be expensive to run. How can a country with a national debt running at more than 100 percent of GNP deal with this? One answer is: *il supplemento*.

If to take an Interregionale to Milan costs €6.82, to take the faster Intercity costs €11.05, or rather the base ticket of €6.82 plus a supplement of €4.23; the even faster (just) Eurostar will cost a further 50 cents. Once upon a time the supplement formed only a small percentage of the ticket, but since basic rail fares are taken into account to calculate national inflation rates, while Intercity rail fares are not, or not until recently, the supplement has tended to grow in relation to the basic ticket. A great deal of inflation can be hidden with such ruses. But what do you get for this extra money? The Interregionale takes fourteen minutes longer than the Intercity and twenty-four minutes longer than the Eurostar. Do I value fourteen minutes of my time at €4.23?

It's more complicated than that.

To encourage people to pay the higher fare, the Interregionali tend to disappear for certain periods of the day, especially if you're making a long trip. On the other hand, following a logic that runs exactly contrary to notions of supply and demand, if you travel with the living dead, as I am often obliged to, the *only* trains will be Interregionali, to cater to the poorer commuters, the damned, those who could not, on a daily basis, pay the higher fare, all this thanks to that rather pious though always welcome Italian commitment to a certain kind of popular socialism (of which needless to say both Catholicism and Fascism are close relatives). The more demand, then, the lower the fare.

So we have the 6:40 Verona–Genova Interregionale in the morning and the terrifying 18:15 Milano–Venezia Interregionale in the evening. Curiously, these humdrum overcrowded commuter convoys with their cheaper tickets traveling at peak times are the most reliable and the most punctual. Covering 100 miles in two hours with a locomotive and rolling stock capable of 110 miles an hour, they have time to play with.

SO ON THE FIRST day of the new academic year I buy my annual season ticket to Milan. There is no special window. You stand in line with everyone else. Four windows are manned, six are not. Fortunately, they recently introduced a single queuing system at Verona Porta Nuova, a long winding snake between rope barriers, this to avoid those frustrating situations where you choose the wrong line and find yourself stuck for hours. We all welcomed this sign of progress and civilization. The ropes were a smart white and red swinging from bright chrome posts; but having set up the snake, they failed to block entry to the windows to people who had not stood in line, people entering at what was supposed to be the exit.

A man leans against a pillar, chewing gum, watching, waiting, then, just as a window becomes free, he strides rapidly toward it and pushes in. The ticket seller knows what has happened but does not protest. The people in the line grumble but don't actually intervene. This has always surprised me in Italy, the general resignation in the face of the *furbo*, the sly one. It is always worth trying it on here. If things get unpleasant, you can protest that you didn't understand the rules.

A notice tells you that you're not supposed to ask for information at the ticket window, just buy your ticket and go, but people are asking for the most detailed information. "How much would it cost to switch from second to first class on an overnight train to Lecce with four people taking into account reductions for the family and the granny over seventy?"

The ticket sellers are patient. They don't have a train to catch. Perhaps they like giving out information, they like demonstrating knowledge and expertise. At the place where the official line emerges from its serpent of ropes, the point where you're getting close to your turn, you'll find it's impossible to see the ticket window farthest to the left, because it's hidden behind a pillar clad (for the World Cup) in a highly polished chocolaty brown stone. This hidden window, I've noticed, is always in use, whereas those directly opposite the line, and hence highly visible, are frequently closed. If you don't know that the window behind the pillar is there, you don't go to it. And the ticket seller doesn't call to you. He has no buzzers to push, no warning lights to attract his customers. Trenitalia does not want to spoil us.

At the window to my right, someone is asking for the timetable for a complicated series of connections to a town in Liguria. The line frets. "On which trains can I take my bicycle?" he asks. Another *furbo* manages to sneak in when the window near the exit is momentarily free. This time the ticket seller protests, but halfheartedly. "I'll be quick," *il furbo* says. "Otherwise I'll miss my train."

Nobody shouts. There is a slow, simmering resentment, as if the people who have behaved properly are grimly pleased to get confirmation that good citizenship is always futile, a kind of martyrdom. This is an important Italian emotion: I am behaving well and suffering *because* of that. I am a martyr. *Mi sto sacrificando.* It is a feeling that will justify some bad behavior at the appropriate moment.

Do these people really need to ask for so much information at the ticket windows? No. There are excellent poster-size timetables showing all departures from the station. The Italians are good at this. There are cheap, comprehensive, and just about comprehensible national timetables available at the station's newsagent. They give you *all* the trains in northern Italy for a six-month period. There is an information office. For some reason the information office is at the other end of the station, perhaps fifty yards from the ticket windows—you have to walk down a long, elegantly paved corridor—and the timetables are *not* displayed near the ticket line. This seems to be true in every station in Italy. It's strange. You cannot consult train times while standing in line, which might be exactly when you want to consult them. Of course you hurry to the line without looking at the timetable, because you fear that if you don't, you'll lose your place and miss your train, but then at the window you have to ask for information. At one window a ticket seller patiently starts to explain the advantages and limitations of a complex promotional offer. The PA system announces the trains about to leave.

TO COPE WITH THIS stressful situation Trenitalia introduced the SportelloVeloce or FastTicket, as it's also called. (Theses could be written about this habit of offering a translation that is not really a translation but as it were an Italian fantasy of how English works directed more at an Italian public, as a marketing operation, than at an English-speaking public on the move.) This is a window that you're only supposed to use if your train departs *within the next fifteen minutes*. Sensibly, they placed the SportelloVeloce in the position where people usually sneak in to beat the main line in its long snake between red ropes and chrome bars.

But what if my train leaves in half an hour? I stand in line for fifteen minutes, I see things are getting tight. Do I switch to the fast line, where there are already four people? What if one of them asks for information? What if everybody decides that they can now arrive only fifteen minutes before the train leaves and use the fast line? This would be a problem, because whereas at least two of the main windows are always open, the FastTicket window is frequently closed.

Or what if I get in line at the SportelloVeloce twenty-five minutes before my train leaves but get to the ticket seller eighteen minutes before it leaves? Will he serve me? Probably yes, but he would be within his rights not to. Immigrants, in particular, tend to get turned away. I mean non-whites. And sometimes tourists. Foreign tourists. So do I have to go to the back of the line? Can I keep him arguing for three minutes, at which point he would no longer be able to deny me a ticket? Unless perhaps my train is suddenly signaled as delayed for half an hour. Not an unusual occurrence. Or, since a standard rail ticket is valid for two months, what if I say I'm getting the Intercity to Bolzano leaving in five minutes, when in fact I'm planning to get it in two weeks? Is anybody going to check that I actually board today's train? These are unanswered questions. FastTicket has not made ticket buying easier. A child could see this. So why was it introduced? The time has come to talk about image.

Use of English is always a clue. Readers will have noticed that only the slow trains now have Italian names, the Interregionale and, slower still, crawling doggedly from one watering hole to the next, the Regionale. These are the trains that need not be presented to the outside world, to the foreign businessman and the credit-card-holding tourist. The rolling stock is old and rattly. In summer you roast and in winter you freeze. The seats are narrow and hard, the cleaning . . . well, best take a deep breath before passing the toilet. But as soon as you start paying supplements you are in the territory of English, or at least international-speak. The proud old categories of Espresso, Rapido, and Super-Rapido have largely disappeared. Now we have the Intercity, the Eurocity, and the Eurostar.

What we are dealing with here is an ongoing Italian dilemma. Are we "part of Europe" or not? Are we part of the modern world? Are we progressive or backward? Above all, *are we serious*? There is a general perception that the Italian way of doing things, particularly in the public sector, is sloppy and slow, compromised by special interests and political considerations; hence an enormous effort must be made to work against the Latin grain and emulate a Teutonic punctuality, an Anglo-French high-tech.

This unease goes right back to the making of the Italian state. It is there in the patriot D'Azeglio's famous line "We have made Italy, now we must make the Italians." It is there in Mussolini's obsession that "our way of eating, dressing, working, and sleeping, the whole complex of our daily habits, must be reformed." To make the trains run on time would be proof that Fascism had achieved this, that a profound change had occurred in the national psyche. *"Abassa la vita commoda!"* proclaimed one Fascist slogan. Down with the easy life! You can understand why elections could hardly be free and fair when the main political party was fielding slogans like that.

But at another level, and quite understandably, Italians have no desire at all to change. They like an easy life. They consider themselves superior to those crude and fretful nations who put punctuality before style and comfortable digestion. A compromise is sought in image. Italy will be made to *look* fast and modern. There will be FastTicket windows even if they make the process of buying tickets more complex and anxiety-ridden than before. At the main station in Milan a member of the railway staff has now been given the task of vetting those who stand in line at the SportelloVeloce. "What train are you getting, *signore*? When does it leave?" But how do we know if the reply a passenger gives to this official is the same as the request he will make at the ticket window? A problem of overmanning is solved, a new job invented, but the gap for the *furbo* remains open.

SUDDENLY I BECOME AWARE that there is a man sitting at one of the five ticket windows that was previously closed. A man in uniform. I'm second in line now. The man sits there quietly, unobtrusively. He has just started his shift. He looks at the line where people are anxiously focused on the windows that are busy. He scratches an unshaven neck and turns the pink pages of his *Gazzetta dello Sport*. He is not shirking work, but he is not inviting it either. He has reading material.

I nudge the man in front: "That window's free." He looks at me suspiciously, as if I were trying to get him out of the way to grab the next free window. "Are you open?" he calls before committing himself. The man raises his eyes to gesture to the electronic display at the top of his window. "It says open, doesn't it?" As a result, just a few minutes later, I find myself going to the window hidden behind the pillar, where I discover that my onetime neighbor Beppe is serving.

Fifteen years ago Beppe gave up a promising and remunerative life as a freelance electrician to take up the dull job of serving at the ticket windows in Verona Porta Nuova. He had applied for the job when temporarily unemployed some years before; he survived a long and complex admissions process and served his time on a waiting list of some scores of men and women. When, years later, the call finally came, it was an opportunity his wife and parents wouldn't let him pass up: a meal ticket *for life*. This is how a railway job is seen. It is decently paid and as irreversible as a place in paradise. In the 1960s there was even the suggestion that railway jobs should be made hereditary, a return to the medieval estates. This might seem laughable, but when most Italians in prominent positions seem to be the children of others in similar positions, when the multitude of small family companies that make up the most dynamic part of the Italian economy are generally passed on from father to son, or indeed daughter in a pinch, one can understand why the unions felt this arrangement could be introduced for an elite group of workers like the railway men.

Another friend of mine, a young man who once specialized in making handmade harpsichords, gave up his little workshop to become a railway carpenter repairing vandalized carriage fittings. Peer pressure to make these sad decisions is considerable. Job security is placed beyond every other consideration. Beppe, I know, finds his work at the ticket window desperately tedious but hangs on with bovine good humor. "These are hard times," he says, though one of the hardest things these days is finding an electrician in a hurry. Handmade harpsichords are not widely available either.

"An annual season ticket to Milan," I tell him.

"Interregionale, Intercity, or Eurostar?" Beppe asks.

I explain that I take the Interregionale going but as often as not an Intercity coming back.

My old neighbor shakes his head, rubs his chin in his hand. "Complicated."

In the early 1990s, as part of an urgent effort to make the railways lean and mean, or at least not quite so bonnie and bountiful, the Ferrovie dello stato (FS) were officially split off from government control and obliged to return, if not a profit, then certainly not much of a loss. However, since the government continued to own more than half the company's shares and to regulate every aspect of company policy, stipulating what lines it was obliged to run with what regularity and at what fares, the move was little more than, well, a formality. Then in the late '90s, to fall in line with European legislation on competition in the transport sector, the monolithic company was split up into various smaller companies under the umbrella holding of the FS; so the Rete Ferroviaria Italiana (Italian Railway Network) would run the lines and the smaller stations, while Grandi Stazioni would run the bigger stations and Trenitalia would run the trains.

Again, since the same people were sitting on the boards of these supposedly different companies, these changes seemed more about theater than substance. What did change things for the passengers was that Trenitalia was now further split into different sections, each under orders not to lose too much money. As a result, the Interregionali and the Intercities are now accounted for separately, and the Eurostars separately again. Hence one can no longer buy a regular ticket plus a separate supplement and decide at the last moment which train to get. No, now you have to tell the ticket seller what train you'll be traveling on (time and day) and he has to locate that train on the computer screen before printing the ticket so that the money you pay can go to one company rather than the other, even though actually they're all part of the same company. Strangely, though, the ticket you buy *is valid for two months* and hence it's perfectly legitimate *not* to get on the exact train you referred to when you bought the ticket. Isn't that weird? So if you buy an Intercity ticket, with its supplement included, you'll be able to travel, if the fancy takes you, on a cheaper Interregionale, though not vice versa, of course.

Is this actually a recognized rule, written somewhere, or just common sense; I mean, that you can use a more expensive ticket for a cheaper train but not the other way around? I really don't know, but recently I witnessed a situation where a rather beautiful young woman, raven hair, the kind of breasts that Italians call *prosperose*, was told she would have to pay a fine for traveling on an Intercity with a *more expensive* Eurostar ticket. Only a mutiny of the surrounding passengers saved her. The whole scene must have lasted twenty minutes and eventually involved five or six people. She was, as I said, an attractive lady.

So to keep things brief, you can no longer buy five or six Interregionali tickets and a few supplements and take whatever train is most convenient, because the Intercity ticket now has the supplement built in. *However*, Beppe tells me, if I get an *annual* season ticket for the Interregionale, I *will* be allowed, as a very special favor for having spent so much money, to buy separate *supplementi*—they do still exist, then—to travel on Intercities for individual trips, *if*, and only if, at the moment of purchase of the supplements, I am able to show my season ticket and a valid ID (I love the expression "*valid* ID"). The ticket seller will then type into his computer (using two fingers) my name and the number (the rather long number) of my season ticket so that the journey can be moved in accounting terms from one service to another, thus making the railways more efficient. Alas, because of the need to show an ID, this special favor supplement is not available at the ticket machines. I'll have to stand in line.

It's a drag, but I agree to this. I can buy half a dozen supplementi at a time, I decide, restricting my trips to the ticket window to a minimum. For €670, then, at the time about $800, Beppe gives me a ticket that looks *exactly* like any other Trenitalia ticket and indeed any other supplement: a piece of soft cardboard about seven inches by two and a half with a pink-and-blue patterned background and faded computer print above. The only thing that distinguishes this ticket from the one that costs €6.82 is the word ANNUALE, which occupies approximately one hundredth of the ticket's surface area. It's clear I'll have to stick a piece of colored tape on this ticket to distinguish it from the *supplementi* I buy. And I'll have to laminate it to stop it from disintegrating in my wallet.

Beppe wanders off to make a photocopy of the ticket in case I lose it. In fact he makes two photocopies, one for me and one for the ticket office. That's generous. They keep a file. He opens an old metal cupboard. All this takes him five minutes and more. The photocopier has to warm up. Then he starts to ask after my family and he's expecting, of course, that I'll ask after his. I do. I'm getting embarrassed because at 6:35 a.m. the line behind me is long and there is a mill of worried people around the FastTicket window. The train of the living dead has been announced as "*in partenza*," about to depart. His son is doing very well at school, Beppe is explaining. I know that if I protested that we shouldn't be exchanging pleasantries in these circumstances, with other people waiting, he would imagine that I didn't want to talk to him. His daughter less so, he says, unfortunately. She doesn't seem to take her teachers seriously. Beppe would never really understand that I was worried about the others in the ticket line. Why should I be? Personal relationships come before civic sense. *Salutami la Rita*, he calls. My wife.

MY TICKET SAYS "*da convalidare*" at one end. For the past ten years or so they've been making us insert our tickets into a little yellow stamping machine before we get on the train. The idea is that if the ticket inspector on the train doesn't manage to check your ticket (with its two-month validity), you still won't be able to use it again, stamped as it now is with one particular time and date: the *convalida*. But the ink in the stamping machines is usually so faded that, assuming the inspector doesn't come along and punch a hole in it, I am sure you could use the same ticket twice at least. The print is illegible. Suspicious as I have learned to be, I wonder who got the contract to install and service all these little yellow stamping machines in every foyer and on every platform in the 2,260 stations in Italy and whether that cost can really be lower than the revenue previously lost to the *furbi* who were able to avoid the ticket inspector as he passed through the train. For nine times out of ten your ticket still gets inspected and punched, even after it has been *convalidato*.

Or—since there is no end to conspiracy theory once you've begun—perhaps rather than guaranteeing that everybody pays for their ticket every time they travel, the idea was to open up new opportunities for fining passengers: if you don't have your ticket stamped you're liable to a fine—€50 or so—even if you merely forgot to have it stamped. Since there is no barrier in Italian stations between ticket purchase and platforms—nothing to remind you, that is, of your duty to have the ticket stamped—forgetfulness is understandable, especially for tourists who don't know the ropes and perhaps are not in the habit of reading the small print on their tickets carefully.

My mother had to pay up some years ago. She was traveling with a friend. You can imagine them: two pale English pensioners in flowery dresses on the line from Florence to Siena. They hadn't realized they were supposed to have their tickets stamped. My evangelical mother is the least likely person in the world to try to avoid a fare. Probably this was the only time in her eighty-odd years that she has fallen foul of the law. Certainly it was the only time she ever had to pay a fine. She felt deeply shamed. The inspector was remorseless: "You foreigners always pretend you don't understand," he said.

But no law in Italy is ever quite watertight, let alone rigidly applied. There are always interesting loopholes. For example, if I forget to have my ticket stamped, or am unable to do so because the stamping machines are not working (an occurrence so common as to be the norm in some small stations), all I have to do is inform the ticket inspector before boarding the train and he will write the time and date on the ticket with his pen, and sign it, and I will be forgiven and allowed to travel without paying a fine. The inspector, who may or may not also be the *capotreno*, the train manager—can generally be found at the door to one of the carriages toward the back of the train, one foot on the platform, the other raised self-importantly on the footplate, waiting to blow his whistle and wave his green cap to tell the driver to close the doors.

Once, riding an Intercity with my Interregionale season ticket, I realized I had forgotten to have my supplement stamped, priced at €4.23. Immediately anxious, I jumped off at the small station of Peschiera, but there was no stamping machine in sight on the platform, so, seeing the ticket inspector already raising his whistle to his lips, I ran to him and asked if he would convalidate (is this a word?) my ticket. He refused. He said he could see from my ticket that I had already been on the train and hence was liable to a fine. I pointed out that now that I had gotten off the train I could stay off and hence avoid a fine. He could hardly fine me if he didn't catch me on the train and I was clearly not intending to cheat if I had jumped off the train to have my ticket stamped.

We argued. It is extraordinary how regularly Italy creates these areas of uncertainty: how is the law to be applied? Whole personalities form around such complications. The *furbo*, of course, will try to get around every rule. But there is also the opposite figure, the *pignolo*, someone who will apply the rules most determinedly, even when, or perhaps especially when, they are the most inappropriate. The *pignolo* always believes that everybody else is *furbo*, the *furbo* that everybody else is *pignolo*.

"I shall refuse to pay the fine if you try to fine me," I told the ticket inspector.

"I will report you to the on-board police," he declared. There are usually two *carabinieri* or *poliziotti*, armed to the teeth, on every train.

"The on-board police are on board," I told him. "And I am not."

Once again he refused to "convalidate" my ticket.

Meanwhile, the Venice–Turin Intercity was being held up. Perhaps a thousand passengers.

Feeling belligerent, I got on the train anyway. "It's clear that I'm in good faith," I declared.

"The rules don't say anything about good faith," he said. This is true. Italian rules and regulations never consider the question of the spirit in which one has behaved. He was going to fine me and that was that.

But though I sat in the same carriage all the way to Milan, he never came to fine me. Perhaps it was only important to have me worried, to assert an authoritative presence. The tax office has also done this to me. They threaten, then don't do anything. Since the inspector didn't stop by to put the date on my ticket, I was able to use my supplement a second time. And I did!

A similar situation once occurred when I traveled to Gorizia, on the Italian-Slovenian border. The inspector examined my ticket with some care and told me that this "document" required me to travel through Pordenone rather than through Udine. I had gone the long way around, he accused. There was a difference of some twenty miles to pay, plus a fine.

The man at the ticket window had told me nothing about this, I protested. I just asked for a ticket to Gorizia and consulted the time-table and got on the most suitable train. I could hardly be accused of gaining anything by taking a train that traveled twenty extra miles.

"Your ticket says via Pordenone," he told me. "Don't you read your *documento di viaggio*?"

I was fascinated. What kind of man is it who imagines that when one buys a train ticket one then stops to *read* it? Or thinks of it as a *documento di viaggio*?

The train stopped in a station. "I'll be back in a moment to deal with this," he said severely; he would have to calculate the exact excess fare and then the exact fine in relation to that exact excess. Everything in Italy is worked out on the basis of cost per kilometer, with no regard to which lines are more heavily traveled or more costly to maintain. The man hurried off in his nice green blazer with its smart shiny buttons and . . . never came back. With an Italian official it may be that the more he insists on a facade of correctness, the more likely it is, if you are determined, that in the end he will let you off. I suspect that this is why Italian soccer players always challenge the referee's decisions. You just never know. And if the man won't actually reverse *this* decision maybe he'll think twice about blowing his whistle for the next foul.

Anyway, the season ticket I have bought at 6:35 in the morning bears the warning: *da convalidare* (to be stamped). But being an annual ticket, of course, there's no need to stamp it. In fact, it would be a mistake to do so. How could I stamp it every time I got on a train for the next year? Italy is not a country for beginners.

ONE OF THE GREAT advantages of the 6:40 is that it departs from Verona. You don't have to hang around on the platform or in the waiting room. Even if you're fifteen minutes early, you can go right ahead and sit on the train. I make for the last carriage. It has a very particular smell that always affects me deeply when, after the long summer holidays, I return to the trains and another year's teaching. It is a mix of urine and disinfectant and tired synthetic upholstery impregnated with the smoke of years ago. You can't smoke on the trains anymore, but the smell lingers. There are smudgy neon lights that offend the eyes without illuminating a book. Here and there a seat is occupied, by a student returning to college with his newly done laundry; a man in overalls constantly clearing his throat; a black girl, plump and exhausted, clearly on her way home after a long night. There is a brisk trade in prostitutes outside Verona station, immigrant girls mainly, Africans and Slavs, living on the edge of slavery, I fear. They use the trains a lot. I'm not sure why. Heads wobble and suddenly nod. The girl, the only non-white in the carriage, is wearing shiny red boots. Someone snores. It's an open plan carriage, no compartments, and I choose a seat as far away from the others as possible. At 6:42 or 6:43 a faint tension is transmitted through the hard seat to the loins and the thighs. No train overcomes initial inertia as gently, as reluctantly, as wearily, as the 6:40 Interregionale to Genova Piazza Principe via Milano Centrale.

Then a late arrival bangs into the carriage and comes to sit down *right next to me.* Her Discman is tinkling, she wears a sickly perfume and has a jewel in her navel, and she carries a noisy paper bag with a sticky croissant. Why does this happen so often? There are people who want to be on their own, to mark out their own territory and be quiet there, and there are people who are eager to invade that territory, to sit close to someone else. There seem to be a disproportionate number of the latter in Italy. You sit in an empty compartment in a whole carriage of empty compartments, a whole train of them, and someone comes banging in and sits next to you.

Once, during a strike, I found a completely empty Intercity at Milan station, a ghost train. Eventually, an announcement said that the train might leave in two hours' time but this couldn't be guaranteed. The voice apologized for any inconvenience. Having no inclination to go and find myself a hotel, I decided to sit in the train and read. I chose a carriage halfway down the long platform. Since it was an Intercity, there were compartments. Suddenly a man was tugging open the sliding door to join me, a rather sad, lanky middle-aged man in a gray raincoat with a slack, worried mouth and thick spectacles. He had a huge suitcase, the sort of suitcase that has you wondering where on earth its owner can be going and for how long. Are these all his worldly possessions? Is he a refugee?

With some effort the man swung the suitcase up onto the luggage rack, sat down, brushed imaginary crumbs from his trousers, looked at me, smiled, and began—I knew I couldn't stop him—to talk: about the strike, about a difficult change of trains that awaited him in Venezia Mestre, about the impossibility of ever knowing what would happen in Italy even when you began the most banal of journeys. Wasn't that so? It's an interesting thing how often Italians like to refer to the country as if it were foreign to them, inhabited by people who are inexplicably unreliable. I barely nodded. *"Ecco il capotreno!"* he suddenly shouted, and he jumped up and hurried out of the compartment and down the corridor to talk to a man in a smart cap walking along the platform.

This was my chance. Furtively, I picked up my own small bag, headed the other way up the carriage, and pushed through the two connecting doors into the next. I must have walked through about four completely deserted carriages, going toward the locomotive, before choosing another compartment. Since the electricity in the train hadn't been turned on, I was looking for a place where one of the big floodlights high up in the station outside would give enough light to read by, even through grimy windows. Here. Good. I sat down. For perhaps ten minutes I read. I was happy. The truth is, I really don't mind sitting on an empty train for a couple of hours and reading. If a book is good enough, it doesn't matter where you read it. There are times when I have even welcomed train delays. After perhaps fifteen minutes, with a sudden wrenching of the compartment's sticky sliding door, breathless and anxious, the same man reappeared.

"There you are!" he cried. He sat down. He resumed his conversation. He began to tell me what the *capotreno* had said. The train would be leaving, but only when they found a co-driver. They were having trouble finding a co-driver. Because of the strike. As for Mestre, heaven only knows. His last train for some mountain destination departed at 8:15. "Who knows where I'll be sleeping tonight?" He seemed quite pleased with this melodramatic reflection. Then, glancing up at the luggage rack, he asked, "Where's my suitcase?"

I shook my head. "You left it in the other carriage."

"What other carriage?"

The man hadn't realized that he was now four carriages nearer to the locomotive.

"Oh." He squinted at me. "I knew something was odd," he said. "But why on earth did you move?"

"I want to be alone," I told him.

Alarmed, he jumped up and hurried back down the train to reclaim his suitcase. For a moment it crossed my mind he might be a ghost; he haunted this train, even when it was parked for days out in empty sidings. That would explain why he was so desperate for company. Taking no chances, I moved again, this time into first class. They can't fine you for being in first class until the train actually starts moving. I felt sure this was a second-class ghost.

IT'S 6:50. THE LANDSCAPE slips away outside smeared windows. To the left is the *pianura padana*, a ribbon of low factories beside the line and beyond them long stretches of vines, orchards, maize. It's flat and dull, foggy in winter, steamy in summer. The replacement of the old wooden vine supports with a harsh geometry of identical gray cement posts is depressing, likewise the huge expanses of protective black netting now stretched over the cherry orchards. No more the white spring blossoms. This countryside has a dogged, industrial, gridlike look, as if nature had been carefully parceled out in discrete units to make it easier to count the cash. We're riding across one of the wealthiest areas in Western Europe.

But to the right of the line, the north, the land rises through the terraced hills of the Valpolicella to the mountains of Trentino. Here the vineyards have a more traditional aspect, and on a clear day white peaks are visible along the whole alpine arc. You can even make out the wolfish pine woods, far away, the gray rock faces and dark, resiny valleys. It's good to glance up from a book and see the mountains, to imagine you can smell them. They afford an illusion of drama and, for

someone who grew up in London, the assurance that I now live far
from home. Then at Peschiera the train begins to fill.

Peschiera and Desenzano, the first two stops, lie on the southern
shore of Lake Garda. Peschiera is where you get off for Gardaland,
the Italian version of Disneyland. The pretty provincial station with
its dark maroon stucco and unkempt flowerbeds is marred by a series
of colorful wooden facades mimicking a street in the American West
inhabited by cartoon characters. *Gardaland, Bus navetta gratuito!*
says Yogi Bear. Free shuttle bus. During the summer holidays, the
train will be packed with adolescents who come here to spend their
parents' money. This morning a police car has parked on the platform,
as if Paperone and Topolino, or rather Mickey Mouse and Scrooge
McDuck, had really been shooting it out.

The train rattles along a low ridge now and you can look down
across old terracotta housetops and the concrete sprawl of hotels,
pizzerias, and *gelaterie* to the big lake, brightly gray in the morning
light, stretching north as far as the eye can see, with terraced hills
first, then darker mountains rising and closing in on either side, turning the water black. A fishing boat trails a long wake but seems to be
fixed there. The surface is very still and solid-looking. A couple of
backpackers clamber into the carriage, arguing in German. The Interregionali have rather cunning swing doors between carriages: you can
never figure whether you're supposed to push or pull, or on which side
of the double door to do it. The backpackers have a tussle and almost
fall over each other coming into the carriage.

To the left of the train are the low hills of Custoza, rounded morainic
mounds of silt and rubble brought down by the glaciers when the lake
was formed. Here in 1866 Victor Emmanuel II led his troops against
the Austro-Hungarians, still masters of the Veneto despite the unification of the rest of Italy. Austria had offered to hand over the territory
in return for Italian neutrality in its war with Germany, but Victor
Emmanuel felt that the honor of his ancient family and new nation
demanded that he win the territory by force of arms. His army of

120,000 was defeated by 80,000 Austrians. Fourteen thousand men died. Their skulls are on display in an ossuary. You can see where the bullets passed through. Most of them were young enough to have excellent teeth.

A significant part of that victorious Austrian army of 1866 was made up of local Italians who were not greatly inspired by the idea of national unity, and even today on walls between Peschiera and Desenzano you can read such graffiti as GOVERNO LADRO, VENETO LIBERO. The *governo ladro*, the thieving government, is always understood to be Roman, not local. And again: CALL ME A DOG, BUT NOT AN ITALIAN. FREE US FROM SOUTHERN FILTH. And so on. Perhaps as a result some tourists and ingenuous foreign journalists may imagine that there is a serious separatist movement here. But this is just a rhetorical flourish, not unlike that slogan FastTicket. People like the idea that there is a separatist movement, they like hating Rome and the South, and then they travel Trenitalia to work in distant towns, or to their favorite holiday beach in Puglia where quite probably they have friends and relatives. In much the same way people like the fact that a pope is against contraception and abortion but then continue with their sensible, hypercontrolled sex lives. In every aspect of Italian life, one of the key characteristics to get to grips with is that this is a nation at ease with the distance between ideal and real. They are beyond what we call hypocrisy. Quite simply they do not register the contradiction between rhetoric and behavior. It's an enviable mind-set.

MOST PEOPLE ON THE train are asleep, and if not, they wish they were. It's not unusual to climb on board and find carriages turned into dormitories. But this can be dangerous. On two occasions recently the train of the living dead became the train of the truly dead. The first time, thank heaven, I wasn't on it. In midwinter, shortly after the carriages had started to roll, there was a smell of smoke. An electrical fire had broken out. In the last carriage, four or five passengers were sufficiently awake to get up and start moving forward through the train. No one had noticed a woman in her forties fast asleep. By the time the smoke cleared she was dead.

As always when there is a fatal accident in Italy, the magistrates moved swiftly to arrest whoever might conceivably be considered responsible, in this case the poor *capotreno* who claimed he was told by one of the escaping passengers that the smoke-filled and hence extremely dangerous carriage had been completely evacuated. After a few anguished days in custody, he was released. A theater of severity in Italy is always followed by lenience and very often indifference. It is hard to end up in jail for causing an accident, though many are briefly jailed for nothing at all.

The second fatality occurred on a morning of thesis commissions. I had to go to Milan and sit behind a table with seven or eight other professors to listen to students defending their graduate theses. Like the *nullaosta*, the thesis commission is a formality. No student I know of has ever failed. It is also a thing of unspeakable boredom: three or four hours in which tedium can be held in your hands and caressed like a small, fluffy animal. But woe onto him who cries off a thesis commission. Because if more than one professor is absent and the legal quorum isn't reached, nobody can get his or her degree, and serious sanctions will follow. Thus the whole university experience depends, ultimately, on a long ceremony of collective tedium. It is interesting that my Italian colleagues for the most part share this assessment, some are far more scathing than I am, yet never feel that something should be done to alter the situation. Thesis commissions are as inevitable as pizza and the pope.

On that particular thesis-commission morning, then, when, fifteen minutes out of Verona, the Interregionale braked sharply and shuddered to a stop, I at once felt nervous. Five minutes became ten. We were in open country just before the village of Sommacampagna. It was raining steadily. After perhaps half an hour the PA announced, "*I signori viaggiatori sono avvisati che il treno sarà fermo per un periodo indeterminato!"*

Stopped for an indeterminate period of time! How fatal those words sounded. As if the planet had ceased to turn. No explanation, no hint as to when the solar system might resume its various orbits. The rain fell and fell. Alarmed, I phoned a colleague in Milan who, I hoped, was an early riser. It occurred to me that if I started missing thesis commissions perhaps the university administration would reconsider my *nullaosta* when I applied the following year.

Meanwhile, the dozen or so passengers in the carriage were getting their hair wet hanging out of the windows trying to understand what was going on. "Suicide," someone knowledgeable decided. How did he know? Because we had braked violently in empty countryside. Because no trains had passed in the other direction. Obviously the line had been closed down, both ways. What else could it be? "This stretch is famous for suicides," he told us.

He was right. At 6:50 in the morning somebody had been feeling so unhappy that he or she had jumped under the first train the rainy morning brought. Not a student bound for the thesis commission, I hoped.

"Then even before they clean things up," our knowledgeable traveler told everybody, "they have to get a doctor out to certify death and a forensic team to photograph the scene in case the driver was to blame."

How could a driver ever be to blame if someone throws himself in front of the locomotive?

After perhaps an hour and a half the train made the strange movement of going backward at a snail's pace for ten minutes before it found a point to switch to a sideline. Our direction was then reversed again and we proceeded with caution through the station of Sommacampagna. Just beyond the platform, on a grassy embankment, I saw an ambulance team pushing a severed leg into a black plastic bag. Other men, in suits, stood under umbrellas. The curious thing was how little impression this made on me compared with my mental picture of the victim throwing himself on the rails, his healthy body meeting the steel wheels. Or maybe her body. That makes me shiver, perhaps because one somehow thinks of doing it oneself. A few days later the newspapers attacked the railways for sending the clean-up bill to the relatives. A *pignolo*, no doubt, trying to balance the company's impossible books.

AT 7:40 THE TRAIN stops in the town of Brescia. This is Lombardy now. Suddenly a middle-aged man a few seats down from me comes to life. He jumps up, slams open the window, and is leaning out, beckoning to friends on the crowded platform. *"Qua, qua. In fretta!"* Here, here. Hurry! He is saving seats for them, a coat on one, a bag on another, a newspaper on the next. In less than five minutes the train is crowded, it's packed. People are standing, pushing. No one can find space for their bags. Worse still, everybody is talking. Everybody seems to know each other.

This is something I have never observed in England. There, on a commuter train, most of the passengers are shut away in themselves, in a newspaper, a book, or trying to prolong the dreams of an hour before. There's a pleasant melancholy to the journey. But not on the Interregionale to Milan. These dead are alive, which is so much more disconcerting. Either the travelers are neighbors in Brescia or work colleagues in Milan. They form knots of animated discussion all down the carriage. Some knots know other knots and intertwine and snag. Students swap study notes. Soccer, politics, and the proper way to prepare an asparagus risotto are urgently discussed. I insert a pair of yellow sponge earplugs.

But it isn't enough. Half a dozen men and women in their early thirties are crowded around me. There is usually one who does all the talking while the others offer occasional confirmations or objections. When the sexes are mixed, the one talking is always a man.

"Juve was let off an obvious penalty again." Juve or Juventus is one of the so-called Big Four soccer teams—Juventus, Inter Milan, AC Milan, and Roma—that invariably win the championship. "Did you see? *Una vergogna*." It's a suit speaking, in his thirties with a nasal voice, a scrubbed bank clerk's face, an earring, a sneer, a bright red tie. He laughs and jokes constantly. The women exchange indulgent smiles. Two of them are standing arm in arm, touching each other. There's a strange collective consciousness to these groups, something quite physical. They like their bodies and they like their accessories, their handbags and laptops and mobiles and tiny designer backpacks. "Look at this I bought. Look at this." They finger the new material and touch their friend's arm.

"Joke," begins the red tie noisily. "Listen up. So, Berlusconi's son asks his *papà* advice about how to lay some girl he's hot for, right? And old Berlusca tells him, 'Stefano, first you buy her a diamond necklace, *va bene*? You take her to an expensive restaurant, book a room in a five-star hotel, and make sure there's a chilled bottle of the finest champagne on the bedside table. And she's yours. Go for it.' 'But *Papà*,' his son protests, 'isn't love supposed to be free? I don't want her to think I'm buying her.' And what does Silvio reply?" The man smiles brightly before the punch line; he's extremely pleased with himself. "What does *il buon* Silvio say? 'Free love?' he says. 'Romance! That was just a story the cheapskate Commies invented so they could fuck for nothing!' *So they could fuck for nothing!*"

The others titter and groan. Someone remembers something a talk-show host said the previous evening about the way referees were selected for Serie A soccer games. I resign myself to an hour of forced listening, albeit with the pleasant muffling effect of the earplugs.

Recently, prompted by God knows what hypersensitive traveler, Trenitalia began to talk about the possibility of a "quiet carriage" for those who didn't want to talk. But before going ahead with this revolutionary project they decided to carry out a survey of passenger attitudes. The newspapers published some responses. Most fascinating were the people who simply didn't understand: "If I don't want a guy to talk to me," one woman says, "I know how to tell him to leave me alone." "People can talk or not talk as they choose," observes a student. They simply could not grasp the idea that some of us might want to be quiet to read and work. "What happens if I'm in the quiet carriage and my phone rings?" somebody objected. With this simple observation he was sure he had demonstrated the folly of the project. No more was heard of it.

ONE OF THE THINGS that indicates the importance of the railways in the Italian psyche is how often they are chosen as a target in political and industrial protest. In the late nineties I remember looking up from my book on the way to Milan—in the company as always of the living dead—and noticing that the train was stationary. It was an unscheduled stop; we were sitting still in flat, open fields, poplars and pylons the only scenery. We could hear vehicles hooting and a rather odd background noise, something like the lowing of cattle. I stood up and pulled down my window. It *was* the lowing of cattle. A group of farmers had filled a field with tractors and driven a couple of cows onto the line to block the trains. Banners protested about EC milk quotas.

Time passed. Hanging out of the window, I saw that a TV camera had arrived. There were policemen, too, who seemed to be chatting to the farmers. Somebody banged down a window in a carriage farther up and started shouting insults. *"Comunisti! Fannulloni!* (Slackers) *Pagliacci!* (Clowns) *Merde!"* The farmers shouted back. There were gestures of the variety that rival fans exchange at the stadium: scorn, derision.

When the ticket inspector came by I asked him why the police weren't clearing the line. With a wry smile, he explained that there was friendly agreement among the railway unions, the farmers, and the police to let the farmers block each train for half an hour. After which they would let it by and block the next one. "It would be dangerous," he pointed out, "to put a cow on the track if the driver didn't know when and where to expect it. The animal could get killed."

So we had the classic Italian compromise, a theater of strife when all was actually agreed. Anarchy is rare in Italy, but legality is always up for renegotiation, especially if you can present yourself as hard done by, something farmers have a special vocation for. For every liter of milk, the EC guarantees European farmers about double the world market price; in return, the farmers must stay inside specific limits and not exploit the high price with overproduction. The farmers of northern Italy had vastly exceeded their EC milk quotas but did not want to pay the resulting fines. To encourage the Italian government to negotiate on their behalf, it seemed a good idea to block the trains passing through their fields.

For the next six weeks it became standard procedure to have the train stop in the middle of fields somewhere while the driver chatted to farmers and cows mooed at the passengers. The protesters put up large tents and sat at camping tables drinking from big bottles of wine while they watched us trapped on our Interregionali or Intercities. At times it was hard not to feel that train drivers, police, and TV cameramen were enjoying the situation. Every evening the TV dramatized our plight and spoke of the damage to the economy while continuing to sympathize with the farmers at the expense of supposedly obscure European rules. Eventually the government caved in, as it always does, went to Brussels, and got what the farmers wanted for them. What they promised in return I cannot recall, but I sincerely doubt they delivered. Italy is the most enthusiastic member of the EU and also the country most frequently condemned by the European Court for breaking EU rules. There is no contradiction. During the farmers' protest, travelers got so used to the whole affair that they took account of the half-hour milk-quota delay when planning their journey times.

———

MORE OFTEN THE PEOPLE holding up the trains will be the railway workers themselves, for there is almost never a time when they do not have an ongoing dispute with their employers.

As always the situation is complicated. Work contracts are negotiated for two- or three-year periods, after which they must be renewed. The government, however, and the large employers rarely renew the contract when it's due for renewal. Perhaps they only start negotiating at this point. So it's common to have situations where, officially, a contract has lapsed for as many as three or four years. The workers continue to be paid at the level of the old contract, and this puts pressure on the unions to accept a lower offer than they would have wanted; otherwise their workers will get no offer at all. The unions understand this and raise their initial demands accordingly.

Throughout the long negotiation period there will be regular one-day strikes to remind the employers that the situation is urgent. The all-out strike is almost never used in Italy; it is not in line with the feeling that everything can be negotiated, that the final weapon must always be held back.

The public is told no more than that the strikes are for renewal of contract, which of course sounds more reasonable than saying that people are striking for a wage rise. Since one is rarely aware of exactly what is at stake—a feeling apparently shared by many of the railway workers themselves—the strikes take on the characteristics of an act of God, something beyond your ken. Or simply a routine annoyance. Depending on people's political sympathies, they either support the workers unquestioningly, or speak about an Italy that will never be as "serious" as France or Germany.

One says "strike," but the word does not quite mean what it would elsewhere: that the trains aren't running, and that is that. Government and unions have negotiated a minimum service to be maintained during strikes. Again there is a sort of complicity in transgression, or rather a cooperation in noncooperation. The result is another of those ambiguous situations that Italians have such a flair for.

The strike is announced a week or two in advance, although it is also announced that it might be canceled or postponed, or that the government could declare it illegal. There is a telephone number you can call to find out which trains are running, but it is always busy. A poster goes up in Verona station, with a list of *i treni circolanti* in the event of strikes, a sort of strike timetable, as if a strike day was like a Sunday or a bank holiday. But the poster includes a caveat that maybe the trains won't be running after all.

Of course the whole thing is studied to cause maximum confusion while pretending to lessen the impact of the strike. My policy is always to go to the station and the hell with it. There's usually something running. In fact, I can't recall a single strike that has actually stopped me getting from Verona to Milan. It's a line with plenty of international trains and, as we've seen, it's important for the Italians to seem serious in the eyes of their French and Austrian neighbors. Most commuters take the day off, though. It's *un'assenza giustificata*, a legitimate absence. So the aim of the strike is achieved anyway, and without upsetting those who really want to travel. All in all, it's a rather elegant solution.

THE HILLS ABOVE BRESCIA are particularly gloomy. Looming mounds of gray-green vegetation scarcely cover a base of chalky limestone, giving the landscape an odd, threadbare look. Here and there the slopes are broken by the white scar of a quarry, its vertical face scored with horizontal lines. Shapelessness alternates with harsh geometry: shopping centers, cemeteries.

On the other side of the train, thousands of new VWs are parked in perfect symmetry across a vast area of tarmac, all covered by what looks like the same black netting they use to protect the cherry orchards. It's because of the hailstorms we get in summer. There are

factories mixed up with modern apartment blocks, the buildings all
askew to each other without managing to look quaint: towering industrial silos, rusting cylinders and storage tanks, kitchen gardens with
canes for runner beans, fig trees leaning on sagging fences.

A fat man in a white vest cleans his teeth on a balcony. There are
sheets hung out to air, terracotta and creosote, solar panels, corru-
gated iron. A tiny vineyard, just three rows of a dozen vines each, is
choked between two cathedral-size warehouses of prefabricated concrete panels. A smaller warehouse is derelict beside. Ivy crawls over
wooden pallets, broken masonry. It seems one doesn't dispose of the
old before getting on with the new in Italy.

A tractor toils in the mud around what must be a pile of hay bales
under a great white plastic sheet, but the thing has the shape and volume of a prehistoric burial mound. Used car tires hold down the plastic in case the wind blows. Just here and there, like postcards stuck on
a cluttered backdrop, fragments of the old picturesque Italy hang on:
a Baroque church facade up on the hillside, the ocher stucco of a villa
glowing in the morning sunshine, an avenue of cypresses leading no
doubt to cemetery gates.

Comes a powerful whiff of burned brake fluid and the train screeches
into Rovato. These are the satellite towns of Milan now. Chiari,
Romano, Treviglio. Chiari has pretty vine-covered facades to the left of
the train and a giant cement works on the other. More people push in.
Whole office staffs have formed at different ends of the carriage. Whole
university classes have assembled. People who are going to spend most
of the day together nevertheless need to talk things through on the
train. Somehow our red-booted prostitute is sleeping through it all.
She's used to difficult dormitory conditions. Again I wonder why she
has to travel like this. Do people not want sex where she lives?

AT ABOUT EIGHT THE phones begin to trill. The group beside me
passes a mobile around, chattering and laughing. The caller is one of

their company who is two carriages up the train but unable to push his way through the crowd to join them. "Excuses!" A bright young woman protests. "Who are you with? Tell the truth!" She's boldly made up, dressed in pink with pink handbag, pink and white sweater, pink and white bracelets. The friend sends a photograph through the phone to show how blocked the corridor is. Even the *capotreno* can't get through! Everybody is pleased to have found this use for the new technology.

Here and there someone manages to unfold a newspaper, the *Manifesto*, *Unità*, *Repubblica*. The left-wing papers are prevalent on the Interregionali. Somebody reads out an article about the iniquities of the present government. There's a general strike next week, so that's one day off work. On Friday, of course.

The train slows as it approaches Lambrate, the first station on Milan's subway system. This is the station where the Gypsies gather, on the southbound platform of the metro, the Green Line. They take over the stone bench opposite the last carriage when it arrives. There are three or four swarthy men, unwashed and unshaven, half a dozen women, one or two with babies in their arms, and a few adolescents, girls and boys. The boys have violins or accordions. Often they have painted nails, sometimes even lipstick. The girls have an infant in tow. As each train comes and goes, one or two Gypsies get on it. They start at the back carriage and work their way forward, the men in scruffy waistcoats playing their musical instruments, the women begging in their long dresses, repeating their mournful spiel over and over in a high-pitched monotone.

"*SIGNORE E SIGNORI! SCUSATE IL DISTURBO!* I AM A POOR IMMIGRANT FROM ALBANIA, WITH FOUR CHILDREN TO FEED, *WITHOUT* A HOUSE, *WITHOUT* A JOB, *WITHOUT* MONEY, *WITHOUT* FOOD, *WITHOUT* DRINK, *PER FAVORE, SIGNORI, PER FAVORE.*"

The word *senza*, without, is given a queer emphasis, almost sung, as if in a dirge. *SENZA CASA, SENZA SOLDI.* But what these Gypsy women are really without is conviction. They beg bored, zombielike, as if not expecting anyone to believe them. This sort of lament is necessary, they appear to be saying, but only insofar as it establishes a narrative that allows some people to part with their cash. The givers need have no illusions that the recipients are telling the truth.

The Gypsy men, too, have little conviction when they launch into the one or two tunes they know on their out-of-tune violins. "Alla Turca," massacred. A little boy sways through the carriage with a collecting cap. He knows exactly how long to stand before each passenger to create the maximum pathos. Sometimes I have seen the same boy playing the violin himself, entirely on his own in the press of the metro, the din of the train occasionally drowning out his abysmal renderings. Then he passes with his cap. On occasion I get out at the first station and move up a carriage to escape the noise, but invariably the Gypsies follow me at the next station and I have to listen to their grim performance all over again. Better just to hear it the first time and be done. As a rule they work the Green Line down to its southern end, then take the train back and spill out onto the platform at Lambrate for a break. No sooner do they stop begging than they cheer up at once.

Sometimes you'll see the same Gypsies begging on the train. They come into your compartment, place some trinket on the seat beside you without a word, then return a few moments later, hoping you will buy it. But on the train they face stiff competition from the new wave of immigrants from Africa, and I get the impression that at least around Milan the Gypsies prefer the metro.

At Verona station there is a local boy in his teens who will climb on the train and start selling you a story about having lost his wallet and needing money to get back to his parents in Turin. The first time I gave him some money. Later, when I pointed out to him that he had tried the same tale on me three times in less than six months and that since his accent was Veronese it was hard to believe he lived in Turin, he became quite aggressive, as if it were unreasonable of me to expect him to think of something new every day, or to pay attention to the kind of detail that might concern a novelist.

The Indian immigrants sell roses at the traffic lights near the station. That's in the evening, when you're returning. They never beg, but offer a bunch of six or seven roses for only €5. It's a bargain. Sometimes I go for it. Sometimes I wonder if there is any connection between this flower-selling and the prostitutes standing on duty nearby. Do some men buy their regular girl a rose?

The Chinese sell a variety of cheap jewelry and pirated designer goods which they spread on sheets and rugs in the entry tunnels to the metro at Milano Centrale. Sometimes there are as many as twenty Chinese peddlers in the tunnels here as you hurry back to the station after a day at the university. They squat on their haunches quietly chatting to each other, ready to gather up their wares in the rug if the police come to bother them. They can be gone with all their clobber in seconds. Sometimes, with all the commuters and all the blankets spread on the floor, it's hard to find your way through.

ONCE, ABOUT TWO YEARS ago, I helped a Chinese man join this little community at Milano Centrale. My wife and I were setting off for a walk in our small village just outside Verona when we saw an Asian man looking anxiously about him in the tiny central piazza. It was the first immigrant we had ever seen in Novaglie. He was tall, in his late twenties perhaps, heavily built, and clearly, to risk a pun, disoriented. He wore a smart gray suit that looked as if it had fallen on him from a great height. His shoes were too big. He carried no bag. As we walked toward him, he looked at us anxiously, undecided whether to talk, then turned and hurried away. We saw him knocking on one of the doors that open directly on the street. Then another. Then another. People were pretending not to be home.

When we returned from our walk the man was still hanging around in what is an amorphous, depressing little piazza: no more than a bus stop, a few containers for recycling bottles and paper, and a low, pre-fabricated gymnasium. The one or two older and finer buildings are hidden, as so often in Italy, behind high walls and cypress hedges. The man looked more anxious now. He was quite dark-skinned for an Asian. I went to speak to him.

"Posso aiutare?"

He didn't understand.

"English?" I asked. "Can I help?"

"Mi-la-no," he said.

"Parlez-vous français? Deutsch?"

"Mi-la-no," he repeated.

"This isn't Milan," I said. "We're a hundred miles from Milan." Then, inspired, I suggested, *"Char.* You want char?" I had remembered that "char," a word we used for tea in northern England as children, actually came from Chinese.

He nodded eagerly.

We drove the man into town. He moved the way I would no doubt move if someone had suddenly asked me to walk around a strange town in a turban or a kimono. In the first bar in the suburbs I bought him tea and a hamburger. I remember being struck by the practiced way he shook the sugar packet before opening it. It was the first gesture he had made with ease. Packets rather. He must have taken four. He ate his hamburger and drank his sickly tea without a word, making no attempt to discover what my plans for him might be, trusting entirely to my good intentions.

There is a small monastery on this side of town known for its charity. "Don't go to the police," the monks said. They will send him straight back to wherever he came from. He had probably been pushed out of a container truck, they thought, driving into Italy from Croatia. "They cross the border in the middle of the night," a monk explained, "drive for a few hours, then push their passengers out one by one in the most deserted places. He's probably walked quite a long way."

"He wants to go to Milan," I said. They shook their heads. They couldn't help. Then my wife said, "Take him to a Chinese restaurant."

There are only two or three Chinese restaurants in Verona. I'm not a fan of Chinese food. I drove him to the nearest, a garish place at the bottom of an amorphous block of flats. The manager was young, smartly dressed in a light gray suit quite similar to that of the new arrival but worn with panache. Immediately the anxious face of my young man became animated and adult. The two spoke together very rapidly in businesslike tones. They shared a language. Suddenly the restaurant owner pulled a €100 note from his pocket and handed it to the man.

Take him to the station, he told me, and put him on a train to Milan.

"But does he know where to go when he gets there?"

"He is to meet some people in the station. They are expecting him. In return, if you take him, I will give you and your family a free meal."

I had no desire to eat Chinese, and the station was twenty minutes' drive away. Nevertheless, I took the new arrival, stood in line with him at the ticket window, paid for an Intercity ticket to Milan, had it stamped for him (the last thing he needed was a brush with the inspector), and took him to the right platform. I wondered if he had any idea how much his €100 note was worth. The generosity of the restaurant owner had surprised and rather humbled me.

As the train came into the station, the man started saying something in his language. He was smiling now from a very round, slightly pockmarked face. He seemed excited. I shook my head. He mimed a person speaking on the phone, and then writing something. I wrote down my phone number for him. He never got in touch. It seems there are scores of Chinese people living in the old service tunnels under Milano Centrale. Everybody complains: these people are stealing our work, our culture. Yet faced with the plight of the individual immigrant, Italians are far more likely to help than to report the man to the police and have him deported. However reluctant Italians are to embrace a multiracial society, the old antipathy to government and authority works in favor of the illegal alien.

———

IT'S CURIOUS; YOU SEE so much of Italy's new immigrant life revolving around the railways, you see Indian families on the move with all their belongings, you see the prostitutes and their pimps with their colorful shirts, you see Arabs and Turks opening kebab joints in station car parks, but you never see an immigrant working for Trenitalia.

As you drive your car along the riverside, the Adige, hurrying to the station for the train of the living dead, you can't help but notice, even as early as six in the morning, a long queue of black, brown, yellow, and, yes, white faces standing by a tall iron gate. It is the Questura, the police headquarters. They are immigrants looking for permits. Enjoying almost full employment, Veronese businesses need immigrants, they need cheap labor. But why do these people have to stand in line so early, even on the coldest of winter mornings? And why do we never see them driving buses, or checking tickets on trains?

The answer to the first question can only be the usual indifference of any branch of the Italian bureaucracy to those they supposedly serve. It's quite normal for public offices to open for only a few hours on only two or three days a week. You are always a supplicant, never a customer.

As to why the immigrants are not working for public transport, the truth is that all state and public sector jobs require an end-of-school certificate, *il certificato scolastico*. From an Italian school, of course. Whenever one admires the homogeneity and apparent dignity of a society like Italy's, a society that has retained a cohesion and identity largely lost in England or the metropolitan United States, one must always remember that it is constructed around such mechanisms of exclusion as the school certificate. Those immigrants who have not studied in Italian schools will not be permitted to collect Italian garbage, or drive Italian buses, or sell tickets for the train of the living dead. The unions, so ready to strike and raise their voices about everything else, do not seem to make a fuss about this. It will be interesting to see what happens in the next few years as the immigrants' children complete their studies. It will be a great day when a black *capotreno* tries to fine me for not having had my ticket punched.

THE RAILS AROUND US multiply and switch over each other as lines from all directions are gathered together for the final mile to Milano Centrale. For perhaps five minutes the train plays at going as slowly as a train can without actually stopping. All around us there are overpasses, gritty playgrounds, tenements. Graffiti everywhere. *"Evviva la figa!"* someone has written. Long live pussy.

As the train pulls into Lambrate, the prostitute sleeps. I put my book in my bag. There's an extraordinary tension for me in these last moments of the journey as the Interregionale grinds to a stop on another ordinary day of my life. The world appears to be suspended; for a few awful seconds you can't help but be aware of the horror of routine, the days and years bleeding into a past as cluttered and unstructured as this railway landscape. Nobody else seems concerned. Two girls are teasing a third over a new tattoo she has, a little rose just above her bare hip. They touch it with manicured fingertips. The flesh is firm and brown. "Let me see," red tie demands, but now the train jolts to a stop and everybody is piling off. Nothing could be slower than the Interregionale on that last half mile into Centrale. Better take the metro at Lambrate.

Chapter 2

MILANO–VERONA

IF COMING TO MILAN I GET OFF MY INTERREGIONALE AT LAM-
brate, returning I board whatever train I take at Centrale. Because it's
convenient, and because I love going through Centrale. In particular,
I love entering it, being outside it, and moving inside, for this is surely
the most monumental railway station in Western Europe. More than
anywhere I know, Milano Centrale gives the traveler the impression
that he really must be setting out on a very serious journey. This is a
trifle comic when you hurry through the colossal central portal and
across the majestic ticket hall as a matter of routine. You should be setting off to Berlin, or Paris, or even some other world or dimension, and
instead here you are worrying about whether the ticket lines are too
long to pick up a few *supplementi* Intercity for Verona Porta Nuova.

Contrary to popular belief, the station was not dreamed up by the
Fascists. The design, by a certain Ulisse Stacchini, dates back to 1912,
ten years before the March on Rome. But the project was interrupted
by the First World War, and by the time the funds were there to resume
it, the Fascists were in power and the look of the thing was somewhat
altered. It's the massive volumes of the stone spaces combined with

the highly stylized ornamentation that create the special Centrale effect. As you approach the main entrance from the piazza, two solemn horses bow their necks to greet you from forty feet above. Inside the ticket hall, and again high, high above your head, dozens of statues and friezes of classical warriors, their swords, shields, and lances in action, alternate with Liberty-like bas-reliefs of trains and planes and buses. It's Fascism's double gesture of looking back to the glory that was Rome and forward to some unimaginably efficient, technological Italy of the future. Aesthetically, at least in this space of grayish-white stone with colored marble and granite inserts, it works wonderfully.

But you see all this beauty only if you lift your eye. And it's amazing how rarely the eye lifts when you are commuting. "Each man fixed his eyes before his feet," T. S. Eliot said of the crowd flowing over London Bridge. It's no different in Milano Centrale. It was years before I noticed the zodiac signs in bas-relief all up one wall of the ticket hall. To make it even less likely that you will really see the building, its grand spaces are being invaded and broken up by aggressive advertising campaigns involving huge poster panels suspended from the high ceiling to swing only a little way above eye level.

At the moment Coca-Cola has taken over the entrance to the station with a score of towering images so brightly colored that the delicate grays and browns of the stone facade seem as invisible as wet asphalt in twilight. Inside the ticket hall, Naomi Campbell mirrors herself everywhere; twenty feet high in various glossily aggressive poses she shows just how long a girl's legs can be when she wears a short, tight skirt. I forget the manufacturer's name. So the archetypal images that were to establish a sense of Italian nationhood, of continuity from past to present and from present to future, are eclipsed by fizzy drinks and fashion goods. A sticky film of postmodern parody wraps around everything that was supposed to be uplifting, majestic. It's curious to think that Mussolini, who was so enthusiastic about this station, was a sworn enemy of international capitalism, and that when the Americans occupied Rome what distressed him most was the thought that black-skinned soldiers should have captured and, as he saw it, defiled the monuments of ancient empire. I imagine Il Duce, after his summary execution, passing through that portal over which is written "Abandon all hope ye who enter here"—perhaps the design (for even the gates of hell must have an architect) is not so different from that of Milano Centrale—only to find an advertising campaign for canned soda featuring the gorgeously dark Naomi Campbell.

IT WAS IN THIS magnificent concourse, some years ago, that I had my bag stolen. Needing to make a phone call, in premobile days, I stopped at a pay phone and put my bag down at my feet. The phones are criminally riveted to the brown marble coping. It's sheer vandalism. I dialed, I listened. Someone was running by. I turned my head to see a young man charging off with a bag, quite a heavy bag to judge by the way it was banging against his leg, the way his body twisted as he ran. *"Pronto?"* A voice inquired. "Rita?" Already the figure was lost in the crowd by the newspaper kiosk, at which point I realized that that bag was mine. Damn! My old black bag!

The following morning, convinced that no one would have wanted to go far with my students' theses, a set of proofs, three volumes of Leopardi's *Zibaldone*, and a change of underclothing, I returned to Milan early to see if, abandoned perhaps, the bag might have been handed in as lost property.

While the lower hall of the station is an austere cathedral space across which a stream of travelers constantly flows from metro to escalators, the upper concourse is an interminable and confused milling among shops and bars and platforms as people wait for trains to appear, or try to find a machine that's working to stamp their tickets, or even a place to lie down and sleep. There's a constant attrition between the commuters who know how to use the station and move with brutal directness between platform and escalators, and the tour-

ists heaving their preposterous bags this way and that in sleepy bewil-
derment. I couldn't find a Lost Property Office.

Eventually I knocked on the window of a glass cubicle with a
policeman behind. Much of Milano Centrale is cluttered with cubicles
and kiosks and nondescript cabins that seem to have been produced
by a later and lesser civilization than the one that built the station, as if
for the past thirty years we had merely been camping in the remnants
of an older, nobler time. But that's true of much of Italy.

Two policemen were smoking, watching a small gray screen. They
allowed me to open the door without their going for their guns.

"Assuming someone found a discarded bag," I asked, "where
would he take it?"

"A bag?"

"My bag was stolen."

They were not so much impolite as uninterested. "Why would anyone pick up a discarded bag?"

"They might feel some sympathy for the person who had lost it," I
suggested.

It was an interesting idea.

"I suppose they might bring it here," one of the two eventually said.
They were southern boys with strong necks and sleek, hard, seal-like
heads. They had a sort of animal arrogance in being young and strong,
and above all native. They had spotted my accent.

And has anyone?

They looked idly about them. The cabin was a tiny space resting
against one of the station's great stone pillars between shops and platforms. There were ashtrays, newspapers, and bits of old-fashioned
electronics.

"Doesn't look like it."

I have learned to wait in these kinds of conversations, not to seem
impatient, just stand and wait. Eventually one of them said:

"Someone might have taken it to Left Luggage."

"Left Luggage? But why would they do that? Isn't there a Lost Property Office?"

The Italian expression is *oggetti smarriti*. Objects mislaid. But *smarrito* can also mean puzzled, bewildered.

Again I had to wait. It's this quiet refusal to go away that seems to do the trick with Italian officials. Insistence breeds opposition, and friendliness, contempt; only a dogged patience allows them to do their duty without feeling put upon.

"*Naturalmente*," one of them told me, as if this were quite a different subject. I should have asked at once. "Platform three, at the end on the left. It's the entrance that says Railway Personnel Only, up the stairs, second floor.

I set off. Platform three is the last platform to the left as you emerge at the top of the stairs at platform level, platforms one and two being almost outside the station proper. Along the side of the platform are a row of tall, elegant stone facades, though you're still well inside the great curved glass roof that shelters trains and passengers. Railway Personnel Only, I reflected; how would anyone ever know to take a lost bag to a place that says Railway Personnel Only?

On the ground floor there was some kind of common room for the station staff. The stone floor, the old glass-and-wood fittings seemed not to have been altered since the station was inaugurated in 1931. But here and there, there were wires tacked and taped to the walls and incongruous light switches, even a flame-red fire extinguisher.

I climbed the stairs. It was the sort of stone stairway you expect to find in an old library or town hall. The plaster on the walls was turning to powder. Sure enough, on the second floor, one of four old wooden doors, all much in need of varnish, bore the legend OGGETTI SMAR-RITI, and a detailed account of opening hours, different, it seemed for every day of the week. When knocking brought no answer, I pushed the door.

A big gloomy space was piled with bags, boxes, suitcases, parcels, umbrellas. There were a few shelves but no apparent order. Some of the bags seemed to have been left where they had been dropped. It was the sort of place horror-film directors dream of, or playwrights of the absurd, a place of the soul, in limbo.

I looked around, eyes adjusting to the low light. The room was very quiet, an effect that seemed to be intensified by the distant metallic announcements of departing and arriving trains. *"C'è nessuno?"* I called. *"C'è nessuno?"*

After a few moments there was a rustling noise. A man emerged from a gray door just visible over piles of old luggage. He found his way through to me, a man in his late fifties perhaps, craggy, in dungarees, defensive.

"I lost my bag."

"What kind?"

I described it.

"There are hundreds of bags like that." He gestured to the quiet piles. Judging by the dust, many of them had been there for some time. "People lose all kinds of things," he said. "You wouldn't believe it."

"My bag was stolen," I told him.

"Well, it won't be here, then," he said. He laughed: "A thief doesn't bring a bag to lost property."

"I thought, if the thief dumped it, someone might have handed it in."

He said nothing.

"Yesterday," I offered.

"No black bags handed in today," he said.

I waited.

"Or yesterday. A bit soon perhaps. Try again."

It wasn't an invitation.

Retreating, it occurred to me that I should have asked how on earth these *oggetti smarriti* came to be handed in, or recovered, for that matter, given that there was no indication of a Lost Property Office in the station. I thought of going back and having it out with him. What on earth was going on? How long had those bags been there? Since the war? But the whole experience had had a troubling effect on me: the lost bags and boxes, the wasted hours and years of their custodian. *"Non esiste,"* I whispered. I decided to forget my bag, trusting that my students would have backup copies of their theses on their computers.

IN CENTRALE'S TICKET HALL, and on the upper concourse, the Slav immigrants, who never sell things like the Africans or the Chinese, or beg like the Gypsies, hang around the ticket machines. I left out the machines when I talked about ticket buying. About the same height and width as a four-drawer filing cabinet, these machines are also advertised with the red neon logo FastTicket, and they always huddle together in groups of three or four, as if for mutual protection. People do tend to get angry with them. For the miracle of these machines with their touch-sensitive computer screens is that they reproduce all, or almost all, the complications that one can come across when purchasing a ticket in Italy.

You touch the screen and are told to choose a language. Images of flags, German, French, British, apparently wrapped round globelike balls, help you make your choice. You touch it again to let it know whether you want information or a ticket. A list of a dozen major destinations are immediately proposed, but if you want to travel anywhere else you must touch OTHER. An alphabet appears. You start touching the appropriate letters. V-E-R-O. With each addition, you home in on a smaller list of stations. Now you must choose between Verona Porta Nuova and Verona Porta Vescovo. There is no indication for the uninitiated as to which might be the main station.

When you have chosen your destination, you are asked what date you plan to travel. Today, tomorrow, or some time in the future. A calendar appears. You can buy a ticket for months ahead. With that choice behind you, a timetable appears, a list of trains of all different kinds at different hours. You touch your train. First class or second? Do you want to reserve a seat? A window seat? A corridor? And what kind of ticket do you want, what kind of reductions are you eligible for? Hesitate too long and the screen will return to its default setting. I have seen first-timers on the brink of tears.

So just as for any bureaucratic adventure in Italy—registering a car purchase, getting a Christmas parcel through customs—there is always some private agency willing, at a price, to step in and remove the anxiety of a direct confrontation with a public service employee, so at the railway station young Slav boys and girls will offer to mediate between you and a ticket machine programmed by a public service employee.

A polite twelve-year-old with a strong accent offers to work the ticket screen for a confused *signora*. She is bejeweled and smart in a frilly, old-fashioned, southern way, with hair permed to a helmet and powdery wrinkles. He has a thin little nose, clear skin, and shrewd, darting black eyes. *"Grazie,"* she says, for he has already stepped in.

"Where you go?"

"Salerno."

How quickly the boy's fingers move over the screen with its rapidly dissolving numbers and colors!

"Train in twenty minutes. You want return?"

His Italian is terrible, but he works the machine so fast it's hard to keep up.

"You want the first class? You pay cash?"

"Si?"

Cash! Incredibly, the woman hands the boy *a €50 note* to feed into the machine. And he feeds it in! I had feared the worst. At the end of all this, he hopes there will be a tip for him, of course. Anyone who understands these machines deserves one. Or perhaps, since you can purchase these tickets with a credit card, he wouldn't be unhappy if someone hurried off leaving an American Express in the slot; the mechanism doesn't oblige you to reclaim the card before delivering the ticket.

The boy feeds in the €50 note, then gathers the change that clatters into the returned coins tray below. Politely, he hands it, *all of it*, to the *signora*. She leaves him €1. He smiles and makes a small bow. I feel humbled by such trust and generosity. Why am I so suspicious? Alas, with all their complications, their apparent covering of every base, the machines don't offer Intercity *supplementi* separate from Intercity tickets, and so a man who has an annual season ticket for the Interregionale but wishes to make his return journey on an Intercity is condemned to the ticket windows. And if the lines are too long he may end up going home on a slow old Interregionale after all.

SINCE I OFTEN ARRIVE at the station shortly before seven in the evening and won't be home till nine, I'm often tempted to grab a bite. What's on offer at Milano Centrale? There's the FREE SHOP, the SELF BAR, the stand-up café (with one counter inside and one counter out), and the traditional, sit-down, table-service café. What the FREE in FREE SHOP refers to is anyone's guess. Perhaps it has the same significance as the star in Eurostar. You enter through a tight, brightly chromed turnstile and at once face one of those Italian situations that are so character-forming. Arranged around a corner is a long counter selling a wide variety of freshly made sandwiches. A crowd forms along the whole counter, or rather mills around the apex of the corner like a busy eddy in a rough river. There is no question of a proper line. Perhaps the FREE stands for free-for-all, you think. Behind the counter are two acned and bewildered youngsters, one replenishing the sandwiches, one serving the customers. He or she who shouts loudest is served first, regardless of when he or she arrived—unless, that is, the person serving takes a dislike to you. You have overdone it. You have offended him in some way. Then you could be stuck here for a while.

The proper approach is to assume the face of one who is harassed, about to miss a train, and yet absolutely understanding of the pressure the server is under. Above all, never waste time with questions about what's in the sandwiches. The short, sharp, polite request, even over the heads of a dozen others, is always rewarded. I have become an expert.

"Ciabatta con crudo!" I shout. *"Per favore!"*

And I'm gone!

The SELF BAR is another interesting use of English. What it amounts to is a posh-looking vending machine—there's one on every platform—about three yards long by six feet high, oval in shape, with food products on one side and drinks on the other. Presumably the designers were aware that the English expression is self-service, but of the two words they clearly felt the positive one was *self.* I have an aversion to buying food from machines. The only thing that seems to get eaten is my money. I pass by. I do not even examine what's on offer. No doubt I'm old-fashioned.

Which leaves the two cafés. For any curious traveler, the large, table-service bar at the end of the upper concourse (on the far right as you emerge from the stairs) is a must for understanding the abyss in Italy between the private and public sectors, a psychological as much as an economic abyss.

I think I can say without fear of contradiction that in general there is no city in the world where the coffee experience is better arranged than in Milan. The barmen in the thousands of small cafés around the town are never temps, or students, or would-be actors going through hard times. They know how to make coffee. That's their life. Above all, they know exactly the consistency and temperature that the foam on a cappuccino should have.

At the small bar on the busy circular road near the university where I teach, the barman sprinkles chocolate on your espresso and with a deft wriggle of his wrist as he pours in the foam has the most elegant patterns appear: spirals, roses, concentric circles. "Every cappuccino I make," he tells me earnestly, "must be the best the customer has ever drunk."

This man—in his early thirties, I'd guess—is at home in his job.

He knows all his customers, their likes and dislikes. He is not studying to become a computer programmer or trying to write a novel or taking days off for theater auditions. He works very fast and can talk soccer or politics as he does so. He's an Inter supporter. When you take your cup from his hands you can feel sure that the next few minutes will be exactly the break you were after. And all this is done without that horrible pretension that hangs around the celebrated coffeehouses of Paris with their silly red awnings and clutter of wicker chairs. In Milan, at street level at least, everything is natural, busy, fast, and right.

The station is different. The large old bar here occupies the whole of one end of the upper concourse. GRAN BAR, it is unimaginatively called. The letters are a yard high and illuminated from behind by neon, but the white plastic is grubby and fading. Beneath the letters is a long horizontal line of neon, with a blue-and-yellow pattern, designed to imitate an awning (actually it took me quite a while to realize that this must have been the desired effect).

Unlike all the other outlets in the station, the Gran Bar does not present itself as an intruder, a kiosk camping in a mausoleum, but as an integral part of the original design. So its floor is the same gray stone floor of the whole upper concourse, and shining down from its ceiling are two huge glass chandeliers, each with thirty or forty lightbulbs, artifacts that might well have been in vogue when the station was built.

It sounds promising, doesn't it? There should be a bar in grand style, you feel, in a station of this grandeur. And why *not* call it Gran Bar, in the end? The waiters wear white uniforms, and this, too, is as it should be. I'm willing to pay a little more for uniformed waiter service, for luxury and comfort and liveried whiteness.

Alas, few experiences could be more depressing than the Gran Bar at Milano Centrale. The last refurbishment, in a reddish-orange with black lines, is looking seedy now. The smeary glass window through which you can gaze out into the station is set in decaying ironwork.

The illuminated adverts for ice cream and soda seem to refer to the products of a decade ago.

For a bar meant for table service there are remarkably few tables over a very large surface area, as if perhaps the important thing was to be able to pass easily between them with some cleaning machine. And the tables are small, with yellow tablecloths and incongruous plastic chairs of a dark plum color. The gray floor dominates. Pigeons slither across it, perfectly camouflaged. The few clients are almost all elderly people on their own. Can they really be here to catch a train, you wonder? They seem to be people who have fallen out of time. Perhaps the ghosts who haunt empty trains are allowed to meet here for their coffee breaks.

As you enter, there's the till to your left. Aggressive notices warn the clients that they mustn't bring their own food into the café, or order at the bar and then carry their drinks over to the tables. But of course everyone knows this anyway. Almost at once you realize that the staff is hostile. A sort of poison gas pollutes the atmosphere. They don't want you to be here. They have nothing to gain by your presence. Sit at a table and you risk waiting far too long. Go to the bar and you find you need to pick up a receipt at the till first. If you want to eat, you must first go to the bar to examine what's on offer, then back to the till by the door to describe it and pay for it, then back to the bar with your receipt to try to catch the attention of barmen who are barely polite.

As I wave my receipt in the direction of two men behind the bar—vainly, alas—a young woman beside me complains that she asked for a macchiato and has been given a straightforward espresso. Instead of apologizing and rectifying the mistake with a quick dash of foamy milk, the man complains that she *didn't* ask for a macchiato. He's a southerner, in his fifties, with a supercilious curl to his lip, and a little white hat worn at an angle that suggests he doesn't want to be wearing it.

"Actually, I ordered from your colleague," the woman says, and he shouted the order to you. "He definitely said macchiato."

The woman is patient, rather pretty, with pale skin, full cheeks, and raven hair.

"Oh, we want to be unpleasant, do we?" the waiter asks. "Had a hard day, have we?"

The woman closes her eyes and very slowly shakes her head from side to side. The waiter's colleague, a greenhorn, hurries for the milk jug.

What's fascinating here is how the same nation produces such contrasting stereotypes: the resentful, slow, station barmen in the shabby, ill-kept public space, where everything is difficult and unhappy, and the bright and bushy-tailed figure, working twice as hard but cheerful with it in the busy street bar. I'm sure, for example, that the same man, if moved from one environment to another, would change his manner entirely. The quality of his conversation, his dress habits, and above all his cappuccino would be utterly transformed.

Perhaps the deciding factor is not just the business of having a public or private employer with all that entails in terms of job security (and hence freedom to gripe) in the public sector, and more cash under the table (assuming you work your butt off) in the private. No, perhaps it's more a question of the kind of clientele the different places attract.

The barman in the small street bar has the privileged feeling of being at the center of a community. He loves to know all his customers' names, and better still, their jobs. He loves to give you a flattering title as you walk through the door, and to call it out loud right across the bar so that everybody will hear. *"Salve, Professore!"* all three barmen cry when I walk into the bar near the university. In this way everybody present knows who they are rubbing elbows with. *"Buon giorno, Prof,"* says the quieter barman on Via Gustavo Modena near where I sometimes stay the night. How he knows I'm a professor I have no idea. They call to other customers, too. *"Buon giorno, Dottore! Salve Ragioniere! Ciao Capo!"* Someone is filling in his lottery card. "Play eleven, Dottore," calls the barman. "The number of the month of the dead always brings good luck." "Not for a cardiologist!" the man replies. Everybody laughs. "*Sciocchezze, Dottore!*" Their voices are a pleasant mix of respect and light irony. And if you greet them warmly and share a word or two about Inter's tribulations and above all never forget to bid them good day when you leave, they will always serve you well.

This leads inevitably to the reflection that the person who is just passing through is always a second-class citizen in Italy. The barmen in the Gran Bar in Centrale resent the fact that they see most of their customers only once. They will never know their names and occupations; hence, in a certain sense, these people *non esistono*, they don't really exist. Only their money proves they were here. Or worse still, their vandalism. For the casual visitor cannot be expected to show the same respect for his environment as the person who must return. Chairs are knocked over, surfaces are scratched and scribbled on.

Away from the bar, in the street and the workplace, this resistance to the bird of passage is one of the greatest hurdles that the immigrant to Italy has to overcome. One of the most common questions still asked me by new Italian acquaintances is, "When are you going back [to England]?" Recently, when the local newspapers felt that I had said something about Verona that I shouldn't have, the mayor of the town publicly declared, "Visitors to our city should be careful what they say." The lady in question is also an MP for the European Parliament. She was aware that I had been living in Verona for upward of twenty years. I pay my taxes.

SO MORE OFTEN THAN not I get my sandwich and bottle of water from the small stand-up bar in the center of the concourse. I don't go inside, where you have to pay first and take your receipt to the three barmen chattering and griping around the coffee machines. Outside there is a small stand with just half a dozen kinds of sandwiches and drinks. No coffee. Nothing fancy. This place is constantly manned by just one busy person. I know all four of the people who work here. It's intriguing how much more generous and cheerful they have become now that they recognize me. *Piadina e acqua naturale*, I ask. But they saw me coming, they already have the bottle on the counter, the sandwich in the toasting machine. The piadina is a round of pita bread folded over a wodge of *prosciutto crudo* and soft Fontina cheese. They smile while they wait for it to heat up. They tell me which are the busy moments and which the slack. There is a tall, vigorous man in his forties, completely bald with a shiny scalp, and three women, all friendly and serious. Some places are so unpromising to look at and so appealing when you become a regular.

OFTEN I TAKE MY piadina to one of the stone benches on the platforms and eat to the sound of the station announcements. Many of the trains have such splendid names—Ludovico Sforza, Andrea Dorea—that it's really a pleasure to listen to them. Leonardo da Vinci, Tiepolo, Giorgione, Michelangelo. These are not the names of the actual, physical, locomotives, nor of any particular carriages, just the name announced when whatever rolling stock is being used for such and such a route at such and such a time approaches the station. The Brenner Express, the Gianduia. It's the name, as it were, of the event that is this train.

The station announcements are prerecorded in segments and then tacked together, presumably by computer, as appropriate. As a result, the words come in little mechanical rushes—*di-prima-e-seconda-classe*—pause—*con-servizio-di-ristorante-e-minibar*— pause—and then a dramatic flourish when one of the big train names is pronounced— *MICHELANGELO!—VIVALDI!* Apparently it was impossible for whoever recorded the initial pool of information not to read out such glorious names without intense and understandable pride.

The same goes for the names of one or two of the big city stations. At the announcement of Genova Piazza Principe or Venezia Santa Lucia, for example, there's a sudden increase of volume and urgency that cuts through the monotonous flatness of the PA system. So a typical afternoon announcement at Milano Centrale, listing the train number, name, and details of its time and platform of departure and destinations, echoes around the huge old building thus:

> *Intercity—Sei—Zero—Otto—***UGO FOSCOLO!***—di-prima-e-sec-onda-classe—delle ore—sedici—e—zero cinque—conserviziodiris-toranteeminibar—per—***Venezia Santa Lucia!***—è in partenza dal binario—***quattordici***—si ferma a—Brescia—Desenzano—Peschiera—Verona Porta Nuova—San Bonifacio—Vicenza—Padova—e—***Mestre***—carrozze di prima classe in settori—B—e—C.*

It's curious in these announcements how one has to listen to all kinds of information that is absolutely standard for all Intercities (first and second class, buffet, minibar, etc.) before they tell you where the thing is actually going. People stand on the platforms in rapt attention, waiting patiently for the only two pieces of information that matter: the destination and the platform. For who has any notion of the code numbers of the trains, or even their names? And since no one pays any attention to this information, but again no one complains about having to listen to it, you can only assume that these formulas have taken on a sort of liturgical function, not unlike the repetition of the names Hang Seng and Dow Jones in more or less every news bulletin, as if any of us cares what the Hang Seng had done this morning or might do tomorrow. This constant, reliable, decorous repetition perhaps transmits to the harassed passenger the sensation that, rather than simply heading home a little the worse for wear after another dull day at the workplace, he is in fact part of some grandiose, never-ending ceremony. This is not such a zany idea in the lofty temple that is Milano Centrale.

Maybe because I spoke almost no Italian when I first came to live in Italy, there are certain words I actually learned from hearing railway station announcements, words that remain forever associated in my mind with le Ferrovie dello Stato. *Anziché*, for example, and *coincidenza*.

Anziché can occasionally be heard at the end of a prerecorded announcement. They'll read out the whole spiel of your train description, its name, number, various services, and stops, and right at the end, just when you thought all was well, you'll hear, "*partirà dal— binario—nove—anziché dal—binario—tre.*" Platform nine *instead of* platform three. What you thought was going to happen, isn't. Routine is interrupted. The folks on platform three begin to trudge back to the concourse.

I don't know why but I have a special affection for *anziché*. There is something elegant and measured about it, like a person who keeps calm in a crisis. I'm always glad to hear *anziché*. I repeat it to myself under my breath. And when I hear it in other circumstances I always think of changing platforms.

Coincidenza is often heard together with *anziché*, but this time the voice will be alive, urgent, a real person speaking into the microphone. Something is happening right now.

Coincidenza is a curious word with a number of meanings. It can mean coincidence, in the sense of two things corresponding in some way, or happening at the same time, though it's not often used in the English way to suggest that a certain potentially significant happening was actually pure chance. For that the Italians say *caso*. *È stato un puro caso.*

When talking trains, *coincidenza* can be the word used for a connection. In Milan the train for Venezia waits for the train from Genova to arrive (maybe!) so that people can make their *coincidenza*. People love to complain about their *coincidenze bestiali*—nightmare connections. But the word is mostly used to announce a sudden and altogether unexpected development that requires an urgent response.

"*Coincidenza, coincidenza!*" Suddenly a young woman's voice is speaking directly to us through the PA. She's husky, anxious. The liturgical calm of the recorded voice is gone. "*Coincidenza! Interregionale per Verona parte da binario sei, anziché da binario quattro. Il treno è in partenza. Il treno è in partenza.*" Since it's not unheard of that they'll announce a train as *in partenza*, about to depart, when in fact it's already moving, it's gone, the *coincidenza* announcement can cause panic and is often immediately followed by this warning: "Passengers are reminded that it is *forbidden* to cross the lines! It is *forbidden* to cross the lines." And in fact four or five young people have jumped down from the platforms onto the lines. They are running across. Every year one or two people will lose their lives crossing rails.

Even more ominous than *anziché* and *coincidenza* is the dreaded word *soppresso*. On strike days, despite the fact that maybe 80 percent of the trains aren't running, they nevertheless broadcast all the mechanical announcements absolutely as usual; the whole daily timetable is sung out as on any other day, with the sole difference that at the end of each train description, the simple word *soppresso* is tagged on, in a rather louder voice than the rest. So you might hear:

Interregionale—Quattro—nove—due—di-prima-e-seconda-classe—delle ore—otto—e—cinquantacinque per—Milano Centrale! —è—SOPPRESSO!

Canceled.

Sometimes five or six trains will be conjured into existence, one after another by the famous mechanical voice, only to be brutally dismissed: *SOPPRESSO!*

It's amusing watching the uninitiated tourist trying to get to grips with this. They hear their train announced. *Treno—Intercity—Otto—uno—tre—Gabriele D'Annunzio!*—they begin to congratulate themselves—*di-prima-e-seconda-classe*—surely no one would announce a train so confidently if it wasn't running—*delle ore—diciassette—e—zero—cinque*—they check their watches, yes, it's on time—*per Bari Centrale*—this is it, kids, we're headed south—*è* . . . and then comes that terrible word—*SOPPRESSO!*

Once I saw a Japanese girl checking the word in a pocket dictionary. I could see her lips mouthing the *s* and the *p*. Consternation. My dictionary gives: *sopprimere*: put down, repress, suppress, abolish, liquidate, eliminate. There is no doubt in my mind that whoever recorded the word did so with a certain vindictive pleasure. At home sometimes when the kids were smaller, I used to announce: *Il gelato*—their eyes lit up—*delle ore—diciannove—e—ventidue*—that's now, Stefania!—*di—pistacchio—e—vaniglia*—yum yum—*con—cono-di-biscotto—è—Soppresso!*

   Cattivo, Papà!

THE EVENING TRAINS ARE *telefonino* time. If I'm early and manage to catch the 17:25. Interregionale, things can get pretty noisy. People are less worried about being overheard in a big open plan carriage than in the more controlled space of a compartment. There are men still involved in business calls, discussing ball bearings and delivery dates. There are mothers telling their children how to prepare dinner: "The fusilli, not the macaroni!" A student complains that she was treated badly in an oral exam: "The professor asked something that wasn't in the book, and he wrote the stupid thing!" Boyfriends and girlfriends are weighing up the advantages of pizzeria and trattoria. "I'll be in Brescia around eight," says a tense, pale man in his late thirties. "Make sure there's a *prosecco* in the fridge."

   As the train pulls out of Centrale the *capotreno*, speaking over the PA, invites the *gentile clientela* not to disturb other passengers with their loud conversations and to turn off, or at least turn down, the ring tones of their phones. The announcement has exactly the effect of a speed limit on the Rome–Naples autostrada. So I have listened at length to a Sicilian man in his forties, quite a few seats away—olive skin, white shirt, gold cufflinks—discussing his ugly divorce with his lawyer, his new girlfriend, his mother, his brother, and a variety of other people whom it was harder to place. This for the whole one hour and fifty minutes from Milan to Verona. To all of these people he repeated with great relish the phrase *"un inferno durato dieci anni—a* ten-year inferno—*un inferno, ti giuro*," glancing around at the rest of us in the carriage as if for approval or sympathy.

Between Peschiera and Verona a funny scene repeats itself on almost every trip. Passing through the low hills at the bottom of the lake, the phone signal begins to break up; it comes and goes for a while, then disappears altogether. *"Ci sei?"* The woman beside me is suddenly asking. Are you there? She raises her voice. "Can you hear me?" asks the man opposite. And then three or four voices in unison. *"Mi senti? Pronto? Pronto? Mi senti. Ci sei? Mi senti?"* All at once they are all looking in each other's eyes, vaguely embarrassed, as if, while they had been speaking on the phone they were invisible somehow, and now, all of a sudden, cut off in the cutting, they must confront each other, and find themselves faintly absurd.

We've crossed the Valpolicella now. The line from Trento joins ours from the north, then the line from Bologna comes in from the south. Already you can see the limestone hills above Verona, the stadium, the ugly round sanctuary of Our Lady of Lourdes, which looks down on the city from the first hilltop. Only the Church could get planning permission for a horror like that. The PA system crackles and an urgent voice announces: *"Avvertiamo i signori viaggiatori che tra pochi momenti arriviamo alla stazione di Verona Porta Nuova, Verona Porta Nuova!"*

When you get off the train in Italy it's a point of politeness to say *buon viaggio* to those who remain. I like these little rituals, however empty and formal they appear. *"Buon viaggio,"* I say to the woman who has been speaking on her mobile for most of the way. I try to mean it. The woman smiles and nods. It's the first time she's noticed me. *"Buona sera,"* she replies graciously.

IF FOR SOME REASON I'm desperate to get back to Verona as early as possible, I'll take a Eurostar. But I have to be desperate, for this is the train I like least. Unlike the Intercity, it doesn't offer the intimacy of compartments. The days of the train compartment are numbered. The existence of trains with compartments suggests a community that is more or less homogeneous and at home with itself, a society where maybe you risk finding yourself saddled with a noisy companion, but not a nutcase who wants to murder you, a terrorist from some country you've never heard of.

The design of the Eurostar screams out, *This is our vision of the future, this is stylish Italy, techno Italy, high-speed Italy.* The long, sleek carriages are made to seem longer and sleeker still with three continuous bands of color running the length of the train, locomotive included: a green band at the bottom, then a white, as if to hint at the Italian flag, and then a long, long line of shiny black, which masks the separate windows and prevents them from interrupting the hypnotic, forward-flung streamline of the thing. As you look at the Eurostar, and even more when you travel in it, you can't help regretting the times when it was still possible to design something without being obliged to create the impression that science fiction is becoming reality and utopia is just around the corner. It isn't. The aisles of the Eurostar are narrow, the seats are cramped. It's true that the so-called Pendolino design of the locomotive, which allows the vehicle to lean (*pendere*) into the bends, means it can travel faster on ordinary lines, without the need of the straighter and smoother rails that French high-speed trains require. But given that these traditional lines are already very busy, it's hard for the Eurostar to exploit this advantage.

But what really makes the Eurostar a nightmare is also its greatest claim to being serious and European, which is to say, un-Italian: as the sleek green-and-white bands slither and hiss into the station, that ubiquitous metallic voice is already announcing. *EUROSTAR!*— *Novemiladuecentotrentasette—per—TORINO PORTA NUOVA—è— in partenza dal binario—sei—PRENOTAZIONE OBBLIGATORIA!*

Prenotazione obbligatoria. The Eurostar is a reserved-seats-only train. You have to book. The idea behind this was that never again would the moneyed traveler find himself having to stand up on his long journey between the Milan stock exchange and Rome's tortuous corridors of power; never again would a Friday evening through the tunnels of the Apennines remind one of the Milan metro in the rush hour, something that can very easily happen on an Intercity, even in the first class. No, for the Eurostar—a train of such beauty, of such speed, of such thrusting, long-distance purpose—a reservation would be absolutely *obligatory*. Away with the riffraff and their Interregionale tickets trying to muscle on at the last minute and buy supplements aboard. Eurostar journeys are serious matters for serious people.

Of course, there are loopholes.

"Please, please, Signor Capotreno"—a man with a pink tie comes panting along the platform—"let me get on the train."

The *capotreno* shakes his head. "This is a reservations-only train, *signore*."

"I know. But I've got an Intercity supplement."

"I'm afraid you need a Eurostar reservation."

"I know, but I wasn't sure at the time I bought the ticket when I'd be traveling. I thought I'd be in the station earlier. *Per favore*. I really need to catch this train now."

Overweight, harassed, reading glasses on a string around his neck, a green cap on his head, the *capotreno* is striding down the side of his shiny train, trailing behind him the smart trolley bag that all capotreni travel with.

"*Per favore*," the pink tie insists, "it's my niece's first communion."

"*Un momento*," the *capotreno* finally says. He stops and looks at the man. No doubt he's heard the first-communion story before. He purses his lips. "Just one place?" he asks.

The *capotreno* caves in. The man climbs on. Inside, the corridors are chaos. Those who got on at the beginning of the ride, when the train was empty, have of course sat exactly where they wanted to sit, understandably choosing places far away from screaming babies and adolescents playing with the ring tones on their Nokias. But now that the train is filling, new arrivals come along and demand the places indicated on their bookings, so the people who were seated are getting up and heading off down the narrow aisle only to find that their proper places too have been taken. Someone else has to be moved. Luggage has to be pulled down from the strangely ungenerous rack. There's an interminable milling and pushing. Finally, the determined traveler will find that two thirds of the way down the train there are carriages that haven't been booked at all, they are almost completely empty. The Trenitalia computer must book up the train a section at a time.

Perhaps the only real advantage of the Eurostar is its dining car. Often when the train is packed, this is the best place to sit and work with a little elbow room, though, of course, you have to buy a coffee if you want to sit. So one evening, harassed by the beep of a Game Boy, I head for the dining car and stand in line at the bar where an elderly *barista* with the obligatory white hat on is taking far too long to make two cappuccini. Why? He has a nice Gaggia for producing coffee and and steaming milk. What's the problem? Then I realize that he is preparing the milk, not in a jug for five or six coffees, but cappuccino by cappuccino in a paper cup. First he puts a shot of espresso in one cup. Then he pours a little cold milk into another, and holds it under the steam nozzle. He's taking forever. Finally I get in my order and he starts the process again, working silently, carefully, intensely.

"Slow business," I eventually put it to him, "to make the foam separately for each coffee in a paper cup."

The machine is quite low, obliging him to bend. He lifts a gray eyebrow in my direction. *"Eh sì, signore!"* he says.

"Not the normal way," I remark.

Patiently measuring milk into a paper cup, he shakes his head. *"Eh no, signore!"*

I wait. He holds the cup under the steam nozzle and starts to froth it. He turns the steam off, examines the froth, turns the steam on again.

"The normal thing would be to use a *bricco*," he says, as if talking to the machine. A jug.

"That's right," I agree.

Satisfied that he has the milk just so, he tilts the cup so that the liquid and froth pour out in a slow trickle into the other paper cup, where the coffee is waiting.

"With a *bricco*," he goes on, "you can make froth for ten cups at once."

"I imagine you can," I agree.

Finally, putting one of the two cappuccini I've ordered in front of me, he looks me in the eye: *"Ma qua, il bricco manca."* Which is as much as to say: here there are no jugs.

"They haven't given you a jug?"

"No, signore," and he repeats, *"Qua, il bricco manca."*

"But why not? How can you make all these cappuccini without a jug?"

Now he is working with the next paper cup, his eye measuring the milk again. There is something wonderfully professional and stubborn about everything he does.

"You ask them. They won't tell me."

"Everybody knows you need a jug to froth milk."

"Sì, signore."

"They certainly have money for other things."

"They have so much money they are arrogant." He is talking to his machine again. It's as if I were overhearing his complaints, quite by chance. "They grow arrogant. They spend money on this, money on that, *ma qua, il bricco manca*. No jug. *No, signore*."

As he finally puts the two cappuccini on the bar, I tell him, "At that point, you might as well bring a jug from home."

For some reason the remark trips a switch. This man, who had been so determinedly taciturn and wry, is suddenly furious: "From home! From home! At that point I might as well bring everything from home. Everything! *Capisce, signore. Qua manca tutto!* We have nothing."

He seems to be asking me to attribute a metaphysical significance to the statement.

"They give us nothing," he repeats. "We're not in a position to work with dignity. *Una vergogna!*"

Disturbed by the negative energy I have stirred up, I pay quickly and head for a table, where I'm struck by the fact that it boasts a carnation. I touch it. Yes, it's a real flower! Where the table meets the wall under the window there's an elaborately designed squiggle of chromed steel, which serves as a flower holder. Every table has one, and every holder holds a flower. It suggests an interesting hierarchy of values in the purchasing department at Trenitalia headquarters. Jug or no jug, the Eurostar must maintain a pretense to elegance.

BUT ASSUMING IT FITS in with your timetable, the best trains to travel on, for comfort and atmosphere, are the old Intercities, with compartments. In Milan it's wise to walk to the very front of the train, which will be emptier, since most people are just too lazy to go so far. You climb up the steps (I like this old-fashioned business of climbing up three or four steps; it gives you the impression you really are boarding the Leonardo da Vinci), and walk along the corridor in search of the perfect seat.

The compartments have glass screens and doors. You move along looking for an empty one. People who don't want you to intrude on their privacy tend to sit right by the door to the compartment, as if blocking the way. These people are practiced travelers. They are thinking about the psychology of the person choosing his compartment, his desire to see emptiness and a way in, not a guardian at the door, as it were. German backpackers, on the other hand, need only push up all the armrests, take off their shoes, and lie across the three seats with their stinking socks on display. Who would dream of joining them?

Many Italian families find themselves overwhelmed by pangs of hunger as soon as they are safely ensconced in a compartment and immediately start a picnic. There will be the noise of crackling paper and the heavy smells of prosciutto and Gorgonzola. If it is a southern family they will try to press the food on you too and seem mildly offended if you don't accept something. In these circumstances it is almost impossible to feel at ease.

Sometimes you'll find that the ocher curtains have been drawn across the glass door so that you can't see inside the compartment from the corridor. All the compartments have these curtains, a strangely civilized touch in our stripped-down, utilitarian world, but irritating when you're out in the corridor and all the other compartments are occupied, or even packed. Why are the curtains drawn? you wonder. There's no low sunshine to irritate anyone. It's hardly an hour for sleeping.

In the past I didn't have the courage to open a door covered by curtains. I had too much respect. Now I hardly think twice. I push through the curtains and more often than not find a teenager, alone, with his Discman in his ears and his feet up on the seat, or a middle-aged businessman studying his financial newspaper. The teenager will pull himself together a little shamefacedly, as if caught masturbating. The businessman is annoyed that you've had the impertinence to catch him hogging the place to himself.

But on more than one occasion I have stepped through the curtains to find couples in various states of undress, in which case it's my turn to apologize. The desire for intimacy does seem the only good reason for drawing the curtains. I've often thought the railways could earn some useful extra money by selling special supplements that would allow people to have a locked compartment where they could make love during their journey. Recently a ticket inspector of the *pignolo* variety, finding a couple having sex behind drawn curtains, reported them to the on-board police for acts of indecency in a public place. This was particularly unkind because they were married, but not to each other. There have been other stories, however, of ticket inspectors of the *furbo* variety supplying travelers with prostitutes and guarding their privacy for the duration of the service. It's hard to decide which kind of behavior is more regrettable.

One person who never has any qualms about opening those ocher curtains is the minibar man, though he is not as dangerous to lovers as the ticket inspector because his arrival will be announced from afar by nasal yells of "Minibaar! MINIBAAAAAR!" and the tinkling of a little bell of the kind you use on bicycles. For in the end the pompously announced *servizio di minibar a bordo* is nothing more than a clunk-ily old-fashioned refreshments cart squeaking along on big wheels with metal spokes and solid white tires. At the front there's a foot that the cart rests on when stationary. The base is bright red, then there are transparent plastic sides allowing you to see a small collection of snacks and drinks, including beers. On top is a steaming metal urn with a little tap at the bottom.

It's always unwise to buy food from the minibar. The sandwiches in particular are as near to tasting of polystyrene as bread and cheese ever can or will. It's unwise to buy the coffee, too. But from time to time, without really knowing why, I do. A mood catches me. He slides back the compartment door, still yelling "Minibar!" I nod my head to tell him he has a customer.

"Espresso?"

The young man pulls a tiny plastic cup from a long polyethylene bag. It's the kind of cup they use to bring you pills in hospital. He rips open a packet, pours in a powder, and opens the tap of his hot-water urn. Obviously he has repeated these movements so often that they have taken on a kind of conjuring-trick swiftness. Italians love to show off these unexpected dexterities, like the barmen in Milan who always send a little Campari bottle spinning in the air before catch-ing and opening it in a single move. Some can spin and catch two simultaneously.

I am handed the tiny cup together with a little plastic envelope containing a napkin, sugar, a nonfattening sweetener, powdered milk, and a stirrer. Finally there is a small square of blue paper, which is my receipt. The boy has five or six little blocks of these differently colored papers cunningly attached to the handlebar of the cart, and for each sale—coffee, biscuits, sandwiches, beer—he must tear off a different-colored receipt and give it to the customer.

Once, when the minibar boy saw me promptly dump my receipt in the ashtray, he warned me that I was legally obliged to retain it for the duration of my journey, as if it was a sort of ticket without which my digestive processes might be subject to sanction. If the *capotreno*, or the Fiamme Gialle, the tax police, he explained, ran a surprise check on the train, it was important that they find that the minibar operator was giving receipts. Otherwise he might just be taking the money and pocketing it—for the coffee, for example—perhaps charging me a bit less so that I came in on the deal. Or he could be serving friends for free. Anyway, it was my legal responsibility, he said, to keep my receipt and be ready to demonstrate that such corruption wasn't taking place.

I confessed to him that I had never thought of this, though at a price of €1 this thimbleful of instant coffee is so expensive I can imagine some people wanting to pay a great deal less. At the end of his working day, the solemn boy went on, the number of colored receipts handed out had to correspond to the quantity of goods sold and the amount of money taken. For example, the plastic envelopes containing sugar, stirrer, and powdered milk all had to be accounted for. He couldn't just give a plastic teaspoon, for example, to someone who wanted it for a yogurt she had brought from home! People were always asking him, the boy complained, without having any idea of the constraints he was working under. He spoke as though he were running a major department store. I sipped my coffee as he set off on his way, ringing his bell, and yelling "Minibar!" It tasted bitter and metallic, as I knew it would.

IMAGINE, THEN, THAT YOU have chosen to travel on the 21:05. Intercity. It's the last of the evening, and as usual about thirty minutes late. Never mind, because tonight you have lucked out: you have found yourself an empty compartment. You check on the little reservations

board by the door and find there are no cards posted there to indicate that anyone has a claim to any of the six places. You have it all
to yourself. You go in, slide the door closed behind you, hang your
coat on one of the hooks provided, and sit by the window facing the
direction of the locomotive. This is great. For a few iffy minutes now
other people walk by, glance into your compartment, weigh you up,
and move on. Clearly you are sending out powerfully misanthropic
signals. Good. You pull out your book or students' work. There is
a little Formica-topped table, or flap, that folds out of the wall under
the window—you can put your papers on that—then an old ashtray,
which has to be tugged open with great caution. Painted battleship
gray and shaped like an old-fashioned cradle, it offers considerable
resistance to being opened, but once the resistance is overcome it can
fly out and dump damp tissues and old banana skins on your trousers
and shoes.

Beneath table flap and bin is the heater, or air-conditioning vent.
Notices warn you to keep the compartment door to the corridor shut
so the air-conditioning can operate efficiently. A tiny flap of window
at the top of the pane can be pulled open for fresh air, though a red
circle on the glass of the flap showing a bottle lying at a forty-five-
degree angle to the vertical and crossed out by a thick red line reminds
you that you shouldn't experiment with squeezing bottles through
this tight space to chuck them out into the night. In any event, your
opportunities for vandalism are limited. The window flap is locked in
winter when it's too cold outside and locked again in summer when it
might interfere with the air-conditioning. If the air-conditioning isn't
working you'd definitely be better off in an Interregionale, whose big
windows can be opened right up. Still, Italians are famous for fearing
drafts and quite capable of traveling with all the windows closed, even
in the most suffocating heat.

So you sit down and check that you have your stamped supplemento at hand to show the inspector when he comes. You open the
book you are reading. The lighting is decent and has three settings—

off, medium, and bright—which can be operated from a knob above the compartment door. The knob has a delightfully old-fashioned design of a lightbulb beside it, with radiating lines to suggest that the bulb is emitting light, though in fact the light source is neon.

There is also an individual lamp clamped to the lower of the two luggage racks above your head. It has a brass, trumpet-shaped shade that looks like it was designed in the sixties. Sometimes there's a bulb inside. But however much you toggle the little stick switch below, it never works.

No, that's not true. Not quite never. These lamps have been out of action for a decade and more, they are not maintained, yet once in a blue moon you do come across one that by a miracle still responds to the click of its old metal switch. The light they cast is negligible; all the same, these rare occasions, when you find something working that shouldn't be, inspire a strange, wistful sort of tenderness. It's endearing that Trenitalia hasn't simply removed all the lamps to have the metal recycled. They are only screwed onto the luggage racks, after all. They could easily have been taken away and sold as scrap. I like to think that someone somewhere has appreciated their ornamental value and sensed that, for the connoisseur, there is this rare delight of occasionally finding one that will turn on, even if its light is no help at all.

Another thing I appreciate is the way the Trenitalia maintenance staff mends the vandalized armrests. Covered in imitation leather, these rests, which fold up into the seat back for those who wish to lie across the seats or to lean heavily against each other with the curtains drawn, are frequently slashed, perhaps by soccer fans, or passengers angry at yet another delay. Instead of replacing them, Trenitalia has a worker somewhere who sews up the tears using a thick orange-colored tape that, applied in a crude cross-stitch, stands out against the dark polished brown of the fake leather and gives the impression that the repair is actually a fashion element. You have to admire this kind of solution.

———

THE TRAIN HAS BEGUN to pull out of the station and you're just settling down to read when an ear-splitting voice erupts from a loudspeaker in the panel over the door, the panel with the knob that adjusts the neon.

"Benvenuti a bordo a treno 624 Svevo per Trieste Centrale!"

This is not the mechanical speak of the station announcements, but the would-be friendly voice of your *capotreno*, who has his hideaway in the last compartment of the front carriage, a sacred space where no passenger is allowed to sit, even if the train is bursting at the seams. He lists the stations you'll be stopping at. He informs you that there's a minibar, something you already knew. He warns you that smoking is now forbidden on Italian trains, corridors included. At a volume that has the compartment wall panels trembling, he encourages you to turn down the volume on your mobile phone ring tone. "Thank you for choosing Trenitalia," he concludes, "and *buon viaggio!*" Who else could you have chosen? you wonder. Still, the voice is silent now. Relax. Then he starts again in another language. **Leddies an gennlmen!** Next it will be *Mesdames et messieurs*, then *Meine Damen und Herren*.

I jump to my feet. Beside the knob that controls the lighting, there are two other knobs above the compartment door—significantly over head height, that is. They are also of quaintly old-fashioned design, black plastic hemispheres sprouting pointy little fingers. One controls heat and cold. Supposedly. You know that because there are two small thermometers designed on each side of the knob, the one to the left colored blue, the one to the right red, with, over the top, a widening curved line to suggest the gradual passage from blue to red—that is, cold to heat—as the knob turns. It is pointless to fiddle with this knob since it just turns around and around and makes no difference at all to the temperature. This service, like the individual lamps, has long been discontinued; the temperature is centrally controlled, though the passenger isn't informed of that, just as he isn't informed, except by this initial announcement, that the image

of a smoking cigarette on the glass door of the compartment no longer means that you can smoke in here. "'Ave a good journey!" The
capotreno winds up his English performance. If I'm quick I can still
escape his French.

The volume control can be recognized by the design of a little
loudspeaker emitting radiating lines and tiny quavers and semiqua-
vers, in a charming reminder of piano teachers and music lessons,
though I can't recall music ever being played on the train PA system.
The knob has three clicks—presumably loud, medium, and off—
though again, you will get little joy from moving it to these settings.
I never found a single knob that functioned as it was designed to.
Yet the volume control does work in its way, in the sense that if you
can get the knob to stick between any two clicks, the sound abruptly
disappears. You have turned it off. The knob has a propensity to slip,
so this adjustment is a delicate one, but it is possible. *"Mesdames et
messieurs! Bien . . ."*

Done it!

Suddenly the voice is only a rumor in the distance, a radio in someone else's apartment. Turning to sit down, I catch a glimpse of my face
in the strip of mirror between seat and luggage rack. I'm looking old
and harassed. Take it easy. Relax, read.

And I do. I sit back and return to my novel. This is bliss. The evening after a reasonably productive day, the sway of the carriage over
the points leaving Centrale, the lights of the city streets sliding by in
the big night, the voice of Thomas Bernhard on the page before me;
above all, the intimacy of a compartment all to myself. Perfect.

For about five minutes.

Just as the train rides through the platforms of Lambrate, where
desultory passengers are still waiting for the 21:15. Interregionale, now
half an hour late, the compartment door is hauled open and with a
great clattering and banging and a frightening fit of coughing in comes
a truly pantomime figure: an extremely tall, bulky man with a huge
head, no neck, a most respectable paunch, and an ankle in plaster up

to his knee. He is walking with the help of a single aluminum crutch but despite this handicap carries a backpack and a very large, very old duffel bag. Panting hard, with the look of a man who has just escaped death by the skin of his teeth, he drops the backpack and bag on the floor and collapses with extravagant theatricality on the seat by the door, his back to the direction of the train.

Without even looking at me, the new arrival starts to moan: *"Dio povero*, how they make you run!" He coughs and splutters. "But *how* they make you run, *Dio santo, Dio povero, Dio santo!"*

His accent is Veneto. He gasps, brings up some phlegm, swallows it, and now pulls a clown's cloth handkerchief from the pocket of his voluminous trousers to wipe the sweat from his forehead. His face is red and steamy and amazingly big. The eyes are glassy. His hair sprouts unkempt from a baseball cap, his whole body exudes discomfort and stickiness. *"Ma quanto ti fanno correre! Ma Dio santo."* Then he stops and holds his breath, his eyes opening wider and wider until, without any attempt to cover mouth or nose, he produces a deafening sneeze, aaaah-**choooo**!

My victory over the PA system is a distant memory.

The sneeze is repeated. He sucks up hard through his nose, which also sprouts thick black hairs, then begins his monologue again. *"Ma quanto ti fanno correre! Bastardi!* If only you knew! *Dio povero*. If you knew. How they make you run!"

I go back to my book. I can sense he is looking at me now, no doubt a little disappointed that I haven't responded. After what might be two minutes, despite all my instinctive resistance, I'm obliged to exchange glances. The width of the man's nose is remarkable. I raise my eyebrows in polite acknowledgment of his presence, but I absolutely refuse to say anything. I must not give him an excuse for carrying on. The expression in Italian is *dare corda*, to give someone string, meaning to offer them the conversational opportunity to go on talking to you. *Non mi dai corda*, you don't give me string, is one of the classic Italian complaints. The refusal to chatter is a breach of etiquette.

With or without my assistance the new arrival goes on talking anyway. I knew he would. He has traveled, he says, *santo Dio*, from Genoa. *Da Genova, Dio santo!* The train was late, *Dio povero*. He had to make this connection with the train to Trieste. Okay, so the Trieste train waited for the Genoa train, as it should, *no, caspita*, as it must! But he had to get from platform seventeen to platform eight in just two minutes. *Dio santo!* With my foot in this state, *Dio povero!* There should be a law, he says, *santo Dio*. There should be damages.

I'm thinking exactly the same thing. There should be a law against intrusions like this. Again he bursts into a fit of coughing. Again, there's something willed and theatrical about it: he's auditioning for a freak show. Then he bends down, unzips his bag, and pulls out a monstrous sandwich wrapped in the noisiest paper ever manufactured. A smell of mortadella invades the compartment. The air is swiftly saturated with spices and fats. Still spluttering, he opens a mouth in which various brown teeth are missing and takes a savage bite with those that, crooked as they are, remain, contriving at the same moment to wipe his nose with one arm and fish about in his bag with the other. For a can of beer.

He belches.

That does it. Ten years ago I would have sat and suffered, I would have listened to the story of how he broke his ankle, of why he was traveling so far, to visit his mother or auntie, no doubt; I might even have expressed sympathy. But times have changed. The repetition of similar experiences in a controlled environment like a railway compartment allows you to experiment with a variety of solutions and techniques. Very calmly I close my Bernhard, I pack it away in my bag, I slip my pen in my pocket, and get to my feet. For the first time he looks at me with curiosity. He is puzzled. *"Ma quanto ti fanno correre, Dio povero,"* he mutters. There are shreds of mortadella between his lips.

"In the state you are in," I tell him, "*signore*, I fear you need a whole compartment to yourself." I pull open the door and step into the corridor. As I do so, I can see him straining to watch me, extreme perplexity on his face. Who is he going to moan to?

TWO COMPARTMENTS UP, I find a pale young man, alone, sitting in the seat near the door, bent forward over a book in such a way as to narrow the corridor between the seats. It is the perfect way to discourage a new arrival. He doesn't want company. This is my sort of companion. I open the door. He sits up. I read disappointment in his eyes. *"E' libero?"* I ask. This is, of course, only a courtesy. He nods. He has a thin, studious face. In his hand he holds a fountain pen with which he has been writing notes on a notepad held under the book he is reading, a rather old book by the looks. I sit down by the window. Despite the rush of the train I can still hear the coughing of that terrible man two compartments away. But the earplugs will eliminate that.

We read. Sometimes I think I should have kept a list of all the books I have read on trains. Certainly most of the books that have been important to me would be there. Perhaps I just read better on rails. A book has a better chance of getting through to me, particularly when I'm in a compartment, and at night. This hiss of metal on metal, the very slight swaying of the carriage, the feeling of being securely enclosed in a comfortable, well-lighted space while the world is flung by in glossy darkness outside, all this puts me in a mood to read, as if the material world had been suspended and I were entirely in the realm of the mind.

Some forty minutes into the journey, having put the trauma of the fat man behind me, I look up and watch my new companion. A pleasant intimacy can settle over two people reading together on a train, even if nothing is said. Finally the young man shifts his book in such a way that I can glimpse the title: *The Confessions of St. Augustine.* He has round, rimless glasses. His hair is that blond that is almost colorless, like grayish honey, slightly curly, tight to his head. He puckers brow and lips as he reads, he has thin lips, and makes sudden rapacious movements when he wants to jot down a note. Perhaps he's studying at a seminary. Sometimes it is wiser, I reflect, to choose a compartment with a single quiet companion, rather than risk the precarious pleasure of the compartment all to yourself. Alone you are vulnerable. Together we two readers will surely discourage any further intrusion.

I turn my head and through the big black pane of the window spy a small walled cemetery on a low hillside. It's uncanny, but I always seem to turn my head exactly as the train passes this cemetery. It's on a low hill near Brescia. What is the mechanism that makes this happen? Do the dead call? There's the glow of our Intercity windows in the night, a dark field, then the old cemetery, then a newer section added on. In the newer section, where the coffins are slotted into cement drawers in the high walls, you can see the flicker of those little red lights that keep the dead company; *lumini*, they're called, as if the tenants of the place were all lying quietly there, reading together as they decay. At Desenzano my seminarian gets to his feet and puts his book away in his little student's backpack. He smiles softly. *Buon viaggio*, he says. *Buona sera*, I reply.

Part Two

FIRST CLASS, HIGH SPEED

2007–2010

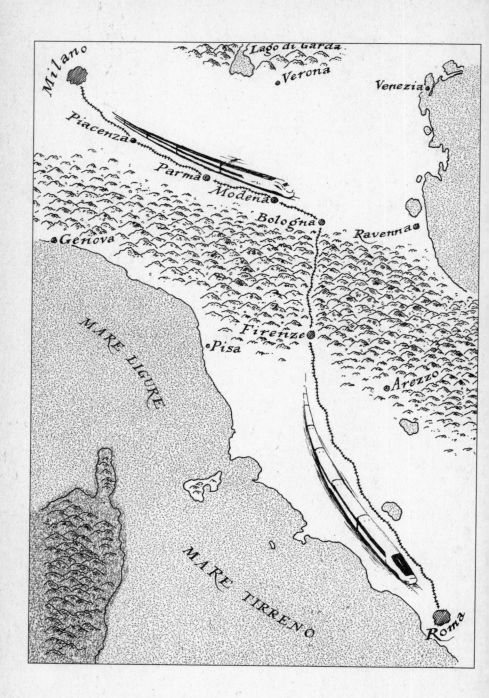

Chapter 3

VERONA–MILANO

I DISCOVERED, OR LET'S SAY I FINALLY STARTED USING, THE TINY station of Verona Porta Vescovo (literally, Bishop's Gate) in 2007. There was an intriguing plaque about Italian soldiers heading for Russia:

DA QUESTA STAZIONE PARTI' LA PRIMA
TRADOTTA DI COMBATTENTI PER IL
FRONTE RUSSO
14 LUGLIO 1941

(The first troop train carrying combatants to the Russian front left from this station July 14, 1941.) But that's not what attracted me to use Porta Vescovo. It had simply become impossible to drive across town to the main station; impossible for me, that is. Not that by normal metropolitan standards Verona is congested; the bottleneck over the bridge taking you from east to west of the river on the circular road can slow things up ten minutes, but no more. All the same, I have begun to feel that the car's pollution is not limited to the exhaust it pumps

out; driving a car pollutes the mind, or at least my mind; it poisons and agitates. Another argument in favor of the train.

All over the city, people get out of their beds far too early. They don't have time to shower and shave, to relax over coffee and a croissant. They leap into their cars and hit the accelerator, racing to the station, knowing that if they don't find that parking space in the roads nearby they may miss their train. Moving from bed to road, soft mattress to hard tarmac in only five minutes, I find myself doing things I shouldn't, overtaking where I shouldn't, crossing lights at the last of last moments, reacting angrily when other hurrying drivers cut me off, loathing the scooters that hover in the mirror's blind spot. My personality, I realize, is bending under the press of a collective stampede, the rush to be first, or at least on time. A wiser person than myself, I know, would not succumb to this contagion. But I'm not wise, and especially not on the road.

One day something happens to tip the balance; it's Monday, I'm leaving home a little late, I'm hurtling toward the light where the *circonvallazione*, the busy circular road from the east, meets the Adige River and turns left and south before the famously congested bridge. This is one of the longest lights in the city; as I approach, it is already on yellow, actually it has long been on yellow, I'm aware of that. Yellows are much longer in Italy than in other countries. Precisely to give you no excuse. At the last of last seconds, the Alpha in front of me hits the brakes. I'm having none of it. I swerve right, overtake on the inside, and cross his path, turning left. As I do so, I see that the light is already red; in fact I'm only a yard or two clear of the cars now accelerating toward me from the right, along the river. Immediately the reason why the Alpha braked so hard is clear. The first car is police.

There are two lanes along the river. We now have five hundred slow yards to the bridge, where the traffic is backed up for another hundred yards across the river to the next light. The *pula*, as Italians call the police, draw alongside. I've got my speed right down now for the simple reason that the traffic here is barely moving. To my right, the police car has space to move ahead, but doesn't. Damn. Blue and white, it simply sits beside me; when I move, it moves; when I stop, it stops.

I could turn and look the officers in the eye, but I don't. I sit in traffic looking straight ahead, both hands sedately on the steering wheel, trying to appear absolutely ordinary and calm. I'm not calm, of course. I'm shaking. The two uniformed guys sitting so close to me know I crossed on red. This is a serious offense. What are they waiting for? Why don't they stop me? Twenty years ago, when I crossed this same light on red at two in the morning and a police car again popped up from nowhere, I solved the problem by simply shelling out the 20,000 lire the men asked for, but those days are over. This could mean losing my license.

We're turning right now, over the river, just a few minutes from the station. I can't get away from them. I can't even park and force them either to get it over with or go away. They stay beside me all the way across the bridge, beneath which, in a completely different manifestation of my personality, I love to play in my kayak on a wave that forms between two bridge pillars. Now the police are playing with me. They drop behind a little. To check my license plate? I'm very aware that the car is old and not a little battered. My daughter had a brush with the garage wall recently. And I rarely clean the car. Correction: I *never* clean it. I don't believe in cleaning cars. Life is too short. How quickly could the police run a check on the plate, I wonder, and find that there is a recent speeding fine? This was actually my daughter again, returning in the early hours from a concert where her band had played. But I accepted the fine and the loss of points on my own license, since I had more points than she to lose and they tend to be harder on young drivers. This was dishonest of me but crucial for my daughter, who at the time was driving all over Italy playing concerts. If they are able to run a check on some computer in their car, some dedicated police iPhone, and see that recent conviction, will that convince them to pull me over now? I can hardly start explaining that it wasn't actually me speeding but my daughter, the rocker.

The traffic inches forward. The police draw alongside again. They're very close, as if they wanted to brush against me. My neck is stiff from looking rigidly ahead. The adrenaline is pumping. I would love to stay cool, but at the crucial moments in life I never can. Five minutes are becoming an eternity. Thank God I'm wearing a nice jacket, which gives at least an air of respectability. Perhaps I could say that I was hurrying because I was on an exam commission and I feel a duty to my students. Would they buy that? They would tell me I should have gotten up earlier. When we finally pass the light and come out of the bottleneck on the city side, the police car stays nailed beside me; I can hardly speed away from it, so the two lanes of traffic stuck behind us now proceed through the underpass with admirable composure. I'm under escort is the truth, and leading a procession. The only thing that feels positive is that so far I've resisted looking at the two men. There are always two in an Italian police car. Perhaps my staring straight ahead, remaining entirely still, has created a sort of protective enchantment, an intimacy almost; if I turned to look at them, thus acknowledging my crime, the spell would be broken and they'd pull me over.

At long last, when I peel off left for the station, the police car accelerates away. They've gone. I feel incredibly grateful to them. What nice guys. They could have enforced the letter of the law, and the spirit, too, for that matter. I really was driving dangerously. Instead they just made me sweat for ten minutes. Turning off the motor, I realize I've made a decision. That is the end of driving for me, or at least of this kind of driving. I've pushed my luck for too long. From now on, however inconvenient it may be, however few trains there are, I will use Verona Porta Vescovo, a tiny station in a sleepy cul-de-sac on my side of town, the Venice side, just three quiet traffic lights from home.

VERONA PORTA VESCOVO IS the kind of station where you hear a bell ring out before a train comes. It's a lovely sound, urgent and old-fashioned as a black-and-white movie. The platforms are very long, very narrow, and generally deserted. To get to platform four, where trains depart for Verona and very occasionally Milan, you have to walk across the lines. I love doing this. It gives a pleasant sense of transgression, of really being in the nitty-gritty.

There are other leftovers from the past here. Above the door outside the station, a yellow sign protrudes perpendicular to the wall just above head height; it's a long, rectangular arm holding up a large disk, which carries the image of an ancient black dial phone with white circular holes arranged in a circle around the circumference of the larger yellow disk to suggest one of those revolving dials you used to put your finger in and turn to form the number. It even has a few holes missing at the bottom right, just as those phones did, where your finger ran into the end stop. Black lettering along the yellow arm supporting the disk proclaims *INTERURBANO AUTOMATICO* (automatic long-distance calls). I presume this advertised the once novel possibility of making long-distance calls without going through an operator. Ever since the mid-nineteenth century, when the laying of train lines went hand in hand with the introduction of the telegraph, railway stations have offered the most up-to-date communication services. They marked the beginning of the world perceived as network. You could send and receive messages through a grid, as it were, like lines on a map, without actually touching the ground anymore, as the train passes over the landscape on its rails without ever really touching anything else. It was a more mental world, more mentally busy and fragmented than the old landscape where a physical message had to be carried on hooves or cart wheels.

Today the young people who use Porta Vescovo station to go to school in Verona or to university in Padua wouldn't even know what an *interurbano automatico* or an operator-assisted call was. They have no idea why the circle of holes is interrupted at the bottom right. They have their mobiles in their pockets, the entire world at their fingertips. But the old yellow sign, the black phone, the dial, reminds us that the yearning for easy communication has always been there, that our grandparents and great-grandparents were already far, far ahead of their grandparents. If "ahead" is the right word for this growing separation between where we are and who we're talking to.

PORTA VESCOVO, I RECENTLY discovered, was actually Verona's first railway station, inaugurated in 1847. At that time the country was still divided, with half a dozen more or less independent Italian states involved in a complex power game with France and Austria over who would control the peninsula. Verona was very much part of the Austro-Hungarian Empire, indeed the bastion of Austrian defenses of its Italian possessions, which then stretched from Trieste in the east all the way to Milan in the west. Almost at once people saw both the military potential of railways and their cultural importance to the Risorgimento movement: rapid, inexpensive travel between the different parts of Italy would surely help to unite the country. The Piedmontese, who were trying to harness Risorgimento enthusiasms to their own expansionist ambitions, were particularly active in building railways, linking Turin to Genoa and seeking to connect with Lombardy. Understandably, the Austrians were not impressed. They refused to connect the lines in their territories to other parts of Italy and built the lines between Milan and Brescia, Vicenza and Venice, Verona and Trento mainly to facilitate troop movements inside their own possessions. Eventually these lines were all linked up right here at Verona Porta Vescovo in 1854, forming one single east–west railway line across the northern margin of the Po Valley beneath the foothills of the Alps. A small siding ran out of Porta Vescovo directly into what is still the large military barracks at Camp Marzo nearby. Soldiers could spill out of their fortress in Verona to be sent off by train to whichever border of the Austro-Hungarian Empire was under threat.

The railways certainly played their part in the Risorgimento wars. The Franco-Piedmontese victory over the Austrians at Magenta in 1859, one of the few important victories the Piedmontese achieved, came largely thanks to a recently completed rail bridge that allowed Piedmontese troops to cross the Ticino River, then the boundary with Austrian territories, rapidly and in force. A year later, Garibaldi crowned his triumphant conquest of the South by riding into Naples on a train. That same year the learned journal *Politecnico* remarked that Italian unity was to be completed and maintained by "armies and railways."

THIS HIGH PROFILE FOR railways wasn't always positive. The first major corruption scandal of the newly unified Italy involved the trains: it came out that ministers had awarded lucrative railway contracts to a company in which they themselves were major shareholders. In general the attempt in the 1860s and '70s to bring the country together very quickly by building more and more railways led to shoddy workmanship and many rail companies failing when it turned out that there was little demand for the lines they had so enthusiastically laid. In 1893 the cultural magazine *Nuova Antologia* observed,

> the determining criteria in Italian railway construction from the unification of the Kingdom until the present day, have overwhelmingly been more political than technical and economic. Financial questions played only the smallest part. But while in the beginning those political criteria were grandiose and national, just and even necessary, later they were to become pettier and pettier, to the point that they were almost always more regional than rational.*

Much of the rail building was done in response to the mythical success of railways elsewhere, above all in England. The anxiety to compete with northern European rivals, a constant need to prove

---

* For these quotations I am indebted to Stefano Maggi's excellent book *Le ferrovie* (Bologna: Il Mulino, 2003).

themselves equal if not superior to their neighbors, is still an important factor in Italian decision-making today. The emotions that fueled local *campanilismo* had carried over onto the international scene, as if collective identity for the Italians could only be asserted through competition. Copying the English model, as they did, buying locomotives and machinery from England and coal from Germany, Italian companies forgot that in England the railways had been introduced into a booming industrial economy where demand for transport was intense and coal and steel readily available. In Italy, on the other hand, many railways were soon being seen as cathedrals in the desert. Fewer people or goods were moving around, and since salaries were low, fares too had to be kept low. Train use per person in Italy remained far below that in England, Germany, or France right into the mid-twentieth century. One problem was the complex ticketing, with so many different companies each having their own byzantine rules. In *Le ferrovie*, Stefano Maggi quotes this letter written in 1869 by a member of Parliament to the minister for public works:

Last week, coming back from Florence to London, I found myself sitting with a number of English and American travelers, some of whom were returning from the Orient, via Brindisi. It's not an exaggeration, Minister, to say that the trip was a constant series of complaints about Italian railways; these travelers were simply amazed that a smart, modern people like the Italians could put up with so many vexations. . . . With regard to paper money, they told me an incredible story. A traveler wanting to buy a ticket costing 15.75 lire handed over 16 lire in National Bank notes. The people at the ticket office refused to accept them insisting that 1.75 lire should be in silver or coppers and the rest in bank notes. Since the traveler didn't have 1.75 lire in coins he said it was fine if they kept the 25 cents change from the 16 lire: he was told that the Company was not in need of charity and they wouldn't give him a ticket.

It all sounds dreadfully familiar.

In the 1880s the Italian Parliament, irritated with the poor show-ing of the private companies that held concessions to run the railways, actually debated the possibility of making the late arrival of a train a criminal offense. It is hard not to sympathize, though one might as well legislate against the rain. In Luigi Bertelli's 1907 children's novel *Il giornalino di Gian Burrasca*, translated as *Diary of a Bad Boy*, the nine-year-old Gian Burrasca, running away from home on a train, remarks, "Dad was really right when he bad-mouthed the rail service!"

But these were also years of heroic achievement, tunnels through the Apennines, tunnels under the Alps, feats of engineering beyond anything that had been done in England or Germany. Indeed, it was this explosion of activity in building the railways that led to the development of the engineer as a figure distinct from the architect, but equally respected in Italian culture, to the point that *Ingegnere*, Engineer, is a form of address in Italian equal to Doctor or Professor. And it was through constructing a network of railways across some of Europe's most arduous terrain that the newly formed Italian nation won a reputation for ingenuity and adventurous construction proj-ects. In the 1860s three Italian engineers invented a blast-hole drill-ing machine that used waterpower to compress air that then turned the drill bit; previous drills had been steam-driven, which meant that when digging tunnels vertical shafts had to be sunk to the tunnel face to remove the coal smoke. It was this Italian invention that made it possible to dig the Moncenisio tunnel under Fréjus in the western Alps in 1871. More than eight miles long and taking forty minutes for a train to cross, the tunnel reduced north–south travel times across the Alps by twelve hours and allowed British companies trading with India to get their goods from London to the port of Brindisi in just forty-seven hours. Italy thus began to attract trade to its ports that had hitherto gone through southern France. But 177 workers died building the Moncenisio. And more than 600 died of lung diseases after work-ing on the nine-mile-long San Gottardo tunnel, completed in 1882.

The longest Alpine tunnel was the Sempione; at twelve miles and five hundred yards it would be the longest tunnel in the world until 1979, when the Japanese went a mile longer. So whatever one says about punctuality and ticketing bureaucracy, you always have to take your hat off to the courage and expertise that built these railways. When a man is introduced to you with the title Ingegnere—*Buon giorno, Ingegnere Rossi*; *piacere, Ingegnere Bianchi*—you have to show a little respect.

Alas, all this hard and brilliant work rarely paid monetary dividends and certainly not in the short term. Railways really are the ultimate test of whether a capitalist model can ever be adequate in the sphere of public transport. If we want railways, we have to pay for them, and if we ask those who are traveling on the trains to pay the full price of the financing in the first few years of their use, then no one will travel on them and we will never have trains at all. This is an investment amortized over decades; centuries, even. The newly constituted Kingdom of Italy wanted railways and wanted the prestige that railways brought at a time when rapid, punctual train travel was the most visible indicator of collective wealth, progress, and modernity. But they didn't want to pay for them. They didn't have the money to pay for them. This will be a familiar set of circumstances in many countries; one thinks of Britain when the Channel Tunnel was dug. The companies to which the Italian government gave the franchises to build and run the various lines, companies often owned by ministers' friends and relatives, found they couldn't after all make the handsome return on investment that the English had made; they had imagined they were doing something *furbo* and would clean up and instead they had done the country a great service and were looking at serious losses. But if they weren't to get rich, they could hardly be allowed to fail either, for trains had become part of the social and economic landscape and to lose them would mean dreaming up a quite different vision of the future. As a result, all kinds of clever accounting had to be invented for the government to prop them up. It was to be, and still is, an absolute staple of the Italian railways, whether public or private, that in some way or other, acknowledged or unacknowledged, they were/are being paid for, or hugely subsidized, by the state, a state that was/is itself greatly in debt. As early as 1869 Mark Twain was puzzled by the phenomenon:

> There are a good many things about this Italy which I do not understand—and more especially I can not understand how a bankrupt Government can have such palatial railroad depots. . . . As for the railways—we have none like them. The cars slide as smoothly along as if they were on runners. . . . These things win me more than Italy's hundred galleries of priceless art treasures, because I can understand the one and am not competent to appreciate the other. . . . But . . . this country is bankrupt. There is no real foundation for these great works. The prosperity they would seem to indicate is a pretence. There is no money in the treasury, and so they enfeeble her instead of strengthening.

By the end of the nineteenth century Italy was indeed in deep trouble, facing hunger marches and large-scale protests, at least in part because of the careless public spending that had so amazed Mark Twain. In 1905, now in a period of severe economic depression and unrest, the government was finally forced to nationalize the railways. Italy was the first large state to do so (only Switzerland had gone earlier), and the railways were the first industry to be nationalized in Italy. Negotiations were marked by the first national strike involving a large and influential union, this because the railway workers refused to accept the no-strike clause in the contracts of state employees.

At this point there were 102,000 railway personnel, more than the total number of Italian civil servants and by far the largest body of organized labor in the country. They were also a closely knit workforce, wearing uniforms, forced by long and unsociable working hours to develop an esprit de corps, proud of their technology and responsibilities. Through the coming years, and particularly during the First World War, in which the railways played a huge role, these men would become more and more militantly socialist and then Communist. After nationalization they won themselves an eight-hour day, which forced their new employers to more than double the number of railway workers, to 226,000. Add to that the large pay increases necessary to keep this dangerously powerful group happy and it was clear that the railways would be a severe burden to the taxpayer for decades to come. In 1914 the legal expert Giuseppe Cimbali, contributing to a wide-ranging document on aspects of public administration in Italy, wrote:

> Aware of being a crucial part of the central and miraculous movement of modern life, railway personnel reckon themselves a cut above all others and believe they are owed every kind of indulgence and privilege. Feeding on the violence unleashed by steam engines and electric dynamos, they refuse to accept any bridle or limit. Accustomed to racing along at vertiginous speeds, they react at once to any attempt to hold them in common chains.

Reading this, one appreciates why, even today, whenever a *capotreno* approaches you to check your ticket, you have the impression you are dealing with a police officer or even a soldier. Public notices warn that "The ticket inspector is a public official," and announcements in the stations declare that "refusal to show him a valid ID is a criminal offense." It also explains why it is still illegal to take photos in Italian railway stations; apparently they are essential to national security.

1,196 railway men died in wartime activities between 1915 and 1918, and 1,281 were decorated. After the armistice Italy annexed the railways of Trentino, the South Tyrol, and the northern Adriatic as far as

Trieste, more than six hundred miles of lines. The railways were also central to the huge patriotic ceremony arranged for the entombment of an unknown soldier that was to give a cathartic closure to this first traumatic national war fought on national territory: on October 29, 1920, a coffin bearing the soldier's corpse was loaded onto a train in Aquileia, a small coastal town east of Venice and in an area that had seen fierce fighting among Italian, Austrian, and German troops; from there, stopping for ceremonies in every station and cheered at every level crossing it was taken down to Rome, where it arrived four days later, on November 2, the Day of the Dead. In triumph and grief, the image of the train was fused with mass patriotism.

Two years later almost to the day, another train traveler heading north to south was greeted with noisy celebration on his arrival in Stazione Termini: Benito Mussolini. The 1922 March on Rome was greatly facilitated by Fascist elements among the railway workers who arranged special trains for the marchers from northern Italy down to the capital. Mussolini himself hung back, waiting to see if his coup was going to succeed before finally boarding a regular night train that left Milano Centrale at 8:30 p.m. and arrived in Roma Termini at 10:50 the following morning, an hour and a half late. Over the next twenty years Il Duce would make train punctuality a test case for Fascist efficiency. Brutally hard on left-wing unionism, he cut the workforce by more than 50,000 men, making sure that the most militant were among those to go and introducing a railway militia to monitor workers' behavior. This heavy stick was then balanced with a paternalist carrot: health care, cheap food, and cheap housing made the railway workers a highly privileged group. Recreational spaces and organizations were encouraged, in particular the famous Associazione Nazionale Dopolavoro Ferroviario (After-Hours Railwaymen), which promoted group holidays and sporting activities. In 1928 the Baedeker was able to reassure foreign tourists that the trains in Italy were running mainly on time.

Yet it was during fascism that the long decline began. A drastic downturn in the economy in 1929 cut the numbers of passengers and the volume of freight. The roads were now beginning to offer serious competition and a radically different vision of the future. Some smaller lines were substituted with buses. The regime responded with a program of hi-tech investment. Since coal was an expensive and politically sensitive import, a resource foreign governments might easily withhold from them in the event of sanctions, the Fascists speeded up the process of electrifying the main lines, particularly in the northern mountains, where they were able to exploit the territory's hydroelectric resources and hence alleviate the problem of coal smoke in tunnels. Italy was and still is ahead of other countries in railway electrification. New lines were laid between many main stations to shorten the distances. In 1937 an Italian electric locomotive achieved the world speed record for a train in commercial operation with an average speed of 106 miles per hour on a regular passenger trip from Bologna to Milan.

The problem was to get people on board the trains and hopefully paying for their tickets. Foreign tourists and businessmen would always use the main lines, and commuters were more or less condemned to using the suburban lines. But what about the provinces? Mussolini, who liked to be personally involved in everything to do with the railways, tried to kill two birds with one stone, inventing the so-called *treni popolari*, made up entirely of third-class carriages, which would take working people to seaside or skiing destinations on public holidays at a fraction of the regular price. People were to be endeared to the regime and encouraged to live healthier lives, getting out into the country on weekends. In 1934 the *treni popolari* shifted more than a million passengers and gave many Italians their first experience of train travel.

On June 14, 1940, just four days after Il Duce declared war on France, an armed Italian train running along the Costa Azzura began shelling French naval vessels. Throughout the war the trains moved troops, refugees, armaments, and prisoners in huge numbers. Eventually the railways were bombed by the Allies and blown up by the retreating Germans. After the Italian surrender in 1943, the Germans, who were occupying the center and north of the country, made Verona their main transport hub, lying as the city does on the intersection between the east–west (Milan–Venice) and north–south (Rome–Berlin) routes. So it was from Verona, from those same platforms where I catch my train of the living dead, that Jews and other undesirables were shipped north in stifling or freezing freight wagons over the Brenner Pass and onward to the gas chambers of Auschwitz and Birkenau. One such wagon is still preserved in Verona Porta Nuova and displayed every year on the Day of the Shoah in Piazza Bra, the city's central square. Auschwitz survivor Primo Levi wrote: "No diary or story written by those of us who came back is complete without its train, the sealed wagons, transformed from freight trucks to mobile prisons or even instruments of death."

2,104 railwaymen died in the Second World War, 407 of them in partisan actions. To their great credit, some workers did attempt to sabotage the German war effort by damaging switching systems and locomotives. At the end of the war, in one way or another, 4,500 miles of line had been destroyed, together with 4,750 rail bridges. Paradoxically, even though the full extent of the prewar network was never entirely restored, by 1950 the number of passengers had doubled in comparison with the late 1930s, though the amount of freight being carried was falling off fast. The roads were winning that contest. Through the 1950s there was a frenzy of road building. No one was thinking of global warming. No one was worried that gasoline might be a limited resource. Traffic congestion was not a concern. Nor were the thousands of road deaths. All that mattered was individual freedom and the dream of door-to-door service. In April 1961 the automobile magazine *Quattroruote* (*Four Wheels*) promoted a race from Milan to Rome between the new, fast electric train, the Settebello, and an Alfa Romeo Giulietta. The train made it in six hours, thirty-seven minutes. The Alfa did it in five hours, fifty-nine minutes. Game over.

As the autostrada construction program moved into full swing, the Ferrovie dello Stato began to hemorrhage passengers.

It was at this point, no doubt, that you started to see the distinction between two kinds of rail travel that is becoming more and more evident today. Most train transport would be a service for the carless poor, for commuters with no choice, for backpackers and hobos, the living dead, or for eccentrics like me who loathe driving any distance at all. Cheap, slow, poorly serviced night trains, the so-called *treni di speranza* (trains of hope) would take workers, students, and later immigrants the six hundred miles from south to north at dirt-cheap prices. Filthy commuter trains would bring low-paid workers into Milan, Rome, and Genoa on annual season tickets that wouldn't pay for a month's travel in countries north of the Alps. Ancient rolling stock wasn't even dusted off to carry soccer fans to away games. Here, alongside the acknowledgment that the railways had an important social and economic function, there would be no serious investment and only the absolutely essential maintenance. This was, and is, a soup kitchen approach to rail transport. Any self-respecting person with the price of a car, or an air ticket, would drive or fly. How many times in casual conversation have people shown surprise that I don't drive to Milan?

But then for the business folks, the respectable tourists, and the phobics who can't fly there would be the luxury trains; first the Settebello, then the Rapido and Super Rapido, then the Eurostar, trains that required you to pay double or triple for speed and hygiene. Even here, though, it was hard to compete with a road network that was soaking up 80 percent of public investment in infrastructure. The terrorist bombs that killed twelve people on a night train between Florence and Bologna in 1974 and again eighty-five people in the waiting room at Bologna Station in 1980 did not help. I was in Verona the day of the Bologna bomb, on a holiday with my wife to visit her brother and to check out the possibility of moving there. Though I wasn't aware of it then, when I settled in Italy in 1981, the Ferrovie dello Stato were moving into what might have proved a terminal decline; government investment was low, yet at the same time politicians were once again forcing the railways to take on more workers than they could possibly need or use. Even the nostalgia that began to attach itself to trains was a bad sign. Nothing is more obsolete than yesterday's vision of the future.

In 1985 train ticket prices, after accounting for inflation, were a third of what they had been at the beginning of the century, while the cost of labor had multiplied by six. Train travel was more or less being given away to keep people sweet. At this point, in a flourish of semiseriousness, the rail company was transformed into an independent authority with an obligation to break even. Much was said about freeing the organization from political control and applying market constraints. But the truth was that it was still owned and regulated by the state, so the obligation to break even was meaningless; it was always going to be bailed out, whatever its losses, and thus was always able to secure loans and build up debt, a debt that was really part of the national debt, though it no longer officially appeared as such.

In 1992 the FS, as it is usually called, was transformed again, into a private company, but with the state retaining a majority shareholding. This meant that it now had the freedom to hire and fire and invest, with state money but without any state-appointed authority to control it. Needless to say, the politicians pushed the railway men to do what was politically convenient for each and all of them in their own constituencies, and very soon there were accusations of corruption and legal investigations. In the meantime, to reduce overmanning, the government offered early pensions to all railway men over forty—an uncle of my wife's was a beneficiary—reducing the workforce from 216,000 to 120,000 at ruinous cost to the taxpayer and without helping the railways very much since many of those who went were the more capable workers, men confident they could get work elsewhere to supplement their pension, while those who remained and found themselves working harder immediately went on strike for higher salaries; by the end of the nineties the company was paying the same wage bill for half the workers.

In the mid-1990s the European Community began to press all member states to open up public transport to private competition. So, as I wrote earlier, in 1999 Ferrovie dello Stato became a group comprising Rete Ferroviaria Italiana (RFI), which would run the lines and smaller stations, and Trenitalia, which would run the trains. Theoretically, the aim was to allow other entrepreneurs to compete with Trenitalia for use of the lines; but since top executives from the RFI and Trenitalia continued to sit on each other's boards, this seemed unlikely; for the most part people thought of the development as an ugly tangle of bureaucracy and cosmetics. It was at this point that we began to hear that mocking farewell when each train reached its terminus: "Thank you for choosing Trenitalia."

WHAT WAS THE CHOICE at Verona Porta Vescovo if I was going to use this station to get to Milan? Exactly four slow but direct trains a day—Interregionali—and a fair number of Regionali that ran as far as Verona Porta Nuova and contrived never to connect with onward trains to Milan.

Four penitential trains it was, then: the 6:50 a.m., the 12:36 p.m., the 16:36, and the 18:37.

There is no ticket office in Porta Vescovo, but in the waiting room you have to pass through from road to platform there is one ancient gray machine issuing regional tickets only, that is, for destinations within a range of something less than a hundred miles. There's no touch-sensitive screen here, just a few sticky old buttons. Everything is coded in numbers. In particular, each station, and there are hundreds of them, is represented by three digits that you have to check on an interminable list to the side of the machine and then punch in with the buttons. Not to worry, though: five days out of seven this machine is not working. In which case you can buy your ticket in the station café.

Porta Vescovo has the most charming railway café I know: old wooden chairs and tables with red-and-white-checked tablecloths, windows with lace curtains looking out onto the platform; two bustling, shrill-voiced women who know their customers of old, for no stranger would ever come to catch a train from Porta Vescovo; then their two shapely daughters (I presume), both with attractively and very differently lopsided smiles, plus an ancient, plaintive old man whom the women trust only to move boxes and perhaps take the money, but certainly not to make a cappuccino or operate the ticket machine they have behind the bar. Get in here at 6:00 a.m. and the girls will have a coffee in front of you in thirty seconds, together with an obscenely calorific croissant full of sticky custard. Return around seven in the evening and the two *signore* will pour out a chilled Custoza and slap a bowl of potato chips in front of you for just a couple of euros. Most of the conversation is strictly in local dialect, with guys working in the nearby bus depot dropping in for robust salami sandwiches and glasses of red wine at any time of day.

But on Sunday the café is closed. And on Sunday the ticket machine *never* works. Sunday afternoon is when I now travel to Milan, to be there on time for a lesson Monday morning. Since I now make only one journey a week, sleeping over in the city for a couple of days, I no longer buy a season ticket. So the malfunctioning machine is a problem.

Loud announcements ring out along the deserted platforms of Porta Vescovo. My favorite is the one that tells people, two or three people, to spread out along the whole platform to speed up boarding. Another very peremptory voice tells us we must "provide ourselves" (*munirsi*) with a ticket before we get on the train; it is a criminal offense, we are reminded, to board a train without providing ourselves with a ticket.

I look around. Who is playing these announcements? Is there anyone in the station, or are they triggered remotely? If there is anyone, they are presumably hiding in the tiny office to the left of the waiting room on platform one, its glass door protected by venetian blinds. *Dirigenti*, says an ancient sign above the door to the left. Directors. When I knock there is no response. Are the directors aware, if there are any directors these days, that the ticket machine isn't working? I don't feel I can simply push the handle and walk in to force someone to pay attention to me because a notice says, "*VIETATO L'ACCESSO alle persone non autorizzate*" (NO ENTRY to unauthorized persons). It then goes on to warn that "Transgressors are subject to sanctions ranging from a sum of €258 to €1,549."

There is a big difference between €258 ($300) and €1,549 (about $2,000). It gives a judge considerable discretion between oddly precise sums. Could they have been converted from the old lire? There's no explanation of the size of the fine, but as always in Italy we are informed as to the legislation that authorized it; "*art. 19.3 of DPR 753/80, artt.le 2 of L. 561/93, 689/81 and s.m.i.*"

A DPR is a decree of the president of the republic. An L. is just a law, that is, when a decree is voted through Parliament and converted into law. And s.m.i.? I must have asked a dozen passengers over several months before one older man told me with a perfectly straight face, "*successive modifiche ed integrazioni*" (later amendments and integrations).

Integrations!

The fact is that despite all this superfluous information there is no one to tell you what you're supposed to do when you can't buy a ticket. I can't remember this ever happening to me before. I suppose I must head straight to the *capotreno* and confess. However, if you are to enjoy the luxury of a seat on the always crowded Sunday evening train to Milan, you must grab one when people get off and on at Verona. And that is only three minutes from Porta Vescovo. If you're still looking for the *capotreno* after Porta Nuova, you'll be standing for two hours. If you sit before finding him, he'll find you and fine you because you haven't bothered to find him.

Officially, a *capotreno* hangs out at the front of the train; that's where he keeps his stuff, his little travel bag and official papers and personal belongings, so I position myself way up the platform. The train is long. As it grinds to a halt, I wait a moment and look along the carriages to see where he will pop out with his peaked cap and the green flag he waves to tell the driver, who presumably watches in a mirror, that he can close the doors and leave. But of course as soon as people start getting off, it's hard to see where the man has appeared. Certainly not at the front of the train. A number of people have jumped off, lighting cigarettes as they do so to get a few desperately needed puffs before the train departs. Then, just as I'm about to get on, a bunch of Japanese girls start climbing down with their huge suitcases. At once I know these kids are getting off at the wrong place—only locals get off at Porta Vescovo. These girls have seen the big signs along the platform: VERONA PORTA VESCOVO. They know their train is due in Verona at 6:43 p.m. They assume it has arrived three minutes early. Or perhaps it's already 6:50, in which case they rejoice that their train is only seven minutes late. Understandably they start to pile off.

"This is not Verona," I tell them in English.

They look at me and smile vaguely. Behind me is the huge sign: VERONA PORTA VESCOVO.

Every time I board a train here this scene repeats itself, with English, German, American, or Scandinavian passengers.

"This is not Verona. Get back on the train. It's the next stop, Verona Porta Nuova, three minutes."

Some refuse to pay attention. You are one of the thousands of wheeler-dealers taking advantage of tourists in some way. The ladies in the bar tell me that the only strangers they ever see in Porta Vescovo are people who have gotten off the train by accident and come to ask how to proceed to Verona proper. Why, I wonder, doesn't Trenitalia do something to make it clear that this is not the main station? After all, they tell us which laws authorize fines we're never going to risk paying. The station could just be called Porta Vescovo rather than Verona Porta Vescovo.

"This is not Verona station."

Does the Japanese girl I'm talking to understand English?

She blinks from weak eyes, looks up and down the narrow platform and across at a wasteland of sidings and rusting freight trucks and decides I'm probably right. So now the bags have to be loaded again. I start to help. The *capotreno* is getting impatient and blows his whistle. Where is he? The shrill sound is coming from far away—the other end of the train, no less. I'm done. I'll be standing all the way.

THIS SITUATION COULDN'T GO on. Since tickets for regional trains are valid for two months, the only sensible answer seemed to be to buy a bunch of tickets at once, whenever I was near a ticket window in any station, so as never to be without. It was January when I came to this conclusion. Carnival was around the corner. At carnival time the trains returning from Venice are packed with masked ladies and tiny penguins and D'Artagnans. The worst season to travel. I decided not to be miserly for once and bought first-class tickets to be sure of a seat.

The truth is I have always thought of myself as a second-class passenger. No doubt this is something that comes from early infancy when my carless parents rarely had the price of a train at all, let alone a first-class ticket. Later, when I had the cash to travel how I liked, I decided that people were more interesting for a novelist in second class. What basis I had for thinking this, I do not know. Perhaps it was a question of the kind of novels I was writing. In any case the second-class ticket to Milan was €9, the first €15. I lashed out and bought six tickets, imagining I was treating myself.

You cross the rails to platform four. There are about ten people spread along a platform of a couple of hundred yards. The first-class carriages are toward but not actually at the front. Other passengers on the platform can see you're standing in the first-class area. You're the only one. It's simultaneously embarrassing and gratifying. The bell begins to ring out with its urgent, insistent tone. The train hoves into view from the Venice direction. The big, filthy blue locomotive squeals and labors along the rails. The old rolling stock is smothered with graffiti. The windows show that the carriages are packed. People are standing, many of them masked in the silliest outfits. How smart of you, you think, to have bought a first-class ticket!

As the train finally grinds to a halt, you move to the nearest door, pleased to be an insider who knows *exactly* where his carriage will be. The door opens and a group of Australians begins to climb down. "Wrong station, mate, you want the next," you tell a strapping boy in a cavalier cloak. "This is just a provincial watering hole." They laugh and climb back up. So now you've done a good deed on top of all your other smart decisions. You hurry after them, your stamped first-class ticket all legal and correct in your pocket and . . .

First class is full. It's packed. It's asphyxiating. There's not a seat to be had. People are standing all down the aisle. The heat is on maximum and the air is unbreathable. Dismayed, there's nothing you can do but push your way to the middle of the carriage and laugh at yourself for having thrown away the cash.

I stand and try to read. There are people who, however packed a train is, always believe that it is worth moving along from one carriage to the next, even if other people are moving in the other direction in the same vain hope. I try to make myself very slim as backpacks push behind me. The train does not empty at Verona Porta Nuova as I hoped it might. Nobody gets off at Peschiera fifteen minutes later. Rather, there are more getting on, families who've taken advantage of a bright cold day to go to Gardaland.

Then just before Desenzano there's a sudden stirring. People are standing up. People are pushing down the carriage toward the door behind me. How odd, I think, that so many people would be getting off at the small lake station of Desenzano. There must be some event on, some carnival occasion.

No, it's the ticket inspector. The man with the green cap has just appeared up the aisle.

Two minutes later, I'm sitting comfortably in a half-empty carriage. "Passengers are advised to check," runs one regular recorded announcement, "that the class indicated on their *documento di viaggio* corresponds to the class of seats they are actually occupying." The appearance of the inspector has inspired a good fifty people to take that advice and flee.

If ever smug self-righteousness were tangible, it is now. There is a grim satisfaction on the faces of those who remain, the faces of the good citizens who have actually paid for their first-class ticket. For myself, I'm relieved to be sitting and able to work, but not sure that I'm entirely happy with the spirit of this. The rest of the train will now be even more packed and asphyxiating. Those who fled included the aged and infirm. Now I'm feeling guilty for the luxury I have paid for. However, some minutes after the inspector has gone, people begin to drift back from second class. It's a scandal, an elderly lady remarks complacently as she settles herself beside me, to leave these seats empty while people are standing.

This scenario was repeated on three of the five remaining occasions when I used my first-class tickets. On the other two, the ticket inspector never passed by and I stood the whole way.

On one trip I met someone who had an interesting take on the situation. Having bagged a seat at Verona Porta Nuova, I offered to help the girl opposite me put her big bag up on the rack, since it was occupying the space between us, preventing us from stretching our legs. She shook her head. "Hardly worth it," she says. She doesn't have a first-class ticket, she explains, so will probably have to move on soon. "Just that there's nowhere else to sit in the entire train." She says this as if she had checked every single carriage herself. In the meantime other people around us are standing, some of whom perhaps do have first-class tickets. But the girl is pleasant and I choose not to comment.

"They should have more of these Interregionali," she goes on, not by way of justification; she's merely remarking that the demand is there and should be satisfied. "The Intercity costs twice as much," she explains, as if someone with a trace of foreign accent could not know that.

"The reason they don't have more," I point out, "is that they wouldn't make any money at all if everybody traveled to Milan for nine euros."

"That's true," she says equably.

"I suppose that's why people pay a bit extra for first class," I observe, pointedly, I hope. "To sit."

"If they can afford first class," she says, "I can't see why they don't get the faster train."

"Maybe it doesn't stop at their station. It doesn't stop where I get on, for example."

"Right, it must be that," she agrees. Nothing I say seems to undermine her confidence in what she originally said, despite her acknowledgment that I have a point.

The inspector appears, but the girl doesn't get up and hurry off with the others. Very calmly and naturally she shows the inspector her ticket.

"This is a second-class ticket, *signorina*," he observes, "and you are in first class."

The girl looks around with an air of vague surprise.

"Is it?"

But she isn't really trying to fool him. The naive gesture is sketched; it's just enough to allow the inspector to act *as if* she hadn't understood.

"Well, *signorina*, you'll have to move," he says. He likes calling her *signorina*. The girl half stands and the inspector moves on down the now pleasantly free carriage. All those remaining are handing him regular first-class tickets with affable smiles. The girl continues to fuss with her bags, pulling things out and putting them back in and arranging this and that until quite suddenly she sits down again, slumps low in the seat so her blond head is beneath the top of the backrest, and closes her eyes.

"He's gone," I tell her after another minute. She opens one eye, smiles, opens the other, laughs, pushes a hand through her lovely hair, then fusses in her bag and brings out an economics textbook. She has to study.

I ask, "What will you do when he comes back?"

She frowns. "It'll take him a while to get down the train. It's very crowded."

"He'll have his assistant working up from the other end."

"We'll see," she says.

"Theoretically he could get nasty."

"Theoretically," she agrees. "But I don't think so."

I realize that I'm dealing with someone more integrated in this society than I can ever hope to be.

"Why not?"

"They're not serious about first class, are they?"

I raise an eyebrow.

"When you travel on a bus without a ticket, what happens? If an inspector gets on, he blocks the doors of the bus and anyone freeloading is fined. That's serious. They could easily get the two inspectors to arrive at the opposite doors of first class and fine everyone with a second-class ticket."

"They could." I had never thought of this.

"If I went into first class in a Eurostar, they'd fine me at once."

"But not here."

"They're not serious."

"But why not?"

She frowns. Clearly she is a serious student.

"I think they would rather all these people paying for first class moved to the faster trains. The *poveretti* here and the *benestanti* there."

Poor and rich.

I ask, "So why offer first class at all?"

"They have the carriages. Someone is always stupid enough to pay, even when they don't get a service."

"*Grazie.*"

"*Prego,*" she says with a laugh.

IF THE FERROVIE DELLO STATO are not serious about class distinctions on the Regionali, when you arrive at Milano Centrale it becomes all too obvious what they do care about. Here a revolution is under way. Inside the station a major refurbishment has just been unveiled; immediately outside, a dramatic year-long countdown is nearing its end. And in every aspect of these changes you can savor what was implicit in that smart girl's observations: the determined division of the railways into the haves and the have-nots, those who travel on Regionali and those who travel on Eurostar, or something even better.

I have described the grandeur of the place, a building with almost twice the cubic volume of the great Gothic Duomo in the center of the city, but I didn't get over the deep melancholy of its neglect before 2008. In particular, I remember the black nets strung like funeral drapes from end to end of the huge entrance hall (the so-called Sala delle Carozze) about thirty feet aboveground, presumably to prevent pigeons from flying into the vaulted spaces above. Sagging as they gathered filth, these nets robbed the passengers of the exhilarating elevation the original architects had planned, that cathedral feeling that invites you to see a spiritual side to every journey. In fact, everything about the station at that time, its cluttered newspaper kiosks and dilapidated prefab sandwich bars, exuded an atmosphere of defeatism. Routine maintenance is never a strong suit for the Italians. They are good at putting on the initial splash, building the building, laying out the roads, arranging the flower beds; they love opening nights and ribbon cutting. But it's hard to keep the great spectacle fresh and gleaming; its very splendor becomes a burden hardly sustainable on a day-to-day basis, like a romance too wonderful to survive the meaner intercourse of marriage. With a collective shrug, what was a wonderful show is allowed to fall apart. There's even a sort of grim satisfaction in its debasement. It was too much work. It wasn't *that* important. You let grass grow, dust gather, cataracts fall over the eyes. Scurrying back and forth from metro below to train platform above, no one wants to remember the vision when the founding stone was laid, no one wants to be reminded of the intoxicating rhetoric of the unveiling.

Until the day comes when something really has to be done, or when someone has finally managed to come up with the €120 million it's going to cost. In 2006 they began the long-overdue renovation. The scaffolding went up, large areas of the station disappeared under drapes. Suddenly my favorite sandwich stand and all the staff I'd gotten to know over so many years were gone. I do hope those people weren't just fired. For two years we were channeled this way and that between boarded walls and splattered hangings. Some 350,000 people pass through this station every day. It's a miracle they kept it up and running while completely redesigning the very core of the place, and above all, as we shall see, the movement through it.

In the meantime, the big open piazza outside the station, Piazza Duca d'Aosta, was also being torn up. This is one of those classic urban spaces set aside for anarchy, demonstrations, drunks, soccer fans, travelers without the price of a hotel, peddlers, pickpockets, prostitutes, and drug dealers; a muddle of ill-kept grass, cigarette butts, and powerfully unpleasant smells in damp corners. At a push, in daylight and decent weather, it could be okay for a quiet smoke or a sandwich sitting on a low wall, gazing up at the imposing facade of the station with its curious central inscription in letters a yard high: *NELL'ANNO MCMXXXI DELL'ERA CRISTIANA* (IN THE YEAR 1931 OF THE CHRISTIAN ERA), a sly allusion to the fact that back then the Italians were building a new regime they hoped might last longer than Christendom: the Era Fascista. It was year 9.

Two Gypsy women once tried to mug me in Piazza Duca d'Aosta. Thinking about it later, I couldn't help but admire their boldness. They converged on me from left and right, each taking an elbow and asking for money while grabbing hold of the shoulder bag I was carrying. I had to shout and thrash about in a most undignified manner. It was after that that I finally resigned myself to using a little Italian backpack to carry my underwear and students' theses, something I'd always resisted in the past, associating backpacks with schoolchildren and beasts of burden. But they do have the advantage that they're not easily snatched.

Workmen arrived and started redeveloping the piazza. What this means in Italy today is neutralizing it, imposing the well-swept hygiene of large expanses of white paving with occasional steps up and down to assert a rigid, linear geometry. Into this austere mental territory are inserted small, rigorously circumscribed patches of green and even a flower bed or two, nature in its most reduced, unthreatening, controllable form. All of this is functional enough, but it's hard to be enthusiastic, especially in summer, when the sun beats down and there is no shade in which to eat your sandwich, drink a soda, or smoke that cigarette.

Then, quite suddenly, in December 2007, right in front of the station, a monolith had been raised. At least that's what people started calling it on blogs and in newspapers: *Il monolite! Il totem!* Sixty towering feet of polished steel, with two convex faces about ten feet across, bearing a legend, high, high up: SEGUI IL CONTO ALLA ROVESCIA. Follow the countdown! To what? ALTA VELOCITÀ came the answer a little farther down: HIGH SPEED. Exactly 365 days from the moment the countdown started, a high-speed train would leave Milan for Bologna, covering the 134 miles in just an hour, half the present time. An old photo I have of the monolith shows a giant digital counter in the center whose glowing red figures, about three floors up, give 237.5.56.11, meaning 237 days, 5 hours, 56 minutes, and 11 seconds until the departure of that train, which would then arrive in Bologna exactly 60 minutes later, where another totem had been set up in front of that station, counting down to the orgasmic moment of this miracle train's punctual arrival.

It takes courage to predict something a whole year ahead in a country where notoriously *everything* is postponed at the last minute—the deadline for paying your taxes, for submitting your thesis, for applying for a professorship. Looking around you as you cross the sterilized space of the empty piazza and enter the complex building site that the station has become (as I write, work on the metro station approach has been interrupted because the company that won the contract is accused of bribery and corruption), picking your way among the immigrants selling fake designer bags, ducking the little helicopters that Arab vendors launch into the air, avoiding the soap bubbles that two Slav men are squirting from ingenious little machines you wish had been around when you were a kid, averting your gaze, perhaps, from a body under newspapers against a pillar or an ancient woman sitting in her piss selling lapsed pharmaceutical products spread out on a filthy blanket, you can't help wondering if high-speed rail travel is really society's most pressing concern right now.

The truth is that every major Italian city rail station—Naples, Rome, Florence, Turin—is a daily challenge to the middle-class commuter's propensity for denial: will we be able to ignore the spill of humanity leaking into our cozy Italian world from all over the planet? Can we really reassure ourselves that it's none of our business that these men, women, and children wrapped in sacking on the pavement are not our neighbors? Most days, I must say, we rise pretty well to the challenge. We have our iPods, our mobiles. We can walk past the starving to the melodies of Beethoven or the bluster of Bruce Springsteen. Perhaps what has most changed since 2005 are the rising tides of the dispossessed, the unemployed, and the unemployable, and the ever more sophisticated technology that helps us not engage with them, to get from A to B faster and faster without touching anything dirty in between.

In this regard, the glittering monolith outside Milano Centrale is definitely on the side of denial. It raises your eye from the feckless press at ground level. "High speed bringing people together," says a pious promotion, "for a more united Italy." You can look away from the sprawling bodies and feel virtuous doing so. Only 150 days now. Only 100. We will be able to travel faster and faster—up to 250 miles per hour—in luxury, seeing less and less of the landscape as we shoot by, paying prices high enough to exclude those in need of charity.

Talking about luxury and prices, on the western side of the piazza, the side where the Arabs and Africans hang out, is the five-star Meridien Gallia Hotel, a dozen stories of pompous 1930s extravagance. Once, my Italian publisher put me up there for the night. What was he thinking of? No sooner was I in my room than a waiter brought a bottle of champagne, courtesy of the house. Looking around, I saw that every luxury was at my fingertips, things I couldn't even convince myself I wanted, the fluffy slippers, fresh bathrobe, a jacuzzi, polished marble surfaces, linen sheets, quality soaps. I didn't really feel like champagne but opened the bottle anyway and drank, gazing out through the excellent double glazing of crystal clean windows to where brown men were kicking a ball back and forth in the shadow of Centrale. I might perfectly well have been watching them on television. Shaking my head, I mimed a toast: to modern insulation.

But the great day was approaching. The first high-speed train was to coincide, more or less, with the opening of the newly renovated station, including a hundred shops; a new ticket hall; specially rebuilt "high speed" platforms; and, above all, an entirely new system for moving people through the station from metro, tram, or bus to the platforms high above, and vice versa.

Until that fatal day *la mobilità*, as Italians call it, worked like this. First you went from the underground metro platform to street level using two escalators, or running up two flights of stairs. Coming out of the metro there were just a few weather-exposed yards before you were safely in the Sala delle Carozze—the carriage hall—

a magnificent vaulted and porticoed space where taxis could pick up customers without their having to step out into the rain or sun. Then you passed through any one of a string of impressive, ironwork doors into the grand ticket hall of the station proper, whence you could take two central escalators heading up side by side to a mezzanine floor, then again two more escalators up to another vast hall of kiosks and cafés beyond which, at last, were the platforms themselves, all twenty-two of them, stretching away under an arched glass and iron canopy. Alternatively, you could choose the broad granite staircases at the left and right extremities of the ticket hall.

Why, you wonder, would anyone choose those stairs when we're talking about climbing the equivalent of three floors in a regular house, having already climbed two to get out of the metro?

Here we have to mention an Italian trait that appears to be deeply ingrained in the national psyche: Italians do not walk on escalators and only rarely stand to one side to allow others to walk. In the main metropolises of the United Kingdom, Germany, and the United States, people who don't want to climb an escalator will stand to the right so that those in a hurry can scuttle by on their left. Rather than encumber the fast lane, they will place their bags on the step above or below them. This is extremely considerate and civilized of them.

Italians do not do this. Not because they are inconsiderate, but because it doesn't occur to them. An Italian all alone on a broad, long modern escalator will stand to left or right as he or she chooses and invariably place his or her large suitcase on the same step, entirely blocking any swift passage up or down the escalator. Desperate, on one occasion, to get by the only two people on the up escalator at Stazione Centrale—the departure of my train already long announced—I was told by an only slightly irritated voice that if I wanted to rush madly around I really should have used the stairs, shouldn't I, which are so much wider. They were a mild, middle-aged couple with Tuscan accents. They did not budge. When I pointed out that since the escalator had the advantage of *moving* upward while the stairs notoriously *stayed put*, to rush up the escalator was faster than to rush up the stairs, the man observed that the escalator was set in motion precisely to save passengers the effort of climbing from one level to another. It was as if, as far as he was concerned, once one stepped onto an escalator the body naturally, *instinctively* reacted by assuming a position of rest and any other behavior was perverse.

So from the time I started using the station I learned to ignore the slowly rising statues on the escalators and would dash to left or right and race up one of the grand granite stairways—forty-eight steps— with their polished marble balustrades and brass banisters beneath Fascist friezes celebrating an accelerated future as imagined in the 1920s—steamers, planes, and trains, but not escalators.

For many years I taught an evening class that finished at 8:30, leaving me just thirty-five minutes, twenty-five of them on the metro, to make the last Intercity to Verona, at 9:05. After a while I realized I was measuring my aging in terms of the energy with which I tackled those stairs. At thirty-five I could do the steps two at a time from the metro platform to the ticket hall and again from the ticket hall to the platforms—a total of five floors, I'd say—arriving at my train bathed in sweat but barely panting. At forty I was panting hard but still forcing myself. At forty-five I was obliged to take the top section just one stair at a time and still feared my legs might buckle under me or my heart burst. I would collapse into my seat with pulse thumping and a taste of blood in my throat. At fifty I had long given up those evening classes but nevertheless stepped briskly up the stairs, noticing that even when you take them one at a time you arrive earlier than the escalator zombies.

Then one ordinary evening late in 2008, returning from Milan to Verona, I found myself in a labyrinth. The monolith had been counting us down to the departure of that first high-speed train—we all knew exactly when that was going to happen—but the new station was unveiled quite casually. One day the covers were all in place; the next they came down. As I was passing through the ticket barrier from the metro, still one floor underground, a tunnel beckoned to my left where none had been before. STAZIONE FERROVIARIA, the sign announced. Instead of climbing the stairs to street level one could now walk straight through to the station. Who would decline such an invitation? However, at the other end of the tunnel, I couldn't find the escalator that ought to shoot me up to the rail platforms where I and everybody else needed to be. Instead there were shops selling sporting goods, underwear, and cosmetics. The only way to move upward was a very long, very shiny "thing" that was neither an escalator with steps nor the flat Trav-O-Lator that speeds up walking along long airport corridors, but a combination of the two, a sort of conveyor belt rising, slowly, at an angle of no more than ten degrees. Actually, now that I lifted my head and looked around, I saw there were two of these things. The odd part was that instead of moving forward, toward the platforms above, each set off perpendicular to the direction we were headed in, one to the left and one to the right. I went and stood on the one to my left. Despite its extraordinary slowness—I have since timed it out at one minute and fifty seconds—everybody was standing still on both sides; there was no way you could hurry by.

Then this *thing*, usually described with recourse to French as a *tapis roulant*, but which I have also seen translated on the FS website as a "treadmill"—this strange silver and glass thing took its freight of scores upon scores of passengers plus their clutter of luggage only as far as the Sala delle Carozze. That is, having gone through the tunnel and now up the *tapis roulant*, we were still *outside* the main station itself; in the past I could get here in about twenty seconds using the stairs.

Now I hurried through to the station where I needed a ticket. But the last ticket windows beside the stairs in the main hall had been closed. Again a tunnel opened where once there had been only solid walls; it bore the legend BIGLIETTERIA E BINARI: Tickets and Tracks. Intensely fluorescent after the marble-softened daylight of the main hall, this unexpected burrowing was to the left of the main central

escalators, which were now both *coming down* rather than going up.
Weird! How were we supposed to get up to the platforms?

The walls of this new tunnel were formed by sparkling shop windows. There were about thirty yards of this, then a space of thousands
of square feet opened out that none of us had ever seen before; it was as
if we'd been admitted to some fantastic grotto deep inside a hill whose
steep slopes in the past we had simply climbed straight up. Here, two
more *tapis roulants*, again departing perpendicular to the direction
you wanted to move in, headed upward, while beyond them a line of
perhaps twenty glass doors invited you into the ticket office at the very
back of the grotto. So now, once you had bought your ticket, you had
to backtrack through the glass doors to these *tapis roulants*, which
took you up with interminable leisureliness, not directly to the tracks
but to a whole mezzanine floor, another novelty, where you could stop
and explore another line of shop windows or turn around and board
yet a third *tapis roulant*, which doubled back on the second to drag
you up, finally, bewildered, and above all late, to platform level.

In short, a building designed as a magnificent thoroughfare taking
you straight down from train to street or directly up from street to
train and offering you on the way and *without going out of your way*
the simple services of food, newspapers, and tickets, had been transformed into an underground maze of zigzagging conveyor belts moving perpendicular to your intended destination and hiding the most
essential requirements deep in buried dead ends.

Why?

Elementary. To take you past the 108 shop fronts that now invite
you in Stazione Centrale. So while fuming and fretting at the thought
that your train might depart at any moment, you can contemplate
designer sunglasses, ladies' undergarments, bathing costumes, best-
sellers, more ladies' undergarments, the latest Mac, iPhone, iPod, and
PC, running shoes, sportswear, men's suits, yet more ladies' undergarments, and so on. Or alternatively, if weary of images of bright fab-
rics stretched over pert buttocks and breasts (and surely we belong to

the first generation for whom it is possible to tire of such images), you can raise your eyes to where the renovators have indeed done a magnificent job of cleaning the elegant stone arches, sculptures, and mosaics of the 1920s building; though here again, images of provocatively worn underwear hanging on huge placards from the ceiling break up the sober pomp that might otherwise have helped you resign yourself to missing your train.

Is it incompetence?

No. It is desperation.

Trenitalia has a massive overall debt of more than €6 billion. The government's social policy, as expressed in their franchise, doesn't allow them to raise fares to realistic levels and they have already laid off as many staff as is politically acceptable. Something "creative" had to be done. People had to be encouraged to spend the money they weren't spending on tickets to purchase consumer goods, mainly luxury consumer goods, with the FS taking a percentage of every sale. Just as when one doesn't want to pay for website content one has to wait while dull advertisements pop up and fade, so now one would have to factor an extra five minutes into each journey to be transported as slowly as possible past shiny shop windows.

Will it work?

I fear not. On my next visit to Milan I studied the station situation carefully: although the metro stairway I had used to use to reach street level had been closed, there was still one available for people entering the metro from the piazza. So it was possible to ignore the signposting and the new tunnel, to walk straight up to ground level, and then to climb those forty-eight 1920s granite steps to the platforms without being drawn into the commercial labyrinth beneath. In fact, these once-daunting stairs were suddenly far busier than they had ever been; to quite a lot of people stone stairs began to feel like progress. A month or so after the great unveiling, a website was launched offering tips on how not to miss your train at Milano Centrale; the most obvious was: don't stop to buy anything.

Chapter 4

MILANO–FIRENZE

———————

No SOONER HAD WE GOTTEN USED TO THIS REVOLUTION IN *mobilità*, or lack of it, than the countdown outside the station was suddenly over. On December 14, 2008, the much-heralded train departed and, yes, arrived in Bologna just one hour later—right on time. Soon it would be pushing on to Florence, then Rome, then Naples. Soon it would be heading west from Milan to Novara, then Turin. By 2010 hourly trains were departing from Milan and racing three hundred miles *nonstop* to Rome in just two hours, fifty minutes. Imagine Boston to New York, city center to city center, in an hour and forty-five, or London to Edinburgh in three hours, and you have the idea. Forget the train of the living dead. Forget the first-class fiasco on the Venezia–Milano Interregionale. This is serious! All of a sudden Trenitalia was winning back passengers from car and plane.

But how exactly was it paid for? It's reckoned that to lay the six hundred miles of seamless rails that only the high-speed trains can use all the way from Naples to Turin, cutting new tunnels and building new viaducts, must have cost some €150 billion, a simply vast amount of money that was never written into any government budget. At a certain point the European Community intervened to insist that the huge loans taken out by the rail company figure as part of the Italian national debt and not simply as private company debts, since everyone knew that in the last resort they were underwritten by the state. Aside from the loans, it's clear that a significant part of the government grant that was supposed to support humbler rail services through stations like Porta Vescovo was switched to investment in the high-speed project and quite possibly the redevelopment of Milano Centrale into an upmarket shopping mall. So the living dead are pushed deeper into their unquiet graves to breathe life and speed into those who can pay to travel fast enough to have time for a spot of shopping at each end. To him that hath, more shall be given: and from him that hath not, even that which he hath—a halfway decent regional rail service, practical stations with reasonable *mobilità*—shall be taken away.

All the same, as Mark Twain concluded his discussion of mad Italian spending on the railways in the 1860s, "it is an ill wind that blows nobody good." Up and running, enjoyed and used by thousands, the high-speed trains have become their own justification. I for one would never wish they hadn't been built.

THE OLD NAMES ARE GONE. That was inevitable. Gone the Gianduia to Venice, gone the Michelangelo to Rome, gone the Andrea Doria to Genoa. Gone the proud announcements reverberating through the station and the beautiful words appearing on the departures board. Every big change in the railways brings a revolution in nomenclature and ticketing. So these screamingly fast new trains are called *frecce*, arrows. This switch back to Italian suggests a new pride and confidence; the Frecciarossa, or Red Arrow, built in Italy by Fiat and Associates, travels at 200 miles per hour, running exclusively on dedicated rails. After the Red Arrow there is also the Frecciargento, the Silver Arrow, which goes at 150 miles per hour on dedicated and ordinary rails, and the Frecciabianca, or White Arrow, which goes at 125 miles per hour on the old, ordinary rails we know so well. It was the arrival of the Frecciarossa, which takes you from Milan to Florence in an hour and forty-five, and again of the Frecciargento, which does Verona to Florence in an hour and thirty, that made it possible for me, in 2009, to make the major mistake of accepting an invitation to curate an art exhibition in Florence.

Back in 2005 I had published a little book, *Medici Money*, which talked about the way a tension between moneymaking and medieval Christianity had flowered in the ambiguous but indisputably beautiful territory of Renaissance art. The ban on usury, a word that at that time referred to any interest-bearing loans, expressed the Church's rejection of the idea that the mind should focus on money and social mobility. People should accept their position on the medieval estates and concentrate their aspirations on the afterlife. However, the bankers, or some of them, showed everyone that getting rich was not just about counting florins; they also invested in education, art, and architecture, seduced the clergy by financing major Church renovation projects, and in the process commissioned some of the finest paintings and sculptures ever made. So the once cold and austere spaces of a timeless liturgy began to take on a decidedly bourgeois, well-dressed fashion feel, something no one had expected or planned for. In the end the tension between Christian purists who resented the mercenary invasion of their sanctuaries and the wealthy classes who felt that their taste, hard work, and charity should surely get them straight to heaven, exploded first in Savonarola's Bonfire of the Vanities, then in Luther's Reformation.

It's curious. There's a direct link between the medieval Church's objection to social mobility, and to Pope Gregory XVI's 1840s condemnation of the railways as the work of Satan. In the early nineteenth century the Papal States of central Italy were among the most backward and static territories in Europe, perhaps nearer to the world of the medieval estates than to our highly mobile capitalism today. The train, Gregory realized, would allow people to get moving, from home to a distant place of work, or from one town to another. Doing so, they would lose contact with their proper place in the world; free from the watchful eyes of parents, partners, and children, men and women would start living double lives. They would no longer know who they really were or where they should be. Trains, Gregory decided, and in general rapid constant movement from one reality to another, were *contro natura*, against nature, in exactly the same way that usury, blasphemy, and homosexuality were *contro natura* in the world of Dante's *Inferno*. They were pernicious temptations to become something other than what God had planned for us.

Today's pope has his own dedicated Frecciarossa when he travels. A YouTube video shows crowds on a platform in Spoleto, Umbria, waving as the papal train passes through without stopping. This was 2011. It's a strange meeting of ancient and modern. The streamlined nose of the Freccia and its darkened, shockproof windows slide smoothly by while a bunch of celebrants, with Spoleto's mayor at their head, cheer loudly. The camera searches through the windows of the passing train, eventually finding a man in white robes propped in a standing position—these trains can sway dangerously through stations—raising an arm to greet people whom he can't possibly see. For perhaps a second his ghostly salute flashes across the screen left to right, more fugitive and unnatural than any appearance of the Madonna. The good citizens of Spoleto must have wondered whether they had really seen him. For all the derision that met his objections, Pope Gregory, I'm sure, would feel he had understood trains perfectly.

IN ANY EVENT, THIS book of mine had led to an invitation to curate an exhibition in Florence at Palazzo Strozzi, a sort of Donald Trump ostentation of the fifteenth century, built, massively and threateningly, with money from the Strozzi family bank. Since regular trips to Florence would be required, the high-speed miracle made possible something that years before I might have wisely refused, since this was a complete distraction from my ordinary life. All of a sudden here I was a regular traveler on a work of Satan, shuttling back and forth to Florence at demonic speeds, to organize an exhibition on another of Satan's masterpieces, the banking techniques that enabled the Medici et al. to circumvent the usury ban and turn the churches of the Renaissance into extensions of their living rooms, in much the same way that the austere Fascist trappings of Milano Centrale have been turned into a version of Macy's.

It didn't start well. My Frecciargento was scheduled to leave Verona Porta Nuova shortly before seven o'clock on a February morning with the temperature near zero degrees Fahrenheit, a once-a-year occurrence in this part of the world. Finding that many of the trains were delayed due to frozen switches, and in particular that my Freccia was posting a half hour delay, I climbed the stairs to the platform to see if the train was there by any chance and, hopefully, heated. There was no sign of it.

The air was bitter. My overcoat wasn't made for it. I scuttled downstairs back into the station, but the waiting room was not yet open. This waiting room, which was notorious for not allowing eating or drinking, a rule regularly policed by unexpectedly zealous station staff, has since been closed to make way—surprise, surprise—for a small area of shops. In the meantime the station, like many others in northern Italy, has been filled with TV screens, scores of them. They are attractive, flat screens in polished metal frames, placed, for example, above your head as you climb down any of the three staircases on the station's twelve platforms, and delivering not, as you might expect, information about train departures and arrivals, but nonstop advertisements, each of about thirty seconds. So moving through the station shortly before seven o'clock on this freezing morning, looking for somewhere warm to wait out the delay, I was able to observe, as always, luscious close-ups of ladies' undergarments hugging perfect, perfumed flesh, images of pasta disappearing between lusciously perfect female lips, luscious breasts on a perfect young woman changing her clothes in a car, and so on. There were also many large posters of Silvio Berlusconi hanging on thin chains from the high ceiling. An election had been announced. The brief government run by Romano Prodi, a ramshackle coalition of the left, had given up the ghost.

The departures board now told me that my train was delayed for eighty minutes. This meant I could safely sit down for a coffee. There may be no waiting room when you need it, but there is a choice of bars: a regular Trenitalia bar at one end of the station and a McDonald's franchise that combines Italian bar and McDonald's counter at the other. The latter has the great advantage that seating is free, and since eighty minutes is eighty minutes, that's where I headed.

I got my cappuccino and croissant, sat, and began to think about Berlusconi's smile. What a strange mixture it was, I thought, of comfortable self-congratulation (I'm a hugely successful man, you can rely on me) and victimhood (I am a scapegoat who has been treated badly), as if he were both a first-class Freccia traveler *and* a long-suffering victim standing in the corridor of a packed Regionale. Quite how Berlusconi manages to convey these contradictory impressions I'm not sure, but they seem to contain a paradox essential to the contemporary Italian mind-set: we are simultaneously well off and not well off; we deserve excellent services but we are already paying too much for them; we are confident *and* hard done by.

At this point I had to move my seat. The fact is that with the station open but the waiting room closed, all those poor folks who had somehow gotten through the night in the icy waste of the piazza outside were invading McDonald's, where indeed half the tables had been roped off, no doubt to discourage this loitering. I noticed a Gypsy woman at the bar getting a flask filled with hot water and then asking for the key to the bathroom. The station bathrooms cost €1 per person to use, but if you buy something in the bar you can ask for a key to the small bathroom there and then take the whole family in to use it for free. Quite a saving. Not that this woman had bought anything; rather she had asked the favor of a refill of hot water, but she got the key anyway, and who would begrudge it to her? There were four or five children in tow. A world without free public lavatories is a grim world indeed. But maybe it *is* a grim world and that's an end to it. Certainly you can be sure that the Gypsy woman in question is not contributing to the construction of public lavatories. All this stuff was going through my head when an elderly man sat heavily on the chair beside me emitting a smell so powerful that I stood up at once and took my cup and remaining crumbs to another table, where two students were amazingly finding the energy to kiss and fondle at seven o'clock on a freezing Monday morning. I wondered for a moment if I should check the departures board again—for there is no information inside the bar, no announcements, no screens—but I had plenty of time.

Berlusconi, I thought. That smile. Not that he personally is responsible for everything that's happening in Italy today—how could one man ever be, however often he has been prime minister? But you really don't need to think hard to see a connection between the rise to power of a man whose fortune has been made by creating a vast TV and advertising empire and an Italy where one tries to resolve any and every contradiction between what people expect and what they are willing to pay for it by turning public services into advertising spaces and retail outlets. Sometimes, moving through an Italian station or airport today, it feels as though the selling power of cute buttocks, sweet smile, and pert breasts is really all that stands between Italy and economic meltdown. It does seem a lot to ask of the girls.

Brushing the crumbs off my coat, studiously ignoring the antics of the two youngsters across the table, I left the warm bar for the freezing station to check where we were up to with the Frecciargento's delay. Anything over ninety minutes and I would go home, I thought.

I couldn't find the train on the departures board. This was odd. Other trains were posted for Munich, Trieste, Turin, Mantua, but not the 6:55 to Rome via Florence. Puzzled, I hurried up to the platform. There was no one there. The train wasn't indicated. I went down to the main concourse, but the information office didn't open till 8:30, and there were long lines at the ticket windows. Eventually I found a man in uniform who didn't seem to be going anywhere in particular.

What had become of the 6:55 to Rome?

He presumed it had left by now. It was 7:20, after all.

"But they announced an eighty-minute delay."

His eyes narrowed and he became cautious. "If it were delayed eighty minutes it would still be on the board."

"They announced the delay, I went to the bar, and now it's disappeared."

He shook his head. The 6:55, he said, actually started its journey from the station here in Verona. It was thus unlikely that they would signal such a long delay, since the train would have been right there overnight. At most they might have had to run a check on some systems because of the cold.

"They did announce an eighty-minute delay. I didn't imagine it."

Picking up my accent, he shook his head and said in comically poor English, "Perraps you 'ave made the mistake."

"I have been in Italy thirty years," I told him. "There have been periods when I have practically *lived* on Trenitalia. I did *not* make a mistake."

He sighed and began to move away. He had work to do. If I had a complaint to make, there were proper channels.

Furious, but above all bewildered, I drove home, booted up my computer, and opened Viaggio Treno. This is one of the truly great novelties of the past ten years, and I take this opportunity to salute and congratulate whoever invented it: Viaggio Treno is a page on Trenitalia's website that gives you the exact position of all the trains in the country. A map of Italy opens with double lines indicating the main train routes in each direction; you can choose the region that interests you and home in on that. If the line is dark blue there is a train on it; if it's light blue, there isn't. You then click on your dark blue line and a small table appears indicating the various trains on the line, their present positions, any eventual delays. In short, it's as if you had a huge toy train set in your front room with all the Frecce and Intercities and Interregionali moving back and forth on it from the top to the bottom of the peninsula.

Sure enough, the Verona to Bologna line was dark blue. I clicked. The Frecciargento 9461 had now passed through Poggio Rusco and was running just ten minutes late. It must have left just as I settled down in the bar. Unfortunately, my ticket was valid for that journey only. Could I claim my money back for a train that had departed more or less on time? No. Could I ever prove that a delay of eighty minutes had been posted? Probably not. Could I claim expenses from Palazzo Strozzi for a ticket I had bought on a train I had not boarded? Hardly. But the most curious thing of all, I realized now, was that I had appeared to be the *only person* at the station who had missed that train, the only one rushing around in an angry panic at 7:20. There were two explanations for this: first, that the other passengers were perhaps even now in McDonald's waiting out the eighty minutes; second, that the other passengers were not so foolish as to have trusted the delay announcement and, knowing the train started its journey from Verona, had hung around, on the freezing platform, or at least somewhere in the vicinity where they could see the departure board and hear the station announcements and above all the *coincidenze*, which, as I said, you cannot do in McDonald's. Of these two hypotheses I preferred the first, but all my experience told me the second must be true. Never lower your guard with Trenitalia.

THE FOLLOWING DAY I boarded the same train at 6:45, had an uneventful journey, and was able to see for myself that the Frecciargento did indeed complete this trip of about 130 arduous miles in just an hour and a half. The train races south over the open plain and the broad waters of the Po to Bologna, then hurtles under the Apennines through tunnel after tunnel, reaching speeds of almost two hundred miles an hour. Distances that in 1848 took Garibaldi weeks in his revolutionary back and forth across these mountains are eaten up in minutes. It's a fantastic achievement.

The woman sitting across the corridor from me thought so too. When the ticket inspector arrived, shortly before Bologna, she had no ticket to show him. Rather grand, in her sixties, but frayed at the edges, wearing a dark red coat that she hadn't taken off despite the excellent heating, she began to protest that she did have her ticket somewhere. Must have. Her son had bought it for her. She had put it in her handbag. She distinctly remembered. The inspector was patient but something in the woman's voice was beginning to give her away as not quite compos mentis. "You people are always bothering me," she suddenly announced. Her mouth seemed strangely big and ill defined, as if her features were as frayed as her coat. "That's the trouble with this country. The honest people are harassed while the rich get off scot-free, the cheats, the tax dodgers, the presumptuous."

Unnecessarily, the inspector remarked that it was important for passengers to pay for their tickets; otherwise the railway would go broke. The woman met the objection with another tirade of abuse. Why didn't he believe her when she told him she had the ticket? Did he think she was a liar? Her voice strained with righteous indignation. The more animated she became, the more evident was the decay in her face. The inspector began to fill out a form for a fine. It was a long form; €60 were mentioned. Plus the price of the ticket. These inspectors always have to work smoothing layers of carbon paper on a book or bag and touching malfunctioning Biros to their lips while the speeding train packed with revolutionary technologies sways and accelerates and brakes. The woman seemed alarmed and her voice became almost hysterical. She would never pay a fine, she yelled, never never never. Because she *did* have a ticket, if only she could find it. In the meantime, she had given up any pretense of looking.

"I won't give you my name," she told him abruptly when he asked for it. She folded her arms in defiance. "I don't have an ID with me."

By now everyone was watching. I had been trying to work, making notes for the meeting that lay ahead, but it was impossible. The inspector told her in that case she would have to get off the train at Bologna.

She wouldn't, she told him. She had a ticket to Rome. She was going to Rome.

"If you have a ticket, show me," the inspector said.

She couldn't; she had lost it, she told him flatly. "Can't you see that?" Her thick white hair, through which she kept passing one hand, now revealed itself as disheveled, unwashed, uncared for. From seeming quite an ordinary passenger it became clear that she was one of the dispossessed. She should not be among us.

"I will not get off this train!" she screamed.

Perhaps because of this transformation on her part, the inspector passed from being admirably patient to cruelly perverse as he took pleasure in dragging the scene out, explaining at great length the procedure she was facing. If she did not show him a ticket he was obliged to write out a fine. If she couldn't or wouldn't pay the ticket plus the fine of €60 on the spot, she would be obliged to disembark the train at the first station and pay a fine of €200 from home. If she refused to leave the train, he would invite two policemen to get on board at Bologna and remove her forcibly.

The woman began to appeal to the passengers around her. There were people in this country, she shouted, daily stealing hundreds of thousands of euros from the public purse, and this arrogant man was victimizing a poor pensioner traveling to see her sick old aunt in Rome. It was a scandal.

As ever in Italy, the acknowledged lawlessness of the country's ruling class offers an excellent alibi for smaller offenders. One of the reasons for endlessly voting for corrupt politicians is that your own misdemeanors seem trivial by comparison.

"The sharks are all freeloading and then they pick on a poor woman who has lost her ticket," she wailed.

Nobody wanted to get involved. This is a business train for businesspeople.

"My poor auntie is dying." The woman now began to cry. "She's ninety-two." Her face betrayed a desperation that went far beyond any issue of tickets or fines, or even dying aunties. It had to do with dignity and humiliation, pure and simple. "What difference does it make whether I am on the train or not? There are plenty of seats free. It won't cost them any more to get to Rome just because I'm on it."

This was true, of course, but a dangerous road to go down.

"Two policemen will come to remove you," the inspector assured her, impressively unimpressed by her antics. He moved on down the corridor as she shouted after him. I wondered if perhaps he was bluffing. He hadn't actually gone to the trouble of making a call to the police in her presence. However, after huffing and puffing in a loud voice for the remaining minutes to Bologna, the woman suddenly stood up, very efficiently gathered three small bags, and got off the train in a completely relaxed fashion, as if she were just another passenger glad to reach her destination.

"Happens every day," the inspector explained on his return a little later. "They get on, get themselves thrown off at the next station, then get on the next train and get a free ride to the next station and so on, till they get where they're going. You can't throw them out of the window, you can't make them pay money they haven't got, the police can't be bothered to arrest them. Since the fast trains only stop at Bologna and Florence, she'll be in Rome before the day is out, if that's really where she wants to go. But maybe she just wants to keep warm and will get on the first train to somewhere else. Or back to Verona."

On arrival in Florence, I found the train stopped not, as I had expected, at Santa Maria Novella, the town's main station, just five minutes' walk from Palazzo Strozzi, but at the sad suburban station of Firenze Campo Marte. Could I, I asked a *capotreno* hurrying along the platform, use my Freccia ticket on a local train to Santa Maria Novella, or would I have to go to the ticket office for another ticket?

"Platform one," he said as he waved. "Plenty of trains."

"But do I need a new ticket? I just came from Verona on the Frecciargento, but now I see the ticket is just to Campo Marte."

He was already off, speaking over his shoulder. "They won't fine you," he said with an enigmatic laugh.

So, I reflected, my ticket was not officially valid for Santa Maria Novella, but nobody would have the courage to complain, since my investment in the Frecciargento was considerable and was supposed to take me to Florence, not to an outlying station. I was one of the blessed. To him that hath . . .

THE BLESSED UNDERSTAND ENGLISH. They have credit. They buy their tickets online. They don't speak dialect but proper, accentless Italian. Their values are cleanliness and speed. I think it was standing on that platform at Firenze Campo Marte that I first heard the new announcers whose voices you now hear in every station, large or small, from the far north of Italy to the deep south, imposing the new, suave Trenitalia feel on the whole peninsula; first a man's voice, Italian, young, educated, and eager to persuade, without any regional inflections, then a woman's voice, in English. She too seems young, efficient, knowledgeable, and unplaceable.

Unplaceable in England, that is, but *very* English, not American or even transatlantic. The funny thing is that although she reads the Italian names of the stations—Roma instead of an English Rome, Firenze instead of Florence, Napoli instead of Naples—she pronounces them with a strong, even exaggerated, English accent, making no concessions at all to the Italian vowel sounds or rolled *r*'s. So we have, Roe-mah, Na-poe-lee, Mi-lah-noe, Fi-ren-say, and so on. The effect is hilarious, but funniest of all is her pronunciation of Trenitalia, which she manages to rhyme with genitalia. Since we all know that Italy is pronounced with the *a* of "fat," not of "fate," it's hard to imagine how anyone could make a mistake like this; indeed, it begins to sound as if the announcements were deliberately making fun of the Englishman's or in this case woman's famed incompetence with foreign languages. Or maybe some PR man who has learned to pronounce the Queen's English at some upmarket language school has imagined that English people will only recognize the names if pronounced this way, despite the fact that the English announcements are not uniquely for the English, but for every foreign national with no Italian. In any event, I feel sure that this woman knows the proper pronunciations and is hamming it. She's having fun. And you can see a lot of Italian passengers are enjoying it too. For them it has the welcome effect of making the speakers of this globally dominant language seem stupid. Trenitayliah five seven zero to Ve-ne-ziaah . . . Trenitayliah two one nine to Pad-you-ah, Trenitayliah eight six one to Doe-moe-dossoe-lah . . .

NEEDLESS TO SAY, TRENITALIA'S reorganization of the train service into a world of first- and second-class citizens would not be complete without a complete overhaul of ticketing policy, which now entirely conditions these trips of mine to Florence. In the '90s there was a maximum promiscuity and flexibility between trains and people, as if passengers on a Regionale from Bergamo to Treviglio actually belonged to the same species as those *signori* and *signore* traveling on a Super Rapido from Milan to Turin. *All* tickets were valid for sixty days, and *all* could be upgraded with supplements. Now instead we have maximum segregation and rigidity; yet it was all done so stealthily, so gradually, that none of us really saw the logic of it until the operation was complete.

For me the moment of transition, or awakening, definitely came one morning in 2008 on a Verona–Milan Intercity. I was in the perfect situation of sharing a compartment with a man and a woman both as eager as myself to read and work. Then all of a sudden, a clamor of children! English children! There were scores of them. "Quiet, kids! Quiet!" A man in Boy Scout shorts and sandals with socks peered into our compartment. He began to look at a ticket and to compare the numbers on it with the seat numbers indicated outside our compartment. The sticky fingers and red noses of his charges pressed against the glass beside him. But I felt confident. There had been no cards to indicate reservations. I'm careful about that stuff. The compartment was free for the whole ride.

But Sandals and Socks opens the door and tells us in halting Italian that all our places are reserved. "*PREE-NOH-TAA-TEE*," he said. *Prenotati* = booked. The poor man seemed embarrassed to have to tell us this. "*Noy*"—he pointed his fingers at himself and the children making manic faces through the glass, "booked, pree-noh-taa-tee."

I didn't smile. The scoutmaster insisted on showing us their group ticket. Sure enough, they had booked. But how could this be? "It's the new rule," said the woman grimly, packing away her papers. "They don't put up the little reservation cards anymore. As of a couple of weeks ago."

"So how do you know where to sit?" I asked.

"You don't," she said. "You just sit until they move you."

The *capotreno* arrived. I asked him if it was true that we couldn't know where to sit anymore, that they weren't indicating the reserved seats. "You obviously don't read the notices we put up to explain the situation," he said. Squeezing through the crowded corridor from one carriage to another, I now had time to read one of these notices, posted in Italian only. "Seats 71–86 of each carriage (two compartments) cannot be reserved," it said. All the other seats could be reserved, but reservation cards would no longer be displayed. There was no explanation for this change. Passengers were kindly invited to show maximum willingness in giving up their seats to passengers with reservations.

Overnight, then, the person who didn't pay an extra €3 to book had become a second-class citizen. He could no longer know if a seat was free unless he was willing to go to the ghetto of compartments six and seven, which, of course, were always full. A couple of years later even this tenuous existence was denied him. All Intercities, Eurostars, and now Frecce would be *a prenotazione obbligatoria*, reserved seats only. *"La comodità è d'obbligo,"* announced a Trenitalia slogan. "Convenience is a must." The implication, of course, was that the regional trains were not convenient, since there you couldn't book a seat even if you wanted to. It was perhaps to make up for this that the old Interregionale was suddenly renamed the Regionale Veloce, the fast regional. When one thinks of all the expense of respraying carriages and rerecording announcements and reprinting timetables just to make this meaningless change, the mind boggles.

So now you always had to know what train you wanted to travel on, even with an Intercity, and book for that alone, a great loss of flexibility. Since people who travel on expensive trains don't want to stand in line, that meant you were more or less obliged to book online with a credit card. Obviously prices were adjusted to include the old booking charge. Then came what Italians call the *beffa,* a single word that means "the trick that adds insult to injury." If you paid a further 25 percent surcharge for a so-called Flexi ticket you would have the luxury, in the event of missing the train you were booked on, of being allowed to take the first train after that without paying any fine or surcharge. Otherwise there would be an automatic fine of €8; oddly, 25 percent of an expensive ticket is often more than €8.

To recap, then, while in the past one had maximum flexibility for price X at the slight risk of not finding a seat, something you could nevertheless sort out if you knew you were traveling at a busy time by adding a reservation for price X+Y, now you *always* pay X+Y and always have a seat but no flexibility unless you pay price X+Y+Z, when you have your seat and a little flexibility, but nothing like what you had years ago just paying X.

The bottom line is that Trenitalia privileges computer-savvy passengers with credit cards who will occupy reserved seats on clean, fashionable, very fast trains and who will even be permitted to show their ticket as a PDF on their laptops, or an SMS on their mobiles, while those without cards are cast into outer darkness, where there will be weeping and gnashing of teeth. In 2011 the ancient ticket machines in Porta Vescovo were replaced by the new, rather beautiful, and wonderfully efficient credit-card-only touch-screen machines; the speed of operation and discreetly presented range of options are simply remarkable. However, in the station's little bar the charming *barista* tells me that the ticket-selling side of her work has more than doubled since the arrival of these breakthrough machines because none of the passengers using Porta Vescovo—schoolchildren, students, immigrant laborers—have credit cards. But of course these people don't take expensive trains, so Trenitalia is not interested in them. More often than not even these splendid machines are broken because someone has deliberately jammed the place where you slot in your credit card.

HOWEVER, I SHOULDN'T COMPLAIN; a man curating a show about bankers with paintings by Botticelli and the Beato Angelico is clearly among the privileged and the blessed, and hence liberated from the purgatory of ticket machines. Like Cosimo de' Medici & Co. he has bought his place in paradise. Freed from all restraints—disembodied, it sometimes seems—I journey back and forth from Verona or Milan to Florence, from Florence to Milan or Verona, at extraordinary speeds and with remarkable punctuality, showing the inspector my first-class ticket, generously e-mailed to me by Palazzo Strozzi, on my laptop. In first class I have a choice of orange juice, wine, or coffee when I get on. There is also a power outlet for my laptop. The air-conditioning is reliable. The bathrooms are relatively clean. What more could one want?

Naturally, I soon grow accustomed to these blessings. I try a trip to Rome and discover that the train really does make it from Milan to Rome in under three hours. All at once train travel makes sense. This doesn't feel like Italy at all, I tell myself. I have stopped noticing the Regionali and the poor folk who use them. What a relief. I can read,

I can work, but *seriously* work, and I can travel center to center faster than by car or plane at cheaper prices with no, or next to no, hassles.

I can even feel *virtuous*. "Congratulations," my ticket tells me: "By choosing the train you have helped save the planet from CO_2 emissions." It gives examples. Traveling from Naples to Milan I am responsible for emissions amounting to 31.

But 31 what? It doesn't say. Presumably 31 bad things. By car I'd have emitted 76 bad things, by plane 115. It doesn't say whether we're talking about full planes or empty planes, full cars or empty cars. It doesn't say if it makes any difference whether I travel in first class or second. The important thing is that I feel virtuous—wealthy and virtuous—like those old Renaissance bankers. Isn't this what it means to be bourgeois, after all? A state of mind invented in Florence in the fifteenth century: the virtuous, forgivably self-satisfied businessman. While those bankers spent vast sums building splendid churches and commissioned fine paintings, we save on CO_2 emissions and make our small contribution to one of the most expensive railway lines in the world. Either way the money is not going to a lot of people who might feel they have a better claim to it. The same was said of the Medicis and Strozzi's lavish spending on their grand palazzi.

In any event, it must have been all this ease and sophistication that led to my last and greatest bust-up with a *capotreno*. I hesitate to tell the tale, since I come off rather badly, and perhaps the reader feels he has had his fill of *capotreni*. But this was a truly defining moment, both of my relationship with Italy and of my understanding of the new Trenitalia. I shall tell it, and then promise you there will be no more. It will be an easy promise to keep, since this was the bust-up that ended all bust-ups. I will never again allow myself to be drawn into an argument with a *capotreno*.

Basically, the unforgivable mistake I made was to act like a privileged Freccia person on a proletarian Regionale; I tried to mix the two worlds. But let me explain.

Until the summer of 2012 you could only buy Trenitalia tickets online for fast trains on which booking was obligatory. The Regionale or Regionale Veloce tickets had to be bought in the station, were valid for two months, and needed to be stamped on the day of travel. The Intercities had been pretty much phased out at this point, at least up north. So when I returned to my humble Porta Vescovo life, I was still having to deal with the idiocy of ticket machines and ticket windows. Imagine my surprise and delight, then, when sometime in spring 2012 I discover that you can now buy regional tickets online. There has been no advertising campaign for this, mind you, no overt encouragement to use these cheap trains, just that all of a sudden, while checking the online timetable, I notice that there is now the little circle you have to click to show that you want to buy online. Of course you have to specify your train, time, and date, which are then indicated on the PDF they send you, and the "ticket" is considered as already stamped and valid only for that train. So no two months for usage, but who cares if I can buy so easily only minutes before a train departs? I bought my Regionale Veloce ticket at once and put it in background on my laptop for display to the inspector *exactly as I always do when traveling the Frecce.*

Yep, this is truly fantastic; I patted myself on the back, heading for the station. Very soon I shall have to stop complaining about Trenitalia, which actually offers me a wonderful service at very reasonable prices. I'm a lucky man. I like trains, I live in a country that has trains, and at the highest level people are working hard to make those trains easier for us all.

I salute them.

I even salute the mad new announcement they have recently introduced to replace the old warning that a train is arriving:

"Trenitalia Regionale Veloce 2106 proveniente da Venezia Santa Lucia e destinato a Milano Centrale arriva e parte dal binario quattro."

"Trenitayliah Fast Regional 2106 from Veneziah Santa Luciah with terminus at Milanoh Sentralay arrives *and* departs from platform four."

Arrives *and* departs!

Who thought of this? If the train arrives at platform four, could it depart from anywhere else? It seems that high-speed technology, Internet connections, and general modernity in no way inhibit a flare for the absurd.

So I board my train, which does indeed arrive and depart from platform four. Thankfully, I find a seat at once, in second class; I am sitting next to some diligent young students, all bent over their books. Remembering that there is no electricity supply in this train, I decide to write down my ticket code, just in case my computer should run out of battery. I find a scrap of paper in my bag and jot it down: PCWNG2. Again I am filled with pleasure and a deep complacency at the thought that after twenty years I am now *entirely free of Trenitalia ticket lines and ticket machines*. I can always buy online for every train. I am master of the situation, empowered, in control of my life.

The ticket inspector arrives shortly before Peschiera. "Is there anyone's ticket I haven't seen?"

What a friendly way to approach his clientele! Presumably he has already checked this carriage before I got on and so is simply asking if anyone has boarded since he last checked. Our inspector is feeling relaxed. The net has many chat rooms where people discuss the various techniques for avoiding payment on Trenitalia trains. Awareness of the mood of the inspector is considered crucial.

Normally I might just continue my work and pretend that my ticket has been checked. I'm reading, of course. Actually I'm overwhelmed with reading for a literary prize I'm supposed to be judging, the International Booker. But today is a big day: the first day with an electronic ticket on a Regionale. So I say, "You haven't seen mine."

And I show him the code on the piece of paper.

Of course by now I'm familiar with all the inspectors on this line. This is an elderly man—the *capotreno*, in fact—with deep dusty wrinkles and cobwebbed eyelashes, dry papery skin, a shrewd, calculating look. I once saw him being very tough with a Slav girl who claimed that she hadn't bought a ticket because the machine accepted only credit cards. On the other hand, he regularly turns a blind eye to the freeloaders in first class.

"This ticket needs to be *in una stampa*," he says. Printed.

All around me eyebrows are raised. Over the years passengers become connoisseurs of ticket complications, and I may be the first person they have seen who has tried to travel on a Regionale Veloce with an electronic ticket purchased online.

I decide to say nothing.

"I need to see all the details," he says. "Your name and an ID card."

"I always give the booking number on the Freccia. They seem to think it's enough."

"This is not a Freccia, *signore*. Does it look like a Freccia? I don't have a fancy little computer with me to check your booking code. I can't know if the details are correct."

"But I have the details on-screen."

I open my computer, which is in sleep mode, and wait for it to fire up. Everybody is silent, intent. The inspector, who had seemed so relaxed when he merely inquired whether there were any tickets he hadn't checked, now seems disturbingly grim and purposeful, as if he'd encountered an unexpected pocket of enemy activity deep inside home territory. Perhaps he is a traditionalist, entirely against the intro- duction of electronic tickets. He fears that one day these tickets will cancel out his job, as they have already canceled out the jobs of thou- sands of ticket sellers. It occurs to me that maybe I shouldn't have mentioned that I regularly travel on the Frecce. Perhaps the inspector now feels that this well-to-do foreigner has no business cheapskating on his Regionale Veloce, which is a social service for the poorer trav- eler. He's a Communist of the old school, maybe.

Needless to say, the computer takes an unconscionable time to fire up. The train rattles along. Since the air-conditioning isn't working, everyone has the windows open, and the blue curtains are flapping and fluttering all down the packed carriage. It looks like a cinema ver-ité production from the 1950s.

"I need to see a printout," the inspector repeats. "On paper."

Why, then, is he waiting to see what I am going to show him on-screen? Again I choose to say nothing, but realize that I'm getting ner-vous. My right hand is trembling. This is ridiculous! It's just a ticket inspection.

The screen glows and there, at once, ready and waiting, is the PDF. The date and time of travel, the stations of departure and arrival. The class. Second.

"As you see," I tell him, "there's my name, which you can compare with that on my ID."

I pull my ID card from my pocket, my Italian ID, and offer it to him. He refuses to look at it.

"The ticket is only for this train, so I couldn't use it again," I tell him. "How could I be cheating?"

"I need to see a paper printout," he says.

I object that it doesn't say anything about printouts. Surely if there was some major difference between this and the other online tickets they would have warned the buyer.

"Of course it says so. Look at rule three."

He is standing in the corridor bending over the screen, which is on my knee. He is enjoying himself now, absolutely sure of his position, like someone who has a good hand at poker and is just waiting for the pleasure of recording a win and, even better, registering the dismay on his opponent's face.

"Where is rule three?"

He sighs, as though wishing he were up against more experienced opposition.

"Scroll down to the bottom of the page."

I confess I had never done this before. The PDF as it pops up on my screen ends with a long and unexplained code number, KK8-

9EY-U5K-UVJ. I scroll down. Sure enough, written in a much much smaller typeface there is a heading, *AVVERTENZE*. Cautions, warnings.

The first says: "This transportation contract is governed by 'Conditions and tariffs for the transport of persons on the FS,' which can be consulted on www.ferroviedellostato.it and on www.trenitalia.it— Conditions of transport."

The second says: "This ticket is named, personal, and untransferable. It is to be considered as already validated and can be used for four hours from the time and date indicated on this receipt."

The third says: "At the request of the inspection personnel, this receipt must be exhibited together with a valid ID."

It's the first victory to me. "I can't see anything here about printouts," I say triumphantly. "I'm showing the receipt in PDF and I have my ID where, as you will see, the name corresponds to that on the receipt, Timothy Parks."

It's a crass mistake on my part to sound so damn pleased with myself.

"Look at rule four," he says, unperturbed.

I scroll down another click.

Rule four says: "The ticket bearer cannot depart before the time shown on this receipt."

Reading it out, I don't even bother to remark that he seems to have slipped up. I departed exactly at the time indicated on the receipt, though the rule does raise the interesting question of whether one could legitimately travel on a train that left early.

The students are chewing their pencils, nudging each other. They like my style. The thought that a public official is being proved wrong is always sweet to an Italian. It appears to be happening. Only later would it occur to me that the inspector had made me read the irrelevant regulations to drag things out, to build up my hopes and hubris, to have me fall harder when the blow came.

"Look at rule five," he says.

Perhaps the reader could remember here that this man has a job to do checking tickets on an extremely busy train. It must already be absolutely clear that I have paid for my ticket and can't reuse it or cheat in any way. So why isn't he getting on with his job? But of course I know why. Deep down we all know that the rules are invented precisely to create the conditions for these confrontations, and when they occur they are immensely more important than merely checking that people have paid their fare or, in my case, reading some novel.

Rule five says: "The passenger cannot change the ticket or the class of the ticket."

The passengers around me on both sides of the central corridor are beginning to smile broadly.

"Which leaves rule six," the inspector says with a sigh. Something in his voice makes me look up at him. Our eyes meet. His dusty dry lips are twisted in the triumphant smile of bureaucratic Italy celebrating another victory.

I read out rule six; it says: "The passenger who is not able to show this receipt in printed form or does not present a valid ID is to be considered as traveling without a ticket and *regolarizzato*—regularized—according to current norms [ticket price + €50, or a regional fine]."

Again he sighs and says, "You do not have a printout. You do not have a ticket."

From this point on I find it hard to recall the exact progress of the dialogue, for the simple reason that I lost control. I was suddenly trembling and furious, far beyond anything that appeared to be at stake. Why had this crucial change been made, I demanded, without warning the traveler up front rather than in a tiny rule that didn't even appear on the screen without scrolling to the bottom? "A PDF *is* a *stampa*, a printout," I told him. "If I tell my computer to print it asks me if I want to print out a PDF." In what way was the printout on the screen any different from a printout on paper? What piece of information would he get with paper that he wasn't getting on the screen? None. Nothing.

"To me a printout means paper," he said.

"Remember, I actually volunteered this information when you

asked if there was anyone who hadn't had their ticket checked. I could have just kept quiet. Surely that indicates I'm in good faith."

He shook his head. "Without a paper printout I can't accept that someone has a ticket."

My voice began to wobble, perhaps my Italian slipped, my Englishness became more evident. An inspector is used to these confrontations. You're not. You're like the amateur who agrees to spend five minutes in the ring with the professional wrestler. I asked him whether, given that the regulations were new and given that the mistake I had made was understandable, he wasn't willing on this one occasion to turn a blind eye. He didn't even respond. He simply looked at me as if I were becoming too pathetic for words.

"I'm not paying a fine," I said.

"You don't have a ticket," he told me. He had to "regularize" my situation. That was his job.

"I'll get off at the next stop," I said. This, as we have seen before, is one way of resolving a ticket problem without formalizing a fine. Logically the man could have insisted on fining me, but he hadn't actually started writing out the fine.

"Okay," he said. "Make sure you do." Smiling faintly as he turned away, he said, "And make sure you read the regulations before you travel on Trenitalia."

No sooner had he turned his back than the people around me exploded into conversation. The girl next to me wanted to see the PDF at once.

"It doesn't say anything about paper," she said. "Only a *stampa*." A printout.

"There are no *avvertenze* on the online tickets for the Frecce," someone commiserated. "There was no reason why you should have gone and looked for them for a Regionale."

"If you were a pretty girl," the boy across the corridor said with a laugh, "there would have been no problem."

"That guy's one of the most *pignoli*," somebody else agreed.

At this point, the inspector, perhaps hearing the tones of indignation, strode back down the corridor to defend himself. "If you people would only . . ." he began.

"Who the hell *are* you?" I demanded.

I had totally lost it. The kids around me were agog. In particular the boy opposite had his mouth hanging open.

"You're the ticket inspector, right?" The tone of my voice had shifted into an unpleasant treble. "I've agreed to get off your train, right? Conversation over. Go inspect tickets. Isn't that what they pay you for?"

"You people like to complain, but . . ."

"Stop!" I yelled. "You have no right to interrupt a conversation between passengers on the train. We want to talk among ourselves. We can think what we like about you and your rules. *We don't want to talk to you.* I've agreed to get off the train, now *basta!*"

The man looked at me, weighing up the situation, pursing his lips. He had displayed a weakness and he knew it. First he had acted with unreasonable inflexibility, then he had shown that he didn't want to be ill thought of, he wanted to split me off from his regular, as he saw them, Regionale travelers. That was an error.

"You have no right," I repeated. "We do not wish to speak to you."

He looked at all of us. Myself and seven students, all with their books and laptops, abundant hair and scanty summer clothing, all viscerally against him. I had the feeling he was now seeing us all as privileged, whereas he came from a more honest, older world where workers had worked long hours and voted Partito Comunista Italiano and deserved protection from foreigners and electronic tickets. With a mocking bow he said *"Chiedo scusa, signore,"* and stalked off.

The youngsters were all respect. No sooner was the conflict over, however, than I was appalled. Why do I rise to this kind of bait? I wondered. Why had I been so rude, so shrill? I stood up to pull my bag down from the luggage rack. I'm sick, I thought.

"You're surely not really going to get off," someone protested. Everyone seemed amazed when I stood and got my bag down.

"But you've paid for your ticket!"

"You can't be serious. What's he going to do, get the police? They'll take one look at the PDF and laugh at him."

"He won't dare come back the whole trip, he'll just go to the other end of the train and hang out with his assistant."

I sat down with my bag on my knee and thought about it. So, all these young people, young Italians, had understood my offer to get off the train not as a real offer, but as a way of defusing the argument, or creating an honorable standoff, such that the inspector could continue to inspect and I could stay put and everybody would be happy. But I hadn't meant it like that. And I wasn't sure the inspector had understood it like that. Particularly not after his return and my inexcusable outburst. He would surely relish a chance for revenge if I offered it to him.

The train was approaching Peschiera. A few folk planning to visit Gardaland were standing up. Should I stay? Should I go? If I stay and he doesn't come I will spend the next hour and a half in a state of anxiety and won't be able to do any reading for the prize. If I stay and he returns there could be an almighty showdown, perhaps leading to legal action. I was aware that I couldn't vouch for my own responses.

But there was something deeper: this whole culture of ambiguous rules, then heated argument about them without any clear-cut result, seems to serve the purpose of drawing you into a mind-set of vendetta and resentment that saps energy from every other area of life. You become a member of society insofar as you feel hard done by, embattled. Others oppose you, or rally around you, for the entertainment. Almost everyone has some enemy they would like to crush. They become obsessed. They speak constantly about bureaucratic issues. Italian universities are full of such people, people who have been denied promotion because of some obscure regulation, people who have seen others promoted above them officially because they fell foul of some arcane paragraph in the university's constitution, but in reality because the promoted person is a friend of a friend of the vice rector. The whole soccer scene in Italy is a farcical factory of these emotions, a gaudy theater of mimed tribal conflict. To hang on in the train now, so that I could either boast before an appreciative audience that I had outwitted or faced down the inspector, or worse still so that I could plunge into a conflict that would engage my energies for months to come, would be to become more intensely and irretrievably Italian. No doubt about it. And all these young people around me wanted that. They couldn't conceive of my taking any other course of action at this point. They wanted to see the end of the drama, the defeat of the public official, or the confirmation that all the cards are stacked against the individual in his battle with the state. But my dream had always been to buy a ticket, use it, and travel in relative comfort, hopefully getting a little reading done on the way.

The train was slowing down in Peschiera. On the platform Mickey Mouse and Scrooge McDuck were still shooting it out twenty years on. *"Buon viaggio e buona giornata,"* I told my disgusted supporters and headed for the door. In the ticket office I paid twice the price of my original ticket for a seat on the next Frecciabianca, which arrived and departed from platform two only twenty minutes later, and after an uneventful journey spent reading Rohinton Mistry's excellent novel *A Fine Balance*, I arrived in Milano Centrale some five minutes ahead of the Regionale Veloce that I had so ignominiously bailed out of. I thus had a last chance to wait for the train and confront my antagonist again, perhaps to tell him that I planned to write about the incident in a book where I hoped he would come off extremely badly. For thirty seconds I seriously considered this option in the great arrivals hall of Milano Centrale. I looked up to the chalky friezes of warriors hacking each other to death, a huge advertisement for Nike with the ominous slogan, in English, HOW FAR CAN YOU RUN?, and another poster inviting me to gamble for cash on my cell phone. Surely the best thing to do, I decided, was to hurry to the university and get on with my Englishman's life in Italy.

Part Three

TO THE END
OF THE LAND

2012

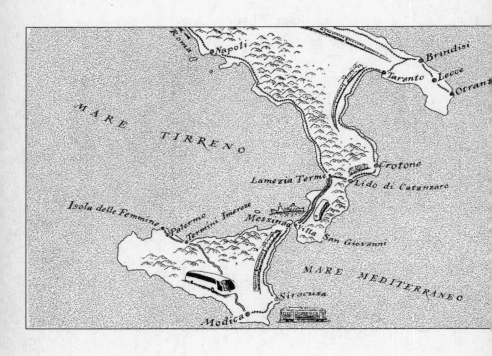

Chapter 5

MILANO–ROMA–PALERMO

I'M SCARCELY SURE WHAT NATIONALITY I REALLY AM THESE DAYS. All I know is that for the past thirty years I've lived and worked in northern Italy, and like most of the people around me I know little of the South, though the South is always present to us as an idea—a bad one, for the most part. The news we get of the South does not endear it to us. It is Gomorrah, it is corrupt, it soaks up our tax money, and when it isn't corrupt it is superstitious, primitive, sentimental, saccharine. In Milan the presence around us on the streets and in the workplace of all the southerners who have escaped to come to a serious place to work only confirms our opinions. And having made the journey north, these southerners are understandably eager to convince themselves they have done the right thing; they rarely speak affectionately of their home without a certain sigh that reminds you that, much as they love it, it was impossible to stay. The fact that so many politicians are southerners doesn't help; Italian politicians rarely inspire confidence. So when a northerner travels south he does so more often than not with a slight sense of trepidation, as if entering a different zone—a different country, even. I remember once, when traveling to see Hellas

Verona play in Naples, as the train drew to a standstill beside police lined up with batons, an older fan warned me, "We use our fists, they have their knives."

But all of a sudden, I had an urge to head south. Perhaps it was the 150th anniversary of Italian unity in 2011 that started it. During the celebrations people in Milan and Verona just could not have been less interested, never mind festive. The Northern League, a powerful xenophobic and separatist faction in northern Italy, was depicting Garibaldi as a bandit, a terrorist, whose 1860 expedition with the glorious Mille to capture Sicily and the South had merely saddled the North with an unwanted burden and a constant source of cultural contamination. Everybody was talking federalism and autonomy. At the same time, David Gilmour's book *The Pursuit of Italy* was making waves. Gilmour's learned conclusion is that the Risorgimento was a huge mistake and that Italy would govern itself better if split up once more into a dozen city-states. Frankly, I think that this is a complete misreading, a textbound academic's misreading, of Italian quarrels, like the friend who imagines a couple should split because they quarrel and talk about splitting. The truth is, you know the Italians are a people because the way they argue with each other is quite different from the way they argue with foreigners. It is their way of being together. Gilmour also underestimates a current of national idealism that runs beneath the surface of Italian cynicism. Garibaldi embodied that idealism. I for one have benefited enormously from the legacy he left, having spent almost all my adult life in a peaceful, united, and, all things considered, relatively prosperous Italy.

But in any event and for whatever reason, fine words aside, I just wanted to head south. July 2012 was the time to do it, and the trains were the perfect way to travel. What better yardstick than the national railway for judging whether the South was really part of the nation? I would head down to Sicily, starting in Palermo, then, combining work and vacation, try to get around the coast of the island, then back to Calabria and right around the toe, instep, and heel of the boot from west to east. That would mean pulling in towns like Reggio Calabria, Crotone, Taranto, and the splendid yellow stone *centro storico* of Lecce, where Trenitalia hits the final buffer in distant Puglia. We would see if the FS of the extreme South was the same old FS I knew on the train of the living dead.

Yet I didn't start the journey on state railways. For at last, at least on one stretch of line, those words "Thank you for choosing Trenitalia" are no longer a mockery: from Turin to Milan to Rome and on to Naples, you can now travel with Italo.

In short, it was the completion of the high-speed line that finally brought a little real competition into being. The reasons are easy to understand: the infrastructural investment had been so huge that the government and the FS were desperate for anybody willing to pay to use it. There was plenty of spare capacity available. The high-speed lines had been equipped with a new form of electricity supply that ordinary freight and passenger trains couldn't use. Trenitalia simply doesn't have enough Frecce to keep the lines busy if they wanted to. It was the perfect space for some ambitious entrepreneur to step into.

But it could hardly start without controversy.

Nuovo Transporto Viaggiatori (NTV) opened its new travel center, Casa Italo, in a refurbished air terminal built beside the railway lines at Roma Ostiense, a secondary rail station in the west of the city. The handsome building, designed by Julio Lafuente for the 1990 World Cup, already housed a new branch of Eataly, the consortium of restaurants and shops selling traditional Italian food products.

The idea was that passengers for the new private rail service would park in the large adjacent car park, or simply emerge from the metro, buy their tickets in this clean, modern building, and step right onto the Italo, NTV's new and rather beautiful maroon-colored train, holder of the present world speed record, which departs from the open platform right beside the building and promises to make the trip to Milan in two hours and forty-five minutes.

Utopia.

However, the night before it opened, an eight-foot-high steel fence went up between the travel center and the train it was providing tickets for. Passengers thus had to, and still have to, go down two flights of stairs, or an escalator, and walk through almost a thousand feet of underground passages before returning to ground level up more flights of stairs or another escalator (on which no doubt everyone is standing still) to reach the train, a few yards away from where they bought their tickets.

Who could have done such a silly thing? Rete Ferroviaria Italiana, of course, the part of the FS group that runs the rail infrastructure and that in fact stands to gain €140 million a year from Italo's use of its high-speed lines. But, of course, RFI and Trenitalia are still very much hand in glove, and though it's nice to get Italo's money, it would be unfortunate if the newcomer were allowed to become more convenient than the Frecce. Accused of raising obstacles to free competition, RFI released a statement speaking of the need for physical barriers between railway property and public streets, a need that only became urgent the day people could buy a ticket for a rival train. The organization then conceded that a gate might be opened in this fence, but this hasn't happened. Italo passengers troll unnecessarily back and forth through the passageways standing behind Trenitalia passengers on the escalators. In any event, it was the erection of this barrier, again so emblematic of how Italy works, or doesn't, together with that miserable clash with the Trenitalia inspector who wouldn't accept that on-screen e-ticket, that made me absolutely determined to take the Italo on the first leg of my trip to the South.

Needless to say, Italo hasn't been allowed to leave from Milano Centrale, but from Milan's ugly secondary station of Porta Garibaldi, about half a mile away. If the revolutionary fighter's story is remarkable for clarity of trajectory, for flamboyance in idealism, for focus and consistency of purpose, as when, having beaten the Austrians by Lake Como, he marched gloriously into Milan right at this part of the city in

1859, Stazione Garibaldi is an amorphous, sprawling mess. And while Garibaldi the hero is immediately acknowledged as achieving a spiritual aristocracy worthy of the grandeur of Milano Centrale, Garibaldi FS is the home of the humdrum, arrival point of tens of thousands of yawning commuters brought in daily from the north and west on endless convoys of miserable *regionali*.

There is nothing here that declares itself as a main entrance. The shapeless building bleeds its travelers into the surrounding streets from any number of open wounds. Running around its glass and concrete facade is Viale Don Luigi Sturzo, a fast, nondescript road immediately linking to faster, more nondescript highways rushing people out of town. Don Luigi Sturzo was the Sicilian priest who in 1919 formed the Partito Popolare Italiano, forerunner of the Christian Democrat Party. As such he championed the notion of Catholics engaging in politics as a group with its own agenda, which, of course, did not necessarily correspond to a national agenda. Garibaldi would have loathed such an idea. It has sometimes occurred to me that the Ferrovie dello Stato are a kind of Catholic Church. It has that suffocating monopoly status of being more important than its supposed principles and goals, "a state within a state," as one politician called it, as early as 1870. In that case Italo might be a hateful, freethinking, nonconformist rebel, bearer of the gospel of real competition. In any event, it feels like a good omen for my trip to Sicily and the South to leave from Stazione Garibaldi.

Comically, to the eastern end of the station, Viale Don Luigi Sturzo runs through Piazza Sigmund Freud. I doubt that the Austrian therapist would have made much progress with the dysfunctional national family implied by the names of Garibaldi and Sturzo. In fact, the piazza is now a mess of rubble in the ongoing process of redevelopment that has made this part of Milan the most modern and the most unlivable and unwalkable. One evening, returning from Florence, my train stopped in Porta Garibaldi rather than Centrale. It was onward bound to Turin, and Garibaldi has the advantage that trains can run through it without having to be turned around. Climbing down on the platform, it was not immediately obvious which way one was supposed to go to exit the station. I set off down a staircase and found a corridor at the bottom but no signs or directions. "Where's the metro?" I asked the girl walking down behind me. Since it was late at night, she seemed anxious that I might be trying to approach her. How could there not be signs for a metro in a major railway station? She looked around and frowned.

Two men now came down the stairs. "Do you know which is the direction to the metro?" They didn't. They also were looking for the metro. "I think it's this way," one of them said. We went down the tunnel, turned a corner, were confronted with other tunnels, escalators. There were the names of roads, there were numbers of platforms, but no signs for the metro. Eventually we climbed stairs to find ourselves on a tarmac sidewalk running beside a wall beneath an elevated highway. All four of us, now united in our contempt for whoever was responsible for *la mobilità* in Porta Garibaldi, decided we had better turn right. After five minutes walking in that direction we gave up, turned around, and walked ten minutes in the other direction, finally discovering the so-called front of the station and the metro some twenty minutes after our train had dumped us on a gloomy platform. Garibaldi, it has to be said, was famous for being able to lead his men rapidly at night through the most arduous and uncharted terrain.

So when I went to catch the Italo I left much earlier than theoretically I needed to. This was just as well. RFI had hidden Italo on an underground platform under a little mare's nest of escalators. As I would soon discover, in all the stations where Italo operates the tension between the new company's desire to give visibility to its services and the old organization's determination that it not be allowed to develop any special profile is everywhere evident. Does a sign indicating where a train leaves from amount to publicity? I suppose if you never wanted the train to exist in the first place, it possibly does. In the same way, Italian taxi drivers are famous for removing signs at airports that indicate where you might catch a cheap bus into town.

I was traveling not in second class, not in first, not in business, but in "Smart." With this English term, whose many nuances and connotations Italians know nothing of, the shame of the word *seconda* has been avoided. Interestingly, though, for first class the Italian *prima* has been kept. Reasons for pride are expressed in our own language; for less gratifying denominations some smart word from some smart international language will do. There is also "Club." For the top of the top we return to airline English. In any event, it's obvious from the price of my ticket, just €45, that I'm traveling in second.

During the trip, I thought I'd make a few notes to establish the peculiarity of these new Italo trains as opposed to the Frecce: the generosity of the carriages, rather wider and higher than the Frecce, with their stylish gray and orange fake leather seats; the extraordinarily clean—indeed, spic and span—bathrooms; the cinema carriage—can you imagine?—where a recent film is projected on decently large screens; in general, a smoother, far more stable, and definitely quieter feel to the train. But very soon I put my pen down. The real difference in traveling on Italo has to do with an absence, a strange lightness: *there are no Trenitalia personnel and no Trenitalia announcements.* The girl who arrived in her smart maroon blazer behaved more like an air hostess than a ticket collector; I even had the illusion that she was there to serve me. As I went to the bathroom, a man going in before me turned to allow me to go ahead. "No, that's fine," I told him. Only then did I realize that what he was wearing was a kind of gray, dungaree uniform. He was carrying out a routine check of the toilets *en voyage.* It was hard to believe.

The Wi-Fi is free, and I went on the Italo website and looked up *personale a bordo*, on-board personnel. They had avoided the Trenitalia categories by using English for the job descriptions: train manager, train specialist (my man checking the bathrooms) and, yes, the hostess or steward. There was no mention at all that it was anyone's duty to look at your ticket. One of the stewards was black; at last.

I ran a quick Google search on Italo and found an *Economist* article mentioning the famous fence down at Ostiense in Rome that keeps Italo passengers from their trains. "Ingrained hostility to competition," the English journalist said, was "something the Italians have to look at." I find this kind of comment so right, but so wrong, as if the government could pass a law to resolve the problem, or as if hostility to competition wasn't part of a deep ethos that is never going to change here without some massive national upheaval. The Italians invariably produce these monolithic organizations, the Catholic Church, the Ferrovie dello Stato, or indeed the state itself, that they both identify with and feel hostile to. Throughout the postwar period the Italian state expanded into so many areas of industry, running some of the largest monopolies in Europe and proving itself one of the most generous sources of pensions and handouts in the whole world. At the local level whole towns are still willing to put their fate in the hands of one man, or company, as was the case with Turin and Fiat, with Parma and the Tanzis, and for a period with Milan and Berlusconi. Beneath all this lies a fear of being exposed to the competitive world and an overwhelming desire for protection; these powerful men, these powerful organizations will look after us. Our identity lies in belonging to them and then loathing them, accepting their bounty and disobeying them, evading their taxes, traveling without tickets, then voting for them, again and again. It is between the need for protection and the dream of liberty that Trenitalia's Freccia and NTV's Italo rush by each other on the high-speed lines between Milan and Rome, taking in Cosimo's Florence on the way. The balance, or imbalance, between the two antithetical impulses can reasonably be measured by the relative sizes of the two companies: NTV has twenty-five trains, albeit of the latest, Italo-French designs. Trenitalia has thousands.

The main founding partner of NTV is Luca Cordero di Montezemolo, heir to a noble family for many generations hand in glove with the Italian royal family of Savoy. Montezemolo is president of Ferrari, has been executive chairman of Fiat and head of the Confederation of Italian Industry, and sits on the boards of various major companies. His junior partner, with whom he holds a controlling interest in NTV, is Diego Della Valle, heir to a shoe manufacturing empire and owner of

Florence's soccer club Fiorentina. This is big old North Italian business, backed to the tune of 20 percent by French railways. Montezemolo
and Della Valle must be old acquaintances with those heading Trenitalia and RFI. In the end the Ferrovie dello Stato has nothing to fear from
them, the same way that the Fascists had nothing to fear from the big
northern industrialists of the twenties and thirties. As long as these men
are allowed a share of the action, they will not upset the applecart.

Still, they must be made to suffer for their profits. Italo has not
been given space to stop at Roma Termini, hub of all mobility in the
city. Instead I stepped down at Tiburtina, a smaller, sadder version of
Milan's Porta Garibaldi. I took a picture of the driver climbing down
from his futuristic locomotive. He seemed happy enough to be photographed with this great hunk of technology. Ten minutes later, shocked
as I always am to see how drab and dingy the Rome metro is, I took
another, contrasting picture. At once a uniformed metro man, invested
with that air of public officialdom, hurried up to me wagging his finger
and warning, in broken English, "No photo, no photo. Forbidden!"

How is it that Italians always know I'm not Italian, *even before I
speak to them?* It's not that there are not quite a few blue-eyed Italians with light brown hair. I can only suppose there must be subtle
signals in the gait and body language that they pick up unconsciously.
What's sad about it is that my accent is never even given a chance to
pass muster, since people have already placed me before I open my
mouth. It's frustrating after thirty years in the country. Whether it is
really forbidden to take photos in metro stations as in train stations I
have no idea. In the end it makes no difference. I waited for the man to
move off, took another couple of pictures, then headed off for a quiet
weekend with friends.

"YOU DON'T HAVE TO explain anything to me." The young man
shakes his head. "Nothing."

About one thing I was wrong. Compartments do still exist. South

of Rome. That was the big discovery on boarding the 11:39 to Palermo from Roma Termini. It would be amply confirmed in the days
to come. In the South they still have compartments; they still have
the old Intercities. They even call them Intercities. In fact, they still
have lots of old things and old names down south that we're rapidly
forgetting about in Milan. For some reason this puts me in an excellent mood, as when you discover that a model of car you owned twenty
years ago, or a word you once used and had forgotten, is still up and
running in a foreign country. Somewhere between Rome and Reggio
Calabria you go through a time warp.

"Think what you like," the boy beside me says, "I don't care."

He's tall and handsome in a languid southern way, his lithe body
spreading over the seat like liquid copper, legs apart, left elbow pushing mine off our shared armrest, right hand scratching idly behind his
neck. The phone is tucked, no hands, under his chin where he talks
into it, as if savoring his armpit.

"But that's my business," he says calmly, "not yours."

His seat is beside the door where three friends now appear, two girls
and a boy all like himself in their late teens, early twenties. They want
him to move into the next compartment where there is a spare seat.
Without explaining anything into the phone, he covers the receiver,
sighs, shakes his head: "I have to speak," he tells them.

Five of the six places are occupied and I'm the only one not on the
phone. The girl to my left is peppy and pleased with herself.

"Did something crazy!" she says. She has sunglasses hitched up
on a fraying perm. She says with a giggle, "That's the million-dollar
question."

The man opposite is overweight and in his fifties, round bald head,
glistening with sweat, his red skin meaty against his damp white shirt.
The Rome metro and the buses are both on strike this morning. Perhaps like me he walked to the station. It's hot out there. It's hot in
here, too. They haven't hooked up the air-conditioning yet; still five
minutes before the Roma–Palermo Intercity is due to depart.

"So Mass is at seven?" the meaty man asks. He has a copy of the financial paper *Il Sole 24 Ore*, plus a black attaché case. As he speaks he seems openly curious about the fact that I'm typing rapidly on my laptop. Italians often seem surprised by people who type with more than two fingers.

"No, the *monsignore*!" he breaks into a laugh and I see he only has one front tooth up top. Oddly, he keeps his eye on me throughout the conversation, as if he wanted me to join in the laughter, as if there were some complicity between us. Is he a priest? Does some subtle intuition tell him that my father was a clergyman? Perhaps he's one of the Vatican bankers, very much in the news these days, for corrupt practices. But then surely he would have kept his teeth in better shape, he would have arrived at the station in an air-conditioned limousine. He wears his watch face, I see, on the inside of his wrist, something I've always found odd, secretive.

"You don't know how much money I spent," the girl on my left says triumphantly.

"It's my decision and I've made it," the boy says quietly. At first I imagined he was speaking to his mother, since I've noticed that many young Italians feel that phoning one's mother is the natural thing to do when boarding a train. Perhaps Trenitalia makes them think of Mamma. But now I see of course he is firing his girlfriend, he is telling her he wants no more discussion about their breakup. "Still harping on about that?" he asks coolly, as if he'd imagined she were smarter. Totally relaxed, it seems he was born to have the kind of conversations that have always terrified me. For a while he studies his left hand, turning it this way and that, as he listens to her lament.

Only the fifth occupant, a middle-aged, well-dressed woman, sitting opposite the young man and beside the one-toothed banker priest, seems rather anxious. She has spoken to someone informing him or her that she made it to the train, that she is now sitting in a sweltering compartment, that she should be home, all things being well, at about 9:00 p.m., though she doubts that all things will be well, knowing

these trains, that she would be grateful, yes, if she could be picked up
at the station, that she has never been more disgusted by Rome than
on this awful trip, that she has never been treated worse in her entire
life, that she sincerely doubts she will be coming back, but yes, she
knows she's said that before. "Yes, yes, I'm sorry. I won't go on."

She hangs up and takes two magazines from her bag. *Dipiù* and
Zero. *Dipiù* is gossip. The cover shows the naked torso of a grinning,
unshaven young man, as if he were surprised to find himself so handsome. The chain around his neck has a ring on it, and a glamorous
woman has been placed in obvious montage beside him. "My Grand-
son in Love with Emma," says the headline. "Actor's Grandfather
Speaks Out." Looking at the picture as the woman opens the magazine with a frown, I have the impression there's something odd about
it, but can't decide what.

"Do what you like," the young man says. His knee is jerking gently.
"It's really not my problem."

"I just *have to* dance," the girl by the window says. "That's the
truth. What can I do?"

The meaty man has a ring of white hair above his ears and more
sprouting out of his shirt, but none on his head. Reading upside down,
on the papers he's now studying, I decipher the letterhead: "Rever-
endo Monsignor Don Andrea la Regine."

Dipiù magazine carries a feature "*Il Mammone più bello*—Best-
Looking Mommy's Boy." Under a postage stamp photo of a young
man with a light blond beard is the subheading "Why I Can't Find a
Woman by Myself."

"Think what you like," the young man beside me purrs.

The train lurches into movement, just a few minutes late. I had been
meaning to do some work on the trip. There are eleven and a half hours
to get through, after all. But suddenly I just feel too happy. How lucky
I am to be in a compartment again! How privileged to be surrounded
by all this *life* and to be able to understand what everyone is saying,
too. People speak so much about the mutual incomprehensibility of

Italy's dialects, but I can understand all five of these people, the boy clearly Sicilian, the girl to my left from Piacenza maybe, around there; she has those vowel sounds. The woman in the corner is also Sicilian. The man clearly Roman. All have their accents but all are understand-able—all, like it or not, Professor Gilmour, very Italian.

And the train, no doubt, the train compartment in particular, has contributed to this slow unification of the language. More often than not it's been on the train that I first heard new accents. I remember in particular the shock of hearing a group of kids from Bergamo. I honestly thought the language was not Indo-European. It was on the trains and buses with the fans of my local soccer team, the *brigate gialloblù*, that I finally learned the finer points of Veronese dialect. No doubt millions of Italians have had the same experience: trapped in train compartments with people from other parts of Italy, they set to work to understand each other.

I close my eyes and soak it up, as if this morning I were getting an unexpected payoff for my thirty years in this country. I'm not above a little sentimentality from time to time. The girl is now complaining that she slept only an hour and a half, between five and six-thirty. "He gave me a really shitty bed. You wouldn't believe it." In the distance I can hear a hawker shouting his wares at the top of his nasal voice:

"*Aranciata, coca, birra, panini, acqua, acqua, acqua, panini!*"

"Still on about the same old stuff," the boy says. He's shaking his head.

"*Caffè, acqua, panini!*"

"I told you the truth, you know."

"*Coca cola, caffè, acqua, birra.*"

The voice is getting closer, the speaker rearranging his five or six wares in every possible sequence, always with the same mad urgency. "*Panini, acqua, acqua, birra, caffè.*"

"I didn't do anything! It was a joke."

A hand taps mine and I open my eyes. It's a young Gypsy woman placing a printed card on my lap. She has a stack of them and goes out and along the corridor to deliver the rest. In a few minutes she'll be back to see if any of us are willing to give. "I'm a poor woman from Bosnia," the card begins, "homeless, with two young children. . . ." It runs on for a few lines. The type is properly justified and there are no spelling or grammar mistakes. Presumably all the Gypsy women in a given group use the same printed card; otherwise it would push up costs.

"That's the third this morning," the woman reading about celebrities remarks.

The man who corresponds with the *monsignor* shakes his head, then pulls out a crumpled white handkerchief to mop up the sweat. I love a man who has a real cloth handkerchief.

"*Vabbè,*" the boy says lifelessly. "Okay. Okay. Okay."

Apparently the call is over because he suddenly pulls the phone from the crook of his neck and looks at it, turning it over in his hands a few times, as a man who has just used a revolver might examine the smoking barrel. Settling even more deeply in his seat, he starts to hum. I recognize the tune. What is it? Ah! "New York, New York."

"You old fraud!" comes a booming voice. Two ticket inspectors are standing outside the compartment, laughing and joking. They are both men, in their fifties, pulling each other's legs in strong southern accents.

"*Coca, caffè, panini, panini!*"

The vendor appears, banging two refrigerated boxes against his hairy legs. He's wearing a white vest and capacious shorts under a proud paunch and grinning.

"*Un abusivo,*" the possible priest remarks, trying to draw me into a conversation. By which he means this is not the official FS vendor with his proper minibar and wad of carefully distributed receipts. All the same, the abusivo exchanges smiles and words with the inspectors and calls them by name. Leaning into the compartment, he has just begun to shout, "*aranciate, coca, birra*" when he sees me.

"Beeah," he says. "Sanwidge. Sohda."

Even an Englishman's refreshment priorities are assumed.

"No grazie," I tell him, keeping my words as few and my accent as perfect as possible.

Why is the priestly pate so interested in me? He's staring.

With the inspectors and the hawker blocking the doorway, the Gypsy woman is having to wait her turn to come into the compartment and get her begging cards back. She doesn't know the two inspectors or salute them, but they tolerate her. Is begging allowed on trains? I don't know, though at a guess I'd say no. The boy buys an orange soda. The worried woman buys a coffee. Nobody gives a cent to the Gypsy woman, yet presumably people do give or she wouldn't be doing this. Does she have a ticket? The inspectors don't ask, but one of them comes in now to examine ours. I'm the only one who has bought my *documento di viaggio* online, the only one to show his ticket on the computer screen. The inspector, examines the PDF, taps the ticket code in his little machine, and accepts it. I'm relieved, though, yes, I did have a paper printout in my pocket this time, though it's theoretically not required. Again the priest looks at me with brazen curiosity. Something about me has roused his interest. But I have decided not to talk to him; I'm not going to tell him whatever it is he wants to know about me.

About fifteen minutes out of Rome we get a welcoming announcement from the *capotreno* listing all our stops, telling us where the dining car is, which carriages will go to Siracusa and which to Palermo, because after we have crossed to Sicily the train will split. His whole spiel is delivered in four languages and always with some panache.

The dropped girlfriend calls the Sicilian boy again. He listens patiently for quite a while before asking, "Did I say something I shouldn't have?" On the other side of me, the girl who had a tough night has settled down to sleep. Her head lolls.

"I just felt like it," the boy says. He's so patient and so ruthless. "I felt like it and I did it and that's that. It's called freedom."

Writing those words down, one's tempted to add a tag like "he said with sudden belligerence" or "finality"; but he didn't. He says everything in exactly the same tone, perhaps with just the slightest hint of the appropriate emotion, a discreet and washed-out color.

"*In bocca al lupo,*" he says now. "Good luck with everything."

Now I can hear a raised voice at the other end of the line.

"*Basta,*" he says. "Enough. I've decided and that's that."

He closes the call, puts the phone in his lap, and flexes his hand open and closed, open and closed, as might a boxer who has held his fist clenched too long. For a few minutes he stretches his mouth from side to side. Then he begins to hum again. Outside, the barren hills of Campania roll by. Thinking of voices and dialects and difficult conversations with girls I remember the last time I traveled this stretch of line in a train and saw these hills. It was that trip with the soccer supporters to see Hellas Verona play in Naples. The three boys I was with spent this stretch of the journey trying to chat up a Roman girl who was going to see her Neapolitan boyfriend for the weekend. They asked her every embarrassing and impertinent question that a group of boys ever could ask a young woman, and she dealt with it all so coolly and wryly, even taking time to say that she found their accents cute.

"*Evviva Verona!*" the boys yelled. "Home of Romeo and Juliet, city of romance." They tried to get her to join in cheers of Hellas, the name of Verona's soccer club: "HEEELLLLLLAAAAS!" They gave her a blue and yellow Hellas flag and asked her if she would lie on it when her boyfriend made love to her. She smiled and said she would. "Then you'll be a *buteleta,*" they said, a little girl (in Veronese), a Hellas girl. She'd like that, she said. She repeated the word *buteleta* in her Roman accent and all the boys laughed and tried to get her to repeat it in the correct Veronese accent. And the more she was game and unfazed, the harsher their dialect and requests became. She had to yell *Hellaaaaaaaaaaaaaaaaaaaaas* when she climaxed with her boyfriend, they shouted. Very gravely she said she might. She'd have to think about it.

"You don't really want to sleep with a Neapolitan," one of them began. "What about me? Can't you fancy me?" The Veronese were such lovers, he said. "Maybe, someday," she said. "Show us a nipple," one of the boys asked. "Just one, please." She smiled and shook her head. "A bra strap then, a bra strap." She thought about it. She was very petite, cute, well made with very small, neatly molded features. "Okay," she said, and she moved the shoulder of her T-shirt to show them a beige bra strap. There was a wild roar.

Thus the trains bring Italians together, I reflect now, thinking back on that conversation that seemed both extremely spontaneous but absolutely scripted, and so terribly easy to remember, as if it had already happened a thousand times and would happen a thousand times again in the future, like this interminable phone call between the boy beside me and the girl he is leaving. She calls back again. He listens. After a while he says,

"But it's normal. People do this."

And then after another few minutes,

"*E vabbè comunque.*" Okay all the same.

This time the conversation was really over because he turned his phone off and in no time at all had fallen asleep. So now I had two young heads lolling, one on each side of me, in cartoon fashion, slowly sinking, suddenly dropping, then jerking up again, then sinking again. Train sleep. The *monsignor*'s friend smiled to show me he had noticed this too and how endearing it was. I frustrated him by opening my laptop again. When she turned a page, I was able to see that the woman beside him was reading an article titled, "Hate Turns Mother-in-Law into Murderer."

SEVEN HOURS INTO THE journey, at Villa San Giovanni, a northern suburb of Reggio Calabria, they split the train in two and put it on the ferry. I had assumed that we would get off the train, get on the ferry, get off the ferry, and get on another train, as we always did as children when we crossed from Dover to Calais. I had not believed it when a student told me they really put the train on the boat; I thought she must be misinformed. But no, they do. The actual ferry crossing from the Calabrian coast to Messina, at the northeastern corner of Sicily, takes about thirty minutes. Splitting the train and shunting the two halves back and forth to roll them into the belly of the boat takes about an hour. Then another hour to shunt them off and attach them to separate locomotives, four carriages for Palermo and four for Siracusa. During these jerky, rail-grinding procedures the air-conditioning is turned off.

We arrived at the dock in Villa San Giovanni at 6:30 p.m. The train sat under full sunshine. The temperature was about ninety-five degrees. The windows were sealed. Very soon, the woman with the gossip magazines opened a large pink fan.

There had been some changes among the passengers. The dancing girl to my left and the gap-toothed banker priest had both gotten off before Naples. Opposite I now had a chubbily handsome woman in her forties who was keeping her husband constantly informed, by phone, as to her *giramenti di testa*—dizzy fits—and our possible arrival time in Messina. She seemed cultured, competent, and entirely focused on the well-being of her large, slightly moist body.

Beside me, on the window side, was another young woman, this time with her boyfriend facing her, in what had previously been the empty seat. No sooner did this happy couple get on than they placed a large food cooler on the floor between them, their heads meeting and nuzzling over it as they rummaged among wrapping paper and Coke bottles and started to offer around crisps, tiny pizzas, ham sandwiches, and little cakes. Everyone smiled and declined, except the boy who had seen off his girlfriend; he accepted a small pizza. With the air of someone used to presiding over intimate dinner parties, the large lady observed that she had realized at once the couple must be southerners because only southerners offered their food to people, not like the mean and miserable folk of the North. She smiled complacently. A more obvious invitation for general chatter and self-congratulation one could hardly imagine, since it was clear that the boy sprawled beside me and the permed woman with the gossip magazines had very southern physiognomies. I was the one odd man out, and she had clearly decided that wherever I was from I wasn't likely to take offense.

From this point on, the compartment was a salon. The young couple, she with a charmingly long neck of the kind one sees on Etruscan vases, he with a young man's beard that he constantly combed for crumbs as he ate, began to explain the foolishness of their trip: an uncle was picking them up in Palermo to drive them to his house on the coast just below Trapani. But they only had the weekend! So on Sunday evening they would be back on the night train from Palermo, which should get them to Naples just in time to be back at work Monday morning. Exhausting!

"The fact is, I can't fly," the girl confided, and she smiled at her boyfriend with such seductive apology for wasting his weekend on the train that he leaned across and put both hands around that long neck to forgive her. To my right the tall, sprawling, now single young man turned his phone over and over in his hand.

Then everyone felt the need to declare why they would do something so eccentric as to take a *train*, of all things to Sicily. The permed woman, who appeared to be studying her magazines as if for an exam, explained that she lived only a couple of hundred yards from the small station at Castroreale, so that it really was the easiest thing for her, even though the bus would be cheaper and quicker, and the plane much quicker. The chubby woman said her blood pressure problems didn't allow her to fly and she found the bus uncomfortable, the seats weren't big enough, the movements too jerky. The boy told us he was doing his training program to be a soldier. He only had three days off. He would normally have gone by bus, but his parents had bought him the train ticket. The other listeners were so pleased to hear that they had a young soldier among them, and a handsome one at that, that they forgot to ask me, or were spared from asking me, what I was doing on this train, which was fine by me, since wherever possible I avoid the dull discussion about my foreignness and my writing habit. The boy described, with an animation he had not shown throughout the long call with his girlfriend, all the ordeals of his boot camp, in particular the marches in high temperatures carrying some eighty-odd pounds of equipment.

"Would you be happy to be selected for Afghanistan?" the woman with *giramenti di testa* asked with obvious concern.

"Yes," the boy said. He spoke with some solemnity now. But it was more likely that he'd be fighting closer to home, he thought. "The revolution isn't far away now," he told us. "With this economic crisis and everything. It's already begun in Greece and Spain."

It wasn't clear from the way he spoke which side of the revolution he thought he would be on, if ever the fighting began, only that he was looking forward to this chance, as he saw it, to become adult. There was a curious curl to his upper lip, almost a sneer; he was eager to feel superior but knew it was something he had to work on, he had to train to become a good soldier, then he would have earned that sense of elevated detachment that had allowed him to blow off his girlfriend so calmly. He had just turned twenty, he said.

"After a while, you could get yourself transferred home to Palermo," the chubby woman advised. "They have a large barracks there."

He'd already had a chance to move back, the boy said, and added proudly, "Lots of my *compagni* would have said yes, but I'm not the kind. I want to live in new places."

"But you're coming home for your leave, even if it's only three days."

"My mother paid for my ticket," he said with a shrug. Everybody laughed.

IN THE LONG HOURS rattling down the coast—Salerno, Sapri, Paola—the dusty hills to our left and the dazzling sea to our right—*Dipiù* and *Zero* are passed around. The sixty-six-year-old actor and director

Michele Placido was marrying a woman of twenty-eight. The model Raffaella Fico had announced that she was pregnant by the mad and maverick Mario Balotelli, the first truly black Italian to play for the national soccer team. Coal black and always in trouble, Balotelli was demanding a DNA test.

"*Furbe, queste ragazze*," remarks the hefty woman, who is presiding over the conversation.

The soldier boy nods knowingly. "You bet." The young couple lean across to each other and nuzzle noses. Her eyebrows are plucked to pencil line arches. Wearing shorts, his legs straddling hers are shaggy with hair.

"If they wait and see when it's born, it'll be pretty obvious if it's his," remarks the woman in the corner.

"He's not the only black in the world."

"The only one Fico has ever been seen with."

"You're well informed," remarks the tubby woman, who throughout has shown a certain disdain for the gossip magazine, as if the publication interfered with her self-appointed role as hostess.

Finally the paper ends up in my hands. My laptop battery ran out long ago. To my surprise I find that there's an interview with former prime minister Romano Prodi and an editorial criticizing the present government's emergency measures to cut pensions and other spending. Then there are articles you feel must be dusted off and reprinted every year: "Mediterranean Diet Improves Your Humor"; "I Want a Girlfriend Like My Mom." I glance through and hand it back to its owner with a smile.

The large woman asks point-blank, "And where are you from?"

I was wondering when this was going to happen. The train compartment really is a unique environment to travel in. It will be a sad day when it is truly extinct. Arranging passengers face to face, three on three, with barely enough space for legs between, it militates against all those gadgets we use to isolate ourselves, the phones, the mp3s, the computer screens. Sooner or later, in a compartment, you just have to acknowledge each other's presence, it's so blindingly obvious that you're a group, in the here and now, for the duration of this journey.

"I live in Milan," I say, smiling her straight in the eyes.

Everybody listens. They all appreciate that the formula I've chosen has avoided saying where I'm from. It's interesting how curious we all become when we spend a little time together, even though it's completely irrelevant to us where the others are from. But then we hardly need to know that Raffaella is pregnant by Balotelli either.

"Are you going to Sicily for business or pleasure?"

I'd like to answer generously, but the last thing a writer should do is say that he is a writer.

"Pleasurable business."

The woman twists her lips into a pout of wry frustration.

"Okay, okay," she says. "He doesn't want to say."

"But where are you actually from?" the young lover asks. I could hug him because he really seems perplexed. He hasn't assumed I'm English.

"London."

We're racing beside the sea. You can see people bathing fewer than a hundred yards away. There are sailboats. To our left the hills are climbing into a blue heat haze. Distant villages glitter. In the compartment the two dull syllables London sound like distant gunshots.

"Thought so," the chubby woman says with a smile.

AFTER HALF AN HOUR'S wait at Villa San Giovanni, the same woman observes, "It's always the same. As far as Naples, announcements, politeness, ticket inspectors, more information than you'd want. After Naples, silence."

This is true. Since they turned the train around at Naples, there hasn't been a single announcement.

"Why is that?" I ask, since I'm now part of the conversation. "After all, it's the same organization. Trenitalia."

"We are abandoned," she says dramatically.

The woman beside her agrees. "The state has abandoned the South."

"It's like they're serving a different customer, who isn't so important."

All the women are fanning themselves now. The woman in the corner has her proper pink fan; the tubby woman has finally found some reason to appreciate *Dipiù*—its pages make a soft flapping noise; the long-necked girl simply invites the air toward herself with beckoning hands.

And our carriage is reversing now. It stops and starts. And stops again. By the time we are trundled into the boat's dark hold the air is unbreathable. Fortunately, you can go up on deck. Everybody stands, apart from the older Sicilian woman in the corner. "I'll look after everyone's bags," she volunteers. She and the fat woman have huge suitcases. Something might be stolen.

"But you won't get to see the sea," I protest. I offer to change places with her for a while.

"I live by the sea."

To get off the train one has to walk down a couple of carriages, to where a train door coincides with steps leading up into the ship. Without a platform it's quite a jump down. The air is full of fumes. The steps are narrow and steep. The space is not well lit. The twists and turns and galleyways and passages are disorientating. On deck the ship is half deserted. There are train passengers, a few people traveling by car, and a group of bus travelers who left one bus in Villa San Giovanni and will get on another in Messina. Strange that they put the train on the ferry, but not the bus. "It's much faster this way," one of the bus passengers assures me. "We walk down the gangplank and it's there waiting to go."

The bar is a dismal affair, two young men utterly disinterested in their jobs selling coffee in plastic cups. The food display is entirely composed of *arancini*, the ball of fried rice with ragout inside that is a Sicilian speciality. I pass.

———

WATCHING THE COAST OF Calabria recede, or rather the uninspir-
ing facades of the San Giovanni's waterfront, and the coast of Sicily
approach, a dark silhouette under a low but ferocious sun, I keep wondering why on earth they put the train on the boat. Perhaps some time
ago when passenger carriages were mixed with freight wagons it had
made sense to put the freight, which couldn't get off and walk, on board.

But why now, when we're all so used to carrying our bags—there
are no porters in Italian stations—and they no longer mix freight and
people?

There must be jobs at stake.

Although the ferry is mostly dismal, a sort of giant Meccano raft,
and the bathrooms, the day I traveled, flooded, the funnel and upper
structure have recently been repainted to blazon the logo RFI on the
funnel: Rete Ferroviario Italiano. Names again. Image. Looking back
over the ship's wake, I can see other, more modern ferries zipping back
and forth, no doubt with plenty of capacity for the rail travelers on this
train. This is only a two-mile stretch of water. A week after this trip I
would discover that in 2010 RFI had ordered a new ferry for the journey, again with the capacity to load rail carriages. The contract went
to Nuovi Cantieri Apuania, a company based in Liguria, near Genoa.
At the time, the managing director of the company remarked on the
achievement of winning the €49 million contract against international
competition and said how pleased he was that his men could now start
working again after a period of idleness and layoffs. One wonders if it
would have won the contract if the commissioning organization was
not so closely allied to the Italian state. In any event, the new ship
was now ready for service, but the shipyard workers were refusing to
launch it until they received guarantees that they would not be laid
off immediately afterward. The obvious solution would be for RFI to
spend another €49 million on another ship.

———

ON THE END OF the harbor wall, beneath a 150-foot column topped with a bronze statue of the Madonna, these words appear in huge letters:

VOS ET IPSAME CIVITATEM
BENEDICIMUS

As I took pictures in low sunlight, a mother beside me explained to her little boy that Messina was a *città Mariana*, and that while still alive the Madonna had met some men sent to Palestine from Messina and she had written them a letter to take back to Sicily that finished with these words, in Latin: "I bless you and your town." One can see how much more attractive such stories are than thoughts about the economics of ferryboats.

I had a bit of a panic getting down to the train again. You would have thought it was easy to find a train in the bottom of a boat, but actually, no. There were an extraordinary number of stairways and corridors and no signs telling passengers where to go, as if perhaps we hadn't been supposed to leave our compartments at all. All the signs there were led you to the car deck. Eventually I did manage to retrace my steps and found a group of people down in the hold uncertain as to which was which of the two segments of train now side by side, one bound for Siracusa, one for Palermo. In the end, I spotted the languid soldier boy and followed him back to our compartment. It was encouraging to think that he could orient himself better than I could.

A long wait began. Our carriage crawled out of the boat into a dock siding and sat there for an hour. There was no explanation, no information. My fellow passengers grew angry. I wondered if my hotel would keep my room. Night fell. "Abandoned," the tubby woman announced again. "Sicily is completely abandoned. They despise us."

Again she called her husband about her *giramenti di testa*, though she had seemed in fine fettle during our afternoon conversations and had said nothing about her health problems despite the suffocating heat in the compartment. Then everybody called relatives to warn them to delay their departure to the station. I was the only one, it seemed, who would be proceeding under my own steam on arrival. Fearing just such a delay, I had booked a hotel a hundred yards from the station.

Eventually the tubby woman lost her patience, jumped to her feet, and with no sign of any dizziness, rushed out onto the platform, where she had spotted the *capotreno*. Rather oddly he then accompanied her back to our compartment, poked his head in, and explained that there was *una collega*, a ticket inspectress, who was late arriving because the train from Palermo was an hour and a half late. Ours was the last train from Messina to Palermo this evening, so we were waiting for her before departing, so she would be able to get back home.

While the man, avuncular and calmly authoritative in his uniform complete with green tie, was explaining this to us, it all seemed entirely reasonable and almost inevitable. Only when he had gone did the young girl, she of the Etruscan neck, wonder why two hundred people had to wait for one person who actually worked for the railways and could presumably be put up in a hotel if necessary.

"When we get to Trapani it will already be time to leave," she wailed.

"*Una collega*," the woman with the pink fan said pointedly. "It's a woman they're waiting for."

"The *capotreno's* wife," I offered.

"Or mistress," the fat woman insinuated.

"Or daughter," someone else said forgivingly.

In any event, it was a scandal.

By the time the train lurched into serious motion, it seemed like the six of us had known each other for years. "My husband's such a bore," complained the woman who lived two hundred yards from the station. "He always tries to get out of picking me up."

The tubby woman smiled complacently, as if to say, Why don't you tell him you get fits of dizziness? The boy beside me took the nth call from his mother asking him for a progress report. "How the hell should I know where we are?" he shouted, peering out into the dark. "It seems they're already on the platform in Palermo," he told us. "They'll be waiting for hours."

Then the train stopped at the tiny station of San Piero Patti.

And didn't set off.

"We're not supposed to stop here, are we?" I asked.

"Waiting for the train to come the other way," the soldier boy commented.

"Oh, the Englishman didn't realize!" the tubby woman was oddly triumphant. "What do you think, mister, that they would give us two lines? In Sicily!"

Thus I discovered that while the Ferrovie dello Stato had been investing €150 billion to build a high-speed line between Rome and Milan, they had not bothered to double up the line to Italy's fifth-largest town, the principal city of Sicily. We arrived in Palermo shortly before midnight, where I witnessed the soldier boy being smothered with Mamma's kisses on a platform with palm trees. The revolution could wait.

"POSSO DARE UN'OCCHIATA ALLA sua mappa?"

There was only one person standing under the departures board in Palermo Centrale Saturday morning, a woman in her thirties, with austere cheekbones and flaxen hair pulled tightly back in a small ponytail. I spoke to her in Italian, out of a respect I myself am rarely shown, but I guessed that if there was any conversation it was going to be in English. Sure enough, when she looked blank and I asked, "May I take a look at your map?" she handed it over.

The problem was that the destinations on the departures board didn't correspond to anywhere I knew. I had planned to go to Trapani, at the western tip of the island; I had checked on Trenitalia's website before leaving the hotel. There was a train departing at 10:39 a.m. that arrived at 1:28 p.m.: two hours and forty-nine minutes to go sixty-five miles. With two changes on the way. It seemed excessive, but I could always read, I thought. Or just watch people. Except that, on arrival at the station, the departures board had no trains leaving at 10:39, nor did any of the destinations posted seem to fit in with a trip to Trapani. I needed to understand where these places were.

The severe blond woman spoke in a bizarre singsong English full of unusual mistakes, in the sense, I suppose, that they were not the mistakes I'm so used to hearing Italians make. She too had been planning to get the train to Trapani, she said, it was the obvious tourist destination. One felt this natural desire to arrive at the land's limit. "I'm from Latvia," she added, as if to explain her disorientation.

The map wasn't very helpful. I scanned the coast north and west of Palermo. There was no sign of Cinisi, to which three trains were headed. But my eye was attracted to a small seaside place to the west called Isola delle Femmine—Girls' Island or Women's Island. It might be a fun place for a swim, I thought.

We looked around for help. Come to any major rail station in northern Italy on a Saturday or Sunday morning and you'll find it fizzing with families off for the weekend, hikers, mountain bikers, raucous soccer fans, the stolid Japanese, the African girls, quiet couples headed for art exhibitions with plenty of reading material for the journey, groups of Boy and Girl Scouts squatting around mountains of backpacks. The information office will be open, there will be plenty of ticket sellers at the windows, plus the lines of expensive new ticket machines. The bars will be full of people grabbing a quick cappuccino, others telling the barman exactly how much *grappa* they want in their espresso *corretto*. You have a strong sense of a community enjoying itself.

Here the only dozen or so people in the fairly large ticket hall were all standing in line at the one ticket window that was open. Beyond them, glass doors revealed a lush little chapel with satiny wood, polished marble, and comfortably upholstered seating for maybe forty; all the dark chairs were directed to a somber crucifix and sugar-white Madonna complete with an array of electric candles at her feet. The investment was considerable, but nobody was worshiping. Nobody was using the two brand-new ticket machines; they were the variety that take only credit cards. Apparently this was not the kind of place where anyone would want to set up a shopping center.

I went to one of the ticket machines, touched the screen, and then tapped in T R A P A N I. Dutifully, the display suggested the same train my computer had proposed, the 10:39. Again I looked at the departures board: there was no 10:39. But there was something rather odd going on. The trains were not shown in strict order of time, earliest at the top, latest at the bottom. An eleven-something appeared above a ten-something. I shook my head and double-checked. Three departures were not in the "right" place. I had never seen this before. Perhaps they had some other ordering system.

I played around a little more with the ticket machine, asking it for times to here and there, and it soon became clear that its data bank referred to some virtual rail network that had little to do with what was happening at Palermo Centrale that Saturday morning, assuming anything was happening at all. It was one of those fascinating moments when you realize that the usual connections between the information systems we live and move in mentally and the real world our feet are obliged to negotiate only come at the expense of great effort. The map is not the territory, as the philosopher Alfred Korzybski famously said.

We went through to the platforms where five or six old regionali were lined up among palm trees in giant pots, as if in some episode of *Thomas the Tank Engine* where the locomotives get to take an exotic vacation. Finally we tracked down two FS employees smoking outside the Left Luggage Office. They shook their heads. "Trapani, by train? At the weekend?" It was amusing that someone had thought of such a thing. "Go by bus," they advised. "There are plenty of buses. Much quicker." They began to give directions to the bus station. I began to understand why Trenitalia had opted for the high-speed Rome–Milan rather than doubling lines in Sicily. Even if they were doubled they might not get used.

We bought tickets for Isola delle Femmine. The severe and severely perplexed Latvian, who was named Zane (pronounced *zah-ney*), asked if I would mind her coming along. She worked in Oslo, she said. On a complete whim she had booked herself on a flight to Sicily, thinking she would enjoy seeing the sights for two weeks. Instead she understood nothing. The heat was killing her. She constantly feared she was being cheated. The shops and public services, she said, reminded her of Eastern Europe before the wall came down. It was disquieting. She was shocked.

Sympathizing, I slipped into the role of "he who knows the ropes" and suggested an orange juice before our train left. Freshly squeezed orange juice is one of the summer pleasures in Italian bars, and all the more so, I imagined, in Sicily, where the oranges actually grow.

"Ice?" the bartender asked.

I avoid ice, I explained to Zane, because it gives the juice a watered-down taste. There was a huge pile of oranges looking very thirst-quenching on the corner of the counter. The man slammed a knife through four or five and began squeezing.

When he handed us our two glasses, the juice wasn't just room temperature, it wasn't just warm, it was positively hot. Like tea. Now it was my turn to be shocked. The Latvian asked if people always drank their juice at this temperature. Her accent got strangely mixed up with cadences of wild incredulity. I stared at the pile of oranges but couldn't figure how they had gotten to be so hot. Had someone just pulled them in from the sun? Or left them in an oven? And I couldn't figure why the barman hadn't explained this. Not that a couple of cubes of ice would have made much difference. Anyway, Mr. Expert was so no more.

Never mind. Orange juice is orange juice. Drink it down. Coming out of the station bar I noticed that right beside it there was a McDonald's, which was doing slightly better business. A McDonald's in Palermo railway station. No doubt they catered to people who wanted their food and drink to be exactly as they expected it. The general atmosphere, meanwhile, was one of a few people taking time out in a lethargic backwater, fully aware that the real action lay elsewhere.

HOWEVER, AND MUCH TO my surprise, the train to Isola delle Femmine was brand-new, a two-carriage model I've since discovered they call the Minuetto. Who thinks of these names? Its bright blue seats were so clean and the floor so spotless it really felt as if the Latvian lady and the English gentleman were the first two passengers it had ever accommodated. Certainly we were the only ones traveling that Saturday morning. The inspector arrived smiling cheerfully, as a man should when he realizes he's being paid for doing nothing. Young, fleshy, and friendly, he was remarkable for the mass of dense black hair exploding from the top of his regulation FS shirt. He hadn't bothered with the regulation red FS tie. Perhaps the rules are waived when the temperature gets into the midnineties.

"Tickets, please," he said at once, in English. He turned them over in his hands and noticed with appreciation that we had had them stamped *regolarmente*. He completed the ritual by punching in two square holes. Then, since he didn't seem to have much else to do, I asked if by chance he knew whether one might proceed from Isola delle Femmine to Trapani, since the two stations seemed to be on the same line westward. At once he pulled a little machine from his pocket, the very kind the *capotreno* from Verona to Milan had told me *regionale* ticket inspectors were not issued. Was it possible that Sicily was ahead here, even if there were no tickets to check? Alternately tapping the screen and scratching his red neck with the little pointing device, then shaking his head, grunting, and beginning again, growing steadily more perplexed, he finally figured out that we could indeed reach Trapani today.

"At 8:55 p.m.," he announced to us at 10:30 in the morning. He seemed pleased that Trenitalia had this service to offer. I didn't trouble him to check whether, assuming we took this opportunity, we would be able to get back to Palermo the same day.

The coast to the north and west of the city would be stunningly beautiful were it not for a suburban wasteland of declining and abandoned industries. Isola delle Femmine, just ten miles away, turned out to be a quaint little fishing village whose transformation into a satellite town had apparently been arrested some years ago. It was languishing. I asked a young man where we might go swimming and was directed beyond the little harbor with its fishing smacks and luxury yachts along a busy road with no sidewalk and no coastal path. Just tarmac, rocks, sea. An endless stream of vehicles, all with Palermo license plates, filed by; presumably their occupants hadn't wanted to spend €2.25 on the train. The heat was overwhelming.

Taking the lead from the way the Americans give names to their hurricanes, the Italians have recently started personifying the anticyclones that push north from Africa and make the summer weeks so torrid. Myth and ancient history provide the name pool. Caronte— that is, Charon, death's ferryman—had paddled up the peninsula coasts a few weeks before. Now we had Crete's cruel tyrant Minos, who was torturing us all with temperatures in the high nineties.

Names for the trains and now names for the weather; this constant desire to give human narrative and drama to all kinds of phenomena, as if ninety-seven degrees with fast traffic on one side and a dazzling sea on the other weren't dizzying enough. I was beginning to feel like it must be quite ordinary in Sicily to suffer from *giramenti di testa*. No sooner had the rocks turned into pebbles and begun to look swimmable than there were bars and hotels whose owners had fenced off the sea approach and proclaimed the "beach" private. We'd gone almost a mile before a small patch of unclaimed boulders and grit looked like a place where we could finally take a dip. There was no shade. The Latvian lady again said that she felt it had definitely been a mistake to come to Sicily.

Returning to Palermo in the early evening, we had to stand. Hence we discovered who it was that really used the trains. Aside from some sun-dazed day trippers, the carriage was jammed with *extra-comunitari* carrying the big red boards, perhaps five feet by five, on which they pin the trinkets that they sell along the beaches: beads, bracelets, hair clips, headbands, cheap jewelry, and small toys, all plastic, all made in China, to be sold by Africans on Italian beaches, all outside any tax net but taking wise advantage of Trenitalia's cheap fares to get their goods to market.

Over the coming week, traveling the coasts of Sicily, Puglia, and Calabria, I was going to see a great deal more of this. Lean black men in jeans and T-shirts humping these heavy boards back and forth for the benefit of the white Italian beachgoers. So although Trenitalia never employs *extra-comunitari*, the African immigrant's initiation into Italy inevitably seems to involve the trains: the prostitutes in the North, shuffled and reshuffled around the various town centers, these hawkers along the coast. Chatting together, trying to stop their boards from entirely obstructing the doors and corridors, all in possession of regularly stamped tickets, the men don't seem too unhappy with their lot. Perhaps there are worse ways to spend the day than stepping between bodies in skimpy bathing costumes.

MY PALERMO HOTEL WANTED cash in advance and didn't give a receipt. But they did warn me that I would have to take a bus if I wanted to go to Modica, on the southern coast of Sicily, on a Sunday. "There are no trains on Sunday in Sicily," they told me. "You should arrive early for the bus because it might be full."

My first thought was that this was nonsense. This hotel was on the fourth floor and run by a couple who might have been a Sicilian Norman Bates and his mamma, moving in a crepuscular, mahoganied light among dusty crucifixes and ceramic Madonnas. They are big on ceramics in Sicily and never skimp on religious icons. I hurried to my room, opened Trenitalia's ticket purchase page, and typed in Palermo to Modica. The road distance is about 125 miles. Sure enough, a train came up, leaving at 8:49 a.m. and arriving at 4:11 p.m., three changes, seven hours, and twenty-two minutes of travel. Damn.

Still, there *was* a train.

Then I noticed the little asterisk after 8:49. The asterisk—and this is something you have to watch out for because it is so small and apparently inoffensive—means that "*la soluzione si riferisce al giorno successivo*"; this possibility refers to the next day. Rather than indicate there was no train on Sunday, they had given me the *only* train on Monday.

One gets so used to the idea that there are trains between cities, at least in Europe, that one rarely actually studies a rail map to see what is possible and what is not. Obviously this had been a mistake on my part. I found a rail map for Sicily on the net and studied it. Immediately it was evident that the scant network in the interior of the island had nothing to do with modern tourist trails or indeed rapid communication between major Sicilian business centers. These lines had been built in the nineteenth century to bring sulfur and salt down from mines in the mountains. Sicily produced almost all of Europe's sulfur in that period, and industrial Britain was the main buyer. Don Luigi Sturzo, whose street passes by Garibaldi's rail station in Milan, had fought to reduce child slavery in the mines, the kind of awful working conditions recorded in Giovanni Verga's story "Rosso Malpelo," about a brutalized and violent young boy who simply disappears down a salt mine. Most of these mines closed in the early twentieth century; since then there seems to have been very little investment in redesigning the rail network for other uses. Sicily simply isn't a train culture. Perhaps an efficient train system requires the presence of a strong central state determined to integrate all areas of a country into its communications network. The absence of state authority that has allowed the Mafia to flourish runs parallel with the weakness of the train service. If I wanted to travel to Modica on a Sunday I was going to have to take a bus run by the Sicilian municipal authority and hence under the attentive patronage of local politicians. As I write, the president of the region of Sicily has just been forced to resign, mainly over the grotesque overmanning in every area of public administration, something that has pushed the region to the edge of bankruptcy.

TOLD TO ARRIVE EARLY, I was at the Big Bus Bar, just a stone's throw from the Palermo rail station, at 8:00 a.m. for an 8:45 bus. Yes, the Big Bus Bar. English is everywhere. Tickets are sold with coffees and arancini. But no, I couldn't use a credit card, the man said, though he had a credit card terminal right there on the desk, wired up and winking. He took cash, gave me a ticket, and was very friendly in coming out of the bar and pointing along the street to where I could wait for the bus.

"That bench," he said. "It stops there."

Buses need so much less infrastructure than trains. No stations, ticket offices, platforms, or dedicated rails. Just an old bench on a broken pavement.

The seat was made of wooden slats bolted onto a tubular iron frame. It was deserted. I thought I would sit and read. Underneath the bench were plastic cups, a banana peel, a blue plastic bag, a rectangular liqueur bottle. To one end of the bench, on the seat, were two broken eggshells and a little white of egg smeared over a couple of slats. The other end looked clean. I sat down, then quickly stood. Someone had pissed. The morning was already warm. King Minos, our friendly heat wave, was up early, though the bench was in the shade. Now that I'd noticed it, the smell was overpowering and I moved off and found a post to lean on ten yards away. If a crowd began to gather, I could move closer later, I thought.

Two women arrived, one older and one younger; they sat on the clean side of the bench, hung on perhaps two minutes, then stood and moved off. Three or four others repeated the experiment. Then a man in fluorescent lime green trousers, blue shirt, and white plastic gloves arrived carrying a witch's broom and dustpan. He began to sweep around the bench, emptying his sweepings into a tall wheelie bin. His manner was neither lazy nor assiduous. He did his job stolidly, but seemed to feel that to be too thorough would be inappropriate. Having swept well enough around the bench and adventured his broom a little way under it—say, six inches or so—he left the other garbage under there right where it was. Perhaps the powerful piss smell was too much for him. It was not his fault that he had no means of washing it away. If he noticed the eggs on the bench, he didn't do anything about them. Perhaps filth on rather than under the bench was another man's territory. In any event, he seemed satisfied with his efforts to the point that he was actually whistling as he moved off with his bin.

The sunshine intensified and the smell with it. A stately old Fiat 132 arrived bringing two nuns dressed in white. The younger of the two, in her late sixties, parked the vehicle about a yard from the sidewalk, a couple of yards ahead of the bench, and right on a corner. Having pulled out a heavy bag, they began to discuss whether the car could be left there. They decided it couldn't. You can't park a car on a corner, and certainly not so far out from the sidewalk. The younger nun got back in the seat, started the car, frowned, turned the motor off, and got out again. They had been wrong, she said; it could be left there. There was a little more discussion about this, but in the end the decision stood, and the two white-clad nuns now took up positions right by the bench at the exact point where the bus was supposed to arrive fifteen minutes later. Even their sandals were white, I noticed. The urine smell did not deter them. Perhaps years of mortifying the flesh made them immune. The driver nun stood with her hands behind her back; her fingers were linked by the car key ring on which she moved the four or five keys back and forth, as if they formed a rosary. I couldn't see if her lips were moving. The more the sun came up, the more the minutes passed, the more I was impressed by their fortitude. A dozen other passengers were hanging well back. But the nuns showed no sign of unease—not, that is, until a young man came and stood on the tarmac in front of them, even nearer to the eventual bus than they were. This got them hopping from one white sandal to another in agitation.

Then, very unusually, the couple to my left asked me, in *Italian*, with local Sicilian accents bordering on dialect, what time exactly the bus was supposed to arrive, and I replied, in my northern Italian, that it should have arrived a moment ago. Then they said thanks, they had thought as much, how typical, and I said yeah, isn't it, but it's early in the day to start complaining. They laughed and agreed *and did not appear to notice at all that I was not Italian.* Was it the now overwhelming smell of urine that had masked my foreignness? The reader will have long reached the conclusion that I am obsessed by this, but it remains a complete mystery to me how people pick up or don't pick up whatever messages I send out. Anyway, I suddenly felt pleased. No, more than pleased, moved. Here I was in my adoptive country, in a remote part of it that I had always felt would be a bridge too far for me, Sicily, the South, danger, the Mafia, calmly chatting away to ordinary folks, understanding and understood, as if I really were Italian. Fantastic. I decided to enjoy watching developments with the nuns and the insolent queue jumper.

The bus arrived fifteen minutes late. A small crowd of about twenty held their collective breath and closed in on the urine-reeking bench. The white door of the white bus began its jerky, automatic-door-opening movement, first pushing outward and then beginning to slide toward the back. The bold young interloper at the head of the line took a step forward to board and . . . exactly as he did so, the older of the two white-clad nuns, she who didn't drive, she who had seemed very much under the care of her more sprightly companion, surged past him, raising her left arm in such a way as to plant an elbow against his chest and thrust him powerfully back. He was checked and stumbled. Already, white on white, the two brides of Christ were up the steps and in command of the front seat.

THE JOY OF TRAINS is that you can read while you travel. In his book *Le ferrovie,* Stefano Maggi claims that the spread of railways in the late nineteenth century went hand in hand with a marked increase in reading as newsagents opened new outlets in all the stations offering books and magazines for the journey. Alas, you can't read on a bus. Or I can't. If I try, I soon start to feel sick. I also start to feel trapped in my seat. It's not that I really want to move around, but I'd like to feel I could, the way you usually can move about on a train. On the Italo, for example, I had very much enjoyed walking right to the front of the train and back.

Having arrived late, the driver was in a hurry. It was a four-and-a-half-hour ride. With no conversations to overhear, since almost everyone was sitting alone, and buses are anyway noisier than trains, I was reduced to staring at the landscape. Low hills; burned brown green grass; bleached white tracks; small, prickly trees; and dusty vines. I was reminded of the only other time I had traveled deep into Sicily. Benetton's promotional department was going to photograph young people in Corleone, in the heart of the heart of the country, to improve the image of a town that had unjustly been presented, they said, as nothing but Mafia, crime, and tax evasion, this thanks or no thanks to the *Godfather* films. Would I come along and write about it? They offered more money than I was used to. I said I would, on the condition that I was free to write anything I wanted, and I told them straight that I had a gut dislike of Benetton's opportunist mix of piety and promotion. They said I was absolutely free to say what I liked; they were modern people in favor of honesty and free speech.

In a suffocatingly hot Corleone, the kids chosen (very carefully) to be photographed were only too eager to feature on Benetton publicity; they hoped this might prove a passport to leaving the place. Over lunch the new mayor, a brave young man who had been elected on an anticorruption ticket, described how a severed goat's head had recently been left on his doorstep. As the troupe moved around the small town's central streets and piazza, old people sitting against the walls on old wooden kitchen chairs did not want to talk to us. At the end of a restaurant meal that seemed interminable thanks to the proprietor's insistence that we try every dish on the menu, we were first given the bill and then asked what sum we would like to appear on the official receipt; if we were claiming expenses they were quite happy to jack up the figure by 50 percent. Of course, such generosity could only mean that many customers were getting no receipt at all; otherwise there wouldn't have been the cash to cover this. "We did tell them," one of the promo girls said to me, "that we were trying to change the image of the place."

"I guess they don't associate a little cooking of the books with crime," I said with a laugh.

About an hour into the ride the bus attacked a series of hairpins, climbing up to a plateau. After a while we began the descent, at speeds that had to be unwise. At the third or fourth bend, the driver braked fiercely, and my head swayed forward to touch the seat in front. I thought nothing of it. He must know the road like the back of his hand. A couple of bends later the bus braked, skidded, then slammed to a stop at the elbow of the hairpin, sending all kinds of luggage, phones, wallets, and books onto the floor. We were inches from a guardrail protecting us from a steep drop into a rocky gully. The hefty woman sitting on the other side of the aisle from me crossed herself. The woman behind me, a serious, professional-looking lady who had been trying to use her computer to do some work, asked me if I was okay. She had seen my head bang forward. I asked her if it was always like this, why was he in such a hurry.

"He's with his wife," she said.

I must have looked puzzled because she added, "The woman in the seat behind him."

"And so?"

"He's eager to arrive and settle down to Sunday lunch."

This seemed to me a very generous explanation of why a man might respond to his wife's presence by driving with mad haste. In any event, the superiority of the train was evident. Modern signaling systems discourage speeding, and there is no place for a wife to sit behind a husband driver in a train cab. Or a husband behind a wife driver, for that matter, for there is one woman who has qualified to drive Trenitalia's Frecce. I have been unable to find the statistics for women train drivers in general, but they do exist and there are even a couple of eccentric websites dedicated to sightings of them. What is certain is that there are more women driving the trains than blacks of either sex.

Occasionally as the bus rumbles on I notice old train lines half hidden in the dirt, overgrown, broken. Here and there disused rail viaducts are crumbling into the stony gulleys. Perched on hilltops, their houses huddled together in protective isolation, the towns here were clearly not built with railways in mind, or indeed rapid communication of any kind. Tormented by the sun, thirsty, craggy, and prickling with cactuses, the landscape does not encourage movement.

Eventually we arrived at Ragusa, a spectacular town toppling over a high ridge, a sort of baroque lava stream tumbling into an arid canyon of dead grass and cactuses toward Modica, then the coast far below. I was puzzled. I knew Ragusa had a rail station connecting with Modica, but how? This territory was just too arduous. I turned to the woman behind me, still amazingly busy with her computer, despite all the bends, not to mention three hours and more of battery time. Had she ever taken the train from Ragusa to Modica? I asked.

"Years ago," she said. "As a little girl with my parents." But it was too inconvenient, too slow, ran too rarely to use now.

"And it doesn't run on Sundays."

"No."

The bus was now zigzagging fiercely again, plunging down the hillside to the plain. To our left the houses of Ragusa seemed to have been built one on top of another, so sharp was the descent.

"Where does the line run?" I asked. "I love trains. It must be quite a ride."

She frowned as if remembering and said, "Yes, it's famous. It goes under the hill in a spiral tunnel."

I didn't understand.

She closed her laptop; the journey was nearly over. The bus was zipping back and forth down the last hairpins in a sort of bagatelle movement. The driver must be smelling his Sunday lunch.

"The tunnel spirals up from Modica and climbs over itself before coming out just before Ragusa. There's a story about it, if I can remember."

I was looking at the hillside. The rough whitish rock was so uneven and rugged, the facades so higgledy-piggledy, it seemed a miracle they had built the place at all, never mind a train tunnel spiraling up to it. In the nineteenth century.

Zipping away her computer, this busy woman in her forties was evidently someone who had escaped the provinces for a professional life in the city and was paying a visit to family on a Sunday. She gave the impression of making the trip on a regular basis, as a duty.

"That's it," she said with a smile. "The tunnel was dug from both ends simultaneously, from the top in Ragusa and the bottom in Modica. On the day the workers were supposed to break through and meet up, the engineer invited all the local dignitaries to see it. Except the ends didn't meet and he was so upset he'd gotten his calculations wrong that he killed himself that night. That's the story, anyway." She seemed puzzled herself as to whether it could be true. "Then the next day the tunnels did meet. People like unhappy stories around here."

What Latin passion, I thought. What pride in expertise, what a foolish sense of personal honor to kill yourself over a mistake. Without even taking the time to check out how big the mistake was.

Another very unhappy story was recalled by the name of the square where the bus reached its terminus on the outskirts of Modica: Piazzale Falcone e Borsellino. Giovanni Falcone and Paolo Borsellino were two investigating magistrates killed by the Mafia in 1992, and any number of squares, streets, buildings, and schools in Sicily and indeed on the Italian mainland are now named after them. The intention is to honor their extraordinary courage and dedication, but I sometimes wonder if the effect might not be to discourage others from following in their footsteps.

Unlike the train to Palermo, the bus to Modica had arrived at its destination a full half hour early. At some risk to our lives. The driver chased us off his vehicle and roared away with his wife. The light was blinding. There was no shade, such as might be provided by the waiting room or ticket hall in even the smallest of stations. I was to be picked up here by a hotel proprietor related to a colleague of mine at the university in Milan. In the meantime, shading my eyes, I was able to gaze at a baroque church facade looking down from a commanding hilltop. All is baroque here because the older towns of Ragusa and Modica were largely destroyed in an earthquake in 1693 and then rebuilt in the style of the time. Waiting, I tried to throw together a few feelings about this Sicilian baroque: a confusion of the ornamental and the devotional, self-satisfied, sentimental, glorying in the pathos of Christ's suffering but ostentatiously rich, flamboyantly affluent. Somewhere or other there was a connection between this style—the bleeding hearts, the weeping Madonnas, the money—and the complacency of the person who announces, "The state has abandoned us, the railways have abandoned us," knowing full well that she is returning to a nice home and a husband waiting in a new car.

No sooner was I in my hotel room than I got online and looked for the history of that tunnel. It was completed in 1896. The engineer *"supposedly"* killed himself, not because he feared he had gotten his calculations wrong but because he was convinced his Sicilian workers had not carried out his instructions to the letter; in fact, he was English. This put the whole matter in a rather different light.

"SO, WHAT ARE YOU doing here, Professor Parks?"

That evening, after swimming and sightseeing, I was invited to dinner on a terrace out in the country. Giuseppe, my hotelier, a man my age, and his wife, Concetta, always ate on Sunday, they said, with the same group of four or five friends. It was a routine that couldn't be broken. Would I join them? "So long as I don't have to eat meat," I said. For another thing that has changed since I wrote the first part of this book is that I have become a vegetarian, though I don't actually like to use the "v" word. People think you are preaching. To say you don't eat this or that merely makes you picky, which I feel is preferable. In any event, as we got together around the table there was some consternation about this refusal of mine to eat flesh. Sicilians are not used to it. "Consider it a mystery," I said. "Sicily is full of mysteries. The railways are full of mysteries. Let's not try to explain it."

The air was warm over hills and dunes. We were near the sea. The walls were giving back the day's heat. There were bats and bougainvillea and june bugs and crickets. Smells, too, of plants and grasses I did not know.

"The railways, you said?"

They wanted to know why I had come to Modica, and above all, why having come I planned to be here so briefly. Giuseppe had told them I was leaving the next morning, shortly after eight. By train! From Modica station! Two of the six other people present weren't aware that there was a functioning station in Modica. Where was it?

"It's not a book about Italy seen from train windows," I corrected. "Not a travel book. And it's not a book about trains as such."

"What, then?"

I realized it might have been easier to explain my vegetarianism.

"Well, I'm of the opinion that a culture, a system of"—I hesitated—
"communication, if you like"—they were looking at me with the wry
skepticism with which one does look at foreign professors—"manifests
itself entirely in anything the people of that culture do. Right?"

They smiled indulgently. I was their guest, after all.

"Like this routine Sunday dinner of yours, every week, the same
friends on the warm terrace, the things you prepare, the way it's
served, the things you talk about, even the way you invite and tolerate
a foreign *professore* like me. All Italy could be teased out from this if we
examined it carefully, the clothes you are wearing, the way you've laid
the table, the pleasure taken cooking, the wineglasses."

Now one of the men, who held a half-smoked but extinguished
cigar between his lips, raised a quizzical eyebrow. A car roared down
the narrow lane beyond the small garden, accelerating and decelerat-
ing fiercely as it approached the bend.

"The way people drive."

Giuseppe laughed. "So?"

"So if you're stupid enough to want to write about a country, a people, the problem is where to start. You could start anywhere, because
everything they do manifests that spirit. I don't know, I cast about. *Le
strisce*, for example."

The *strisce* are zebra crossings, or crosswalks.

"What about *le strisce*?"

"In England when you want to cross at the *strisce* you approach
and stand on the pavement beside them and the cars will stop. Guaranteed. By law they have to stop, and they will. If you just stand by the
strisce in Milan, and I don't suppose it's too different here, the cars
will just keep driving by. Here you have to step onto the *strisce* and
start to walk, and only then will the car stop, right?, maybe braking
hard and cursing you. You need to be courageous."

Heads were nodding now. They agreed on this one. Concetta complained what a disgrace it was. The *strisce* might as well not be there at all, since she always waited until there was a big space in the traffic before taking the risk.

"And in a way that says everything about laws and rights in Italy. They exist, you have your rights, but you have to fight to have them; otherwise, people just ignore you. It's the same when you want an appointment for a medical test. If you don't shout and scream, they'll make you wait until it's far too late."

"You don't want to write a whole book about *le strisce*!"

"No. But you don't want to write generally about a whole country either, because there's so much, and the secret is always in the details, and the way one detail calls to another in a kind of tangle, I mean, the way a woman moves on the beach might connect with the way she genuflects in church. That sort of thing."

There were sighs around the table. Somebody started to fill the wineglasses. But it was their fault; they had asked me why I was there.

"Okay, let's just say I'm writing about the way trains sort of *happen* in Italy. You know?"

It wasn't clear they did.

"Or don't happen," I added, laughing a little nervously.

They smiled generously, forgivingly, eating prosciutto and melon. I had slices of mozzarella. The wine was a strong local red poured from a labelless bottle.

There was a moment's silence. Eventually one of the ladies present announced gravely, "I never travel by train."

"Nor do I," said another.

They were telling me I had chosen a bad subject, I was writing about something that Sicilians couldn't connect with. Giuseppe said he frequently collected hotel guests from the bus stop where he'd come for me, or alternatively he advised them where to rent a car on arrival at the airport. They never arrived by train.

"Never," he repeated. "Not once."

A woman said she went to Rome and Milan regularly for business. She used cheap flights on Wind Jet. Was I aware that Sicily was the home of Italy's first low-cost airline? That was an interesting subject.

Her companion remarked that Wind Jet was run by Antonino Pulvirenti, who also owned the Catania soccer club and the whole Forté empire. The ferry companies and some of the bus companies also were owned by powerful figures who had every interest in the slow death of Sicilian railways.

"So perhaps the interesting thing is that they bother keeping the railways open at all," I suggested, "if hardly anyone uses them."

Giuseppe agreed: "The state likes to pretend it's present when it isn't. They like to behave as if Sicily were like the rest of Italy and everything were under control. It isn't. And, of course, through the railways they can hand out a few jobs, which wins them votes."

I asked them what they thought about the idea of a three-mile bridge over the Strait of Messina to link Sicily directly to the mainland. This is a grandiose project dear to Berlusconi when he was in office; he always loved to pull it out when he wanted to appear as a man of vision, a man who gets important things done. "It's not unfeasible," I said. "There are any number of far longer bridges in the world. Why leave Sicily without a bridge? If the bridge carried trains as well it would revolutionize travel here."

My hosts smiled as one does when humoring a child. It wasn't a question, they said, of being for or against the bridge—who wouldn't want such a thing?—as of simply *knowing* that no bridge would ever happen. It wouldn't be *allowed* to happen.

"They're digging endless tunnels under the Alps," I objected, "at vast expense, not to mention all the viaducts they built for the high-speed Milan–Rome line."

"Precisely. Milan–Rome, Turin–Lyons; *not* Palermo, *not* Sicily."

"Sicily is abandoned!"

There; someone had said it.

"So where is *il professore* Parks headed for tomorrow," someone wanted to pin me down, "so early in the morning?"

"Crotone."

There was a sharp, general intake of breath. Crotone is on the Calabrian coast, but not on the Sicilian side, the toe, but over toward the
Gulf of Taranto, which begins the instep of the famous Italian boot.

"But why? Why not Reggio? Why not Catanzaro? They're near
enough."

Because I'd been to Reggio twice before. Because I didn't have
enough time to go everywhere, and because the ten-hour, twenty-
minute ride with three train changes, a ferry, and a bus link should
push the efficiency of the rail service to the limit.

"Ten and a half hours to go two hundred and fifty miles," one of the
ladies said with a laugh.

"Two hundred and eighty," I corrected.

Then in determined chorus all these good Sicilians told me there
was *no way*; there was no way at all that the Ferrovie dello Stato could
get me to Crotone in a single day. It was unthinkable. It wasn't a major
route. I was crossing Calabria, where everybody else was just going up
or down the coast. Calabria was even less efficient than Sicily. They
were very clear about this. Much less efficient. The famous Internet
that I put so much faith in might *say* I could get to Crotone, but out of
friendship they had to warn me that this was fantasy. I'd end up sleeping in a station, getting mugged, or something worse.

"Let's make a bet," I said. "I will prove you wrong."

Chapter 6

CROTONE–TARANTO–LECCE

ESPITE MY CONFIDENCE OVER DINNER, I HAVE TO CONFESS
that it was with some genuine trepidation that I began my trip to Crotone. The only news I had of the place was negative. The abandoned
chemical works north of the town was supposedly one of the great eye-
sores of the South. It was also famous, infamous, for one of the worst
scandals of toxic waste dumping, 350,000 tons of zinc, lead, arsenic,
mercury, and the like. On the other hand, Crotone, I knew, had also
been one of the great centers of Magna Grecia. Some twenty-seven
hundred years ago, driven by local conflicts and shortages, the desire
for adventure, ambition, and no doubt greed, small groups of men
and women set out from the various Greek cities to form a string of
colonies on the Italian coasts of Calabria and Puglia. Fighting among
themselves, dominating the indigenous peoples, thriving on trade,
exporting grain and all kinds of artisan work and sculptures back to
their communities of origin, these colonies eventually grew so large
and wealthy, so cultured and accomplished, as to think of themselves
as greater than Greece itself, hence the term that they themselves seem
to have coined of Magna Grecia. Crotone in particular, twenty times

winners of the Olympic Games in the fourth and fifth centuries BC, second only in that regard to Sparta, had been home to a huge temple to Hera built on a promontory reaching eastward back across the sea to Hellas, their home. It is curious, with all the admiration heaped on ancient Greece in our schools and universities, that so little mention is made of Magna Grecia; and it was going to be fascinating, I thought, to see how the remnants of that old glory squared with the rare and ugly news that leaks out of the place today.

After first begging me to extend my stay in Modica, with an intensity that had me wondering if there might not be an attempted kidnap, Giuseppe, my hotelier, then insisted on having an early breakfast with me and driving me down to the station at the bottom of the town. When we arrived, he showed an almost childish eagerness to come in and explore the ticket office and the platform, as if this were some kind of oversized toy. The ticket window, a lattice of wood and frosted glass dating back to the fifties by the looks of it, was no longer in operation, having been replaced, as everywhere else, by a smart, new, credit-cards-only machine. Beside this was one of those weighing scales they used to put in stations before people could afford bathroom scales at home. I challenged Giuseppe to think of something less useful in a provincial railway ticket office, but he rightly pointed out that it did once have a use: there was a yardstick on the side of the machine that allowed you to measure your height. The state had used the railways to encourage people to check their weight in relation to their height. Were they malnourished? Were they obese? It was part of a public health drive that had started with the Fascists. In much the same way, since about 2010, each station all over Italy has a fancy waste disposal unit made up of a steel stand and three bins—one green, one yellow, one white—for organic, plastic, and paper, to get people used to *la raccolta differenziata*—waste separation—a concept they have been struggling to get their minds around in Naples. The railways are clearly far more than a transport company; they are part of a process of belonging and the pressure to conform that goes with all community.

Out on the only platform, a nice old clock had a piece of white paper
taped to its face bearing the word *GUASTO* in large computer-printed letters. BROKEN. The station clock is largely irrelevant now, but when the
railways began, time was not synchronized among the various Italian
towns, each one deciding for itself, according to the rising and setting
of the sun, what time it was. The introduction of the train and the con-
sequent need for timetables across the territory led to synchronization,
with a decision made in 1866 that all cities would set their clocks to
the time in Rome, this at a moment when Rome was not yet part of the
kingdom, let alone the capital. In this regard it was a message the newly
united Italy sent to the pope, who still claimed the right to be temporal
ruler of the city, that actually Rome's time was Italy's and the two states
must soon be one.

Aside from the weighing machine and the broken clock, this tiny
station at pretty well the southernmost point of Sicily looked *exactly*
like any small station on the northern border with Switzerland. There
were the same blue signs and warnings you find in all the stations,
all brand-new, all with the same typeface. *Vietato l'accesso* carried the
same fines here as it did at Porta Vescovo. There were the same ugly
metal window fittings, the same yellow line painted on the platform,
with the notice declaring, *Non oltrepassare la linea gialla*, and in English, Do not go beyond the yellow line. In this sense the *ferrovie dello
stato* do indeed unite the country, tying it up in a web whose nodal
points must feel the same from Brunico in the South Tyrol all the way
down to the toe of Calabria. It was both reassuring and disappointing.

A train appeared around the bend. In truth it was only ten minutes late, though it looked like it had come from another age, a single
diesel-driven carriage at least forty years old. The line hasn't been
electrified. On board there was a powerful smell of diesel, and a rattling air-conditioner that just about managed to keep the temperature
bearable. The seats were fairly recent, but everything else had been
left as it was. At the end of the carriage a tiny section of eight seats
behind a glass screen bore the announcement *PRIMA CLASSE*. It was hard

to see in what way it was different from second. On the driver's door, the typeface for the warning *VIETATO L'INGRESSO* was straight out of the sixties and, instead of being first, ahead of the French and German, as it always is today, the English translation was last, reminding you that in those days English was not yet everyone's second tongue. NO ADMITTANCE, it said, instead of today's NO ENTRY. No admittance. The old-fashioned formula and the antique typeface put me in an excellent mood. There are certain train environments that immediately give me the feeling that I am protected, at least for the duration of the journey. I am almost back in my childhood. Nothing can go wrong. Perhaps because this place isn't really part of the modern world.

FROM MODICA THE TRAIN made a generous detour to the south, to Scicli, before turning east along the coast. The ticket inspector spent most of the time ensconced in the cabin with the driver. At each station he emerged, nondescript, in his forties, looked up and down the empty platform, then waved his green flag for the driver, a whole two yards away, to close the doors. Two men and a vehicle from the 1960s to transport half a dozen people forty-five miles in an hour and a half. When eventually he decided to confront me and I showed him the piece of paper with my Internet ticket, which Giuseppe had kindly printed out on the hotel computer, he suddenly grew alert. He looked at it as one finally faced with something he has been warned about but thankfully has so far been spared. He stared at it for a while, then asked me to wait a minute and took it away to show to the driver. Ten minutes later he was back; he frowned, handed over the paper, and made no comment.

The landscape is flat and fertile here in the southeastern corner of Sicily: olive groves, bamboo, kiwis; long gray greenhouses, some in use, some abandoned. Here and there the earth was deeply scored by dry streams—*torrenti*, as the Italians say. I read on my Kindle and photographed obsolete bric-a-brac on the stations. On one platform there was an antique lamppost combined with some sort of pumping device, deeply rusted but somehow dignified and elegant, certainly worth many a modern sculpture. Cactuses of the variety you see in spaghetti Westerns lined the rails, and there were glimpses of the sea across the plain as we cut the corner of the island, turning north. On the wall in a station called Avola somebody had scrawled, *Tanto il resto cambia* (After all, everything else changes). The central platform here was so narrow that the two yellow lines to distance you from the platform edges left no standing room between.

A large woman now boarded the train, a woman of a kind you don't see up north. She was very brown and very tubby, in her midfifties perhaps, but glamorous. Her white hair had been dyed blond and was pinned up with a bright red comb. Her ample dress was a flowery print of green, turquoise, and white, all very bright. On her face she wore large, very modern, almost brash sunglasses, and from her ears dangled the heaviest of earrings, threads of silver holding large red drops of stone. No sooner had she sat down than she produced a black fan with gold trimmings and very slowly, very methodically, as if this was a serious job, began to fan herself.

Although she was sitting across the corridor from me, her presence immediately imposed itself. My set of four seats was empty; so was hers. Trains give you this chance to feel another's presence. She fanned herself and watched me reading. When the train turned a bend and the hot sunshine fell on her shoulder, she promptly shifted across the corridor to my set of seats. I looked up. She smiled deep into my eyes, raising black eyebrows, incongruous against the blond hair, as if giving me the opportunity to say what had to be said. Her cheeks were dark, and some makeup had been used to hide the pores.

"*Buon giorno,*" I said.

"*Il sole,*" she explained. The sun.

"*Già,*" I agreed.

She stretched her mouth a little and set to watch me as I returned to my Kindle and she fanned herself slowly with the same deliberate rhythm. Then the train turned another bend and the sun was on our side again. She wriggled for a moment, sighed, and eventually lifted her bulk to move back across the corridor to the other side. Again I looked up at her and again she smiled. Somehow it felt like a significant and highly satisfactory encounter.

IN SIRACUSA, ON THE east coast of the island, we were already back in serious civilization. The station architecture here is exactly the same as it is in Brescia or a thousand other places, square columns clad in slabs of cheap polished limestone holding up the concrete shelters over the platforms. But it is unusual to find a waiting room labeled Prima Classe and laid out as if for a wake in the 1920s with benches that seem to have been carved from coffins and an austerely framed mirror where travelers can check that they still have a reflection. Outside, where the taxis were parked, the facade had recently been restored in a honey beige stucco with bright white trimmings. On this newly renovated facade I found a plaque that, translated, read:

STATE RAILWAYS
AND THE CITY OF SIRACUSA
To Sebastiano Vittorini, 1883–1972
LITERARY RAILWAYMAN WHO WAS
STATIONMASTER IN THIS BUILDING
WHERE THE WRITER ELIO
MET ROSA QUASIMODO
SIRACUSA 2007

What was charming about this was the assumption that the passerby reading the plaque would know that "the writer Elio" was the celebrated, or once celebrated, Elio Vittorini, novelist, essayist, and translator (of D. H. Lawrence, Poe, and Faulkner). As for Rosa Quasimodo, I myself had no idea, until I checked on the Internet that she was both the sister of the Nobel-winning poet Salvatore Quasimodo, and Elio Vittorini's wife. So this was a plaque for the public, but for a *local* public and a *literary* public, not the uneducated, not the curious tourist who might arrive in this town and wish for an explanation. The railway opened the town to the world, but the plaque celebrated Siracusa among educated Siracusans. Later I did a little research. Rosa's father, it seems, like Elio's, was a railwayman. That was how they met. The two were forced to marry because their parents discovered that they had spent a night in bed together. Such was the rule in those times in Sicily: automatic wedlock. "One August evening," Rosa wrote, "as agreed beforehand, he waited for me at his bedroom window, and I took my shoes off, climbed onto the roof of the station and clambered across to him."

WHY DO SOME PEOPLE have to sit facing the direction of motion while others, like myself, really don't care which way we sit, frontways, backways, sideways? As the Intercity skirted the coast northward toward Catania and Messina—rigorously on time, I was pleased to notice—an elderly couple came into the compartment I was so far sharing with a young man. Both were very small, the man immediately identifiable as a whiner, a miserable soul with deep down-turned lines at the corners of his mouth, a long thin face, white hair combed over a bald spot, a birdlike body, all puffed up, oversized chest, but with meager shoulders and sticklike legs. At first he couldn't figure out which seats were his and his wife's, and he proceeded to get angry about this, assuming that I or the other man in the compartment, who was at the window beside me, both of us facing in the direction of motion, had somehow stolen their seats. They had seats fifty-three and fifty-five, he said. Why weren't the seats clearly marked? He and his wife had specifically asked for seats facing the direction of the train.

I pointed out that the seat numbers were indicated on the glass between the compartment and the corridor. "There's a little *schema*, as you look in from the corridor." He went outside to look. His wife was tiny, frightened, shriveled.

He couldn't figure it out. He could see the numbers but he couldn't see how the little diagram explained where those numbers were. I stood up to help.

"Perspective, *signore*," I said. "The seats close to us are farther apart and the window seats closer together. So fifty-one and fifty-two are the corridor seats, fifty-five and fifty-six the window. That little square between the seats is the window. Odd numbers with their backs to the locomotive, even numbers facing it."

He was furious. Furious he hadn't understood, furious a foreigner had explained it, and most of all furious about the seats they had been given.

"My wife needs to be facing the locomotive! We especially asked for seats facing the locomotive."

The young man to my right remarked that the train would be turned around twice on the journey, so no seat would be facing the locomotive the whole trip.

"Since no one is sitting next to me," I said, indicating the seat to my left, "perhaps *la signora* could sit here."

They were uncertain about this. They apparently had an investment in sitting in the seats allotted to them. What if someone came and sat in their seats while they were sitting elsewhere? On the other hand, his wife could not sit with her back to the train. She just couldn't.

"We were supposed to sit together." The man had perfected a tone of voice that was both belligerent and plaintive.

"I'm happy to move," I said.

But the man did not want this. I was sitting in the seat I was supposed to be in, and I should stay there. He couldn't be responsible for moving me.

As yet the tiny wife had said not a word. He had done all the talking for her. Eventually she sat down next to me while her husband brought in two gigantic, brand-new green leather suitcases, and proceeded to look at them and then to look up at the luggage racks above our heads. Next to me, the young man had gone back to his laptop. A glance at his screen showed he was poring over some highly technical documents.

I offered to help the man put his cases up, but he refused. Watching him struggle, lift the bag, stagger, let it fall again, I'm suddenly reminded of the way, when boarding a plane, the whole overhead locker routine brings out the worst in people. The hostess checks your boarding card and you start toward your seat, only to find the passage blocked for minutes at a time by people trying to fit oversized bags into lockers that the early comers have already stuffed full with coats and packages and guitars and umbrellas. People push, voices are raised. The pilot warns you that we will miss our departure slot if the boarding process is not completed sufficiently quickly. What ought to be the simple matter of getting onto a vehicle and sitting down is protracted into a tetchy trial of nerves.

This doesn't happen on the train, which will depart anyway even if your luggage is all over the floor. But there are times when I fear that someone heaving up a heavy bag will drop it on me or my laptop. This was one of those moments.

"Please let me help you."

Mr. Misery again said no. He now had the huge suitcase at shoulder height but couldn't find the extra push to get it above his head and began to totter backward, then forward again about the compartment, which was now in motion. Suddenly he let it fall on his feet.

The young man beside me offered to put it up for him.

"No." He was grimly determined.

At this moment the ticket inspector came in. He saw that the newly arrived couple still had to put their cases up and said he would come back later.

"No!" the man cried. He began feeling through his pockets. His jacket pockets, his trouser pockets.

"I want my tickets punched," he said.

"I'll come back later," the inspector assured him.

"Please punch my tickets," he demanded.

This was new to me. I thought in thirty years of Italian train travel I had seen it all, but apparently not. Here was a man insisting he have his tickets not just seen but also punched.

While he was fussing in his pockets and the inspector watched him, bemused, the young man sitting next to me put aside his laptop, stood, grabbed the first of the two green bags, and with no apparent effort, swung it up onto the rack. The man glared at him but was now worried that he had lost his ticket.

"*Grazie*," the wife found her voice. Then she said, "Perhaps they're in my handbag."

They were. The inspector punched them.

As soon as he was gone, Mr. Misery announced angrily, "This is a long trip. If we don't have our tickets punched in the first section, when they check them in the second and see they weren't punched, they might think we have been trying to avoid inspection. That has happened to me before."

However fascinated I am by all the things that can go wrong between ticket bearer and ticket inspector, a relationship that has come to take on almost a metaphysical significance for me, I decided not to accept this invitation to converse. Nor did my young computerized neighbor.

But after a few minutes the young man did speak to me. Was I English? he asked. He had seen I was writing in English on my laptop. And he began to explain that in a month's time he would be heading to Australia, to emigrate. His uncle had gone thirty years ago, to Melbourne, and now he was going to join him. He was from Ragusa, he said, graduated in architecture in Rome with a thesis on green buildings that left no carbon footprint.

"So we were on the same train all the way," I said, and explained that I had come from Modica.

He laughed. He wasn't that much of a masochist. He had had his parents drive him to Siracusa. It took half the time.

"Half for you, but not for them."

"True," he agreed.

"Not to mention the carbon footprint."

"*Già*." He confessed that the work experience he was doing in an architect's office in Velletri had left him rather skeptical as to the possibility of the zero carbon footprint. A building that really achieved that would be far too expensive to build.

The train from Modica to Siracusa cost €7.

I asked him if there was no work in Ragusa. Was that why he was leaving? But he said, no, there was work, there was even an architect's office in Ragusa that would take him on, a good one. He hesitated. It was just that, once you had left a place like Ragusa, it became impossible to go back. If he wanted to stay he should have studied nearby, in Catania or Siracusa.

"You can't return to Sicily," he said. "Once you've gone, you've gone."

At Catania, a man got on and claimed the seat next to me, occupied by the timorous wife. She went out into the corridor. I had forgotten her train problem and thought nothing of it for a while, then realized she was standing there, long-suffering and a little uncertain on her feet. Her husband was frowning over his crossword puzzle.

I went out and told her, please, to take my seat.

She hesitated. "But you were talking to the nice young man. I don't want to interrupt you."

"Take it," I told her. "Please."

I STAYED IN THE corridor for a while. I had forgotten how these old Intercities have a bar running along the bottom of the corridor windows about four feet from the floor. This is just right for gripping with both hands as, your back to the compartments and face to the window, you gaze out over the countryside as it flies by.

We were passing Etna. Its perfect volcano shape looked very beautiful in the bright sunshine behind the lava stone city of Catania. "And you feel you can touch it with your hand," Giovanni Verga's short story "Malaria" begins, "as if it smoked up from the fat earth, there, everywhere, around about the mountains that shut it in, from Agnone to Mount Etna." He was born near here, malaria country. It was the disease that smoked up from the bowels of the earth. I use that passage with my students sometimes. Likewise the opening paragraphs of Verga's "Black Bread," which talk about how an old man's greed led him to go on working on fertile slopes below Etna, despite the fact that everyone knew you inevitably caught the disease and died if you worked there for any length of time.

I love Verga. In "Malaria," the local innkeeper, whose five wives have all died of malaria, becomes obsessed with the railway when he realizes that the people passing by on the trains don't suffer from the disease. He associates the malaria with the smoke of the volcano, while the railways become synonymous with wealth and health. But he was wrong there. One of the first studies investigating the link between malaria and mosquitoes was carried out with the help of Italian state railways. They had a problem with workers living in cheap railway men's housing north of Rome; these men were constantly falling ill. Someone had the bright idea of installing nets in the bedroom windows so that when they slept with the windows open in summer the mosquitoes wouldn't get to them. At the time it was just a hypothesis, a hunch. The improvement in the railway men's health was immediate.

Trains were also useful during the 1908 earthquake, which reduced Catania to a heap of rubble. We were sliding through the suburbs right now, a prosaic clutter of concrete and palm trees. Survivors of the quake were housed in hundreds of railway carriages that the newly nationalized railways had rushed to the scene. Seven years old at the time, Quasimodo later wrote a poem about it, recalling nights in freight wagons where herds of children chew almonds and dried apples while dreaming of corpses and rubble.

Thinking of Verga, I suddenly wanted to read him. I went back

into the compartment and Googled "Malaria." This is the first time
I've made a trip with the chance to be online on the move. I hadn't
realized how much fun it would be tapping in instantly to books I
knew describing landscape and places. Moments later I was reading
D. H. Lawrence's translation:

> twice a day he saw the long line of carriages crowded with peo-
> ple pass by . . . sometimes a peasant lad playing the accordion
> with his head bent, bunched up on the seat of a third-class com-
> partment; the beautiful ladies who looked out of the windows
> with their heads swathed in a veil; the silver and the tarnished
> steel of the bags and valises which shone under the polished
> lamps; the high stuffed seat-backs with their crochet-work cov-
> ers. Ah, how lovely it must be traveling in there, snatching a
> wink of sleep! It was as if a piece of a city were sliding past, with
> the lit-up streets and the glittering shops. Then the train lost
> itself in the vast mist of the evening, and the poor fellow, taking
> off his shoes for a moment, and sitting on the bench, muttered,
> "Ah! for that lot there isn't any malaria."

Crochet-work covers! Beautiful ladies with veiled faces. There was
none of that today on Intercity 724, Siracusa to Rome. The frightened
wife was snatching a wink of sleep in my seat. Her husband was huffing and puffing over his crossword. I smiled. It seemed the train not
only served to unite Italy but now also constituted a kind of catalyst
that brought all my thoughts of the country together, all my reading
and traveling over thirty years. As we drew into Messina I remembered that I had once watched Hellas Verona play in the town, and
the Verona fans I was with, no more than a handful, caused outrage
chanting *Forza Etna!*—Go for it Etna!—meaning, bury them in hot
lava. The result was that at the end of the game they had to beg for
police protection to save them from hoards of Sicilians determined to
beat the living daylights out of these barbarous northerners. In the end

we had to wait in the stadium for almost two hours before their rage cooled to boredom and it was safe to go.

BOARDING THE FERRY, MY bet with the skeptical Sicilians was definitely on; we were only a dozen minutes late. Nothing. Likewise when the train pulled into the absolutely nondescript station of Lamezia Terme. Now came the tricky bit. A bus connection. Between Lamezia Terme on the west coast of Calabria and Catanzaro close to the east coast, the Gulf of Taranto, a bridge had come down only seconds after a train passed a few months before. In fact, the train derailed as the bridge came down, a lucky escape for the passengers who found themselves in one of those movie situations with the train just safe, though off the line, and the bridge behind them crumbling away. The official cause was heavy rain that had swollen a mountain torrent and shifted its usual bed so that it ate away the foundation of one of the bridge supports. Perhaps maintenance was also an issue. The bridge was a prewar structure. In any event, almost a year later the line was still closed and a bus connection was operating. On a blistering July afternoon about a hundred people tried to squeeze into a bus for seventy. Buses are not as big as trains.

Fearing that when all the seats were taken they would close the doors and force the rest to wait for the next bus, thus blowing my next and final connection and the bet, which I was rather foolishly determined to win, I made dishonorable efforts to be on board, and indeed I secured one of the last seats. As it turned out, the driver was not at all worried about people standing. Cripples, ancient ladies, pregnant women, everybody was accepted, everybody crushed into the stifling corridor. The journey was made more uncomfortable by a group of wild young Albanians spread out among the seats around me and yelling to each other over people's heads. They seemed vaguely threatening and extremely restless, standing up to shout and sitting down hard again, bouncing and swaying to whatever music each was wired up to.

The road was not of the best. Hugely overweight, the man standing in the corridor beside me rocked from side to side, grabbing at this or that, depending on the direction of the bend. This bus wasn't made for people to stand in, and there were no handles. After a while I realized he was speaking English to two younger men beside him, with an Australian accent. It turned out he had come with his sons from Melbourne to see his father's birthplace at Catanzaro. It seemed odd that on the same day I had met one Italian planning to emigrate to Melbourne, and then the descendants of another emigrant returning out of curiosity. Remembering a week I once spent in Melbourne, I feared the boys might find Catanzaro a disappointment.

At Catanzaro Lido, the outside of the station had been completely restyled to look like a swimming pool or leisure center. Everything had a polished glass and cool, air-conditioned look, but alas without the air-conditioning. Exposed to a day of ferocious Mediterranean sunshine, the ticket hall was truly suffocating. It was 5:45 p.m. My last train of the day was waiting on the platform. I began to wish that bet had been for money.

MUCH OF THE RELATIONSHIP between a town and the railways depends on the location of the station. Ideally, the train should stop just short of the old city center, damaging nothing but allowing the traveler to walk from station to center in a few minutes. The city is plugged into the national network without its intimacy being violated. Italy has many examples of this ideal situation. Venice is perfect. You cross the causeway, step off the train, and immediately you are in old Venice, which doesn't seem to have suffered as a consequence. Palermo also is good, central without being obtrusive, elegant and sober without being pompous. The stations of Turin, Florence, and Rome are all likewise right there, near the civic heart of things but without clotting any crucial veins. A typical solution for smaller towns is the cul-de-sac lined with plane trees and the sleepy station waiting at the end. Porto Vescovo, Peschiera, Desenzano, and scores of other stations follow this charming model. There's a curious analogy with the cemetery here, another departure point for a different journey also to be found, in Italy, behind a quiet wall at the end of a tree-lined cul-de-sac. You can book your place in advance or leave matters to chance as the fancy takes you. But if you're not carrying a valid *documento di viaggio* there's no question of getting off at the first stop to avoid the inspector's ire. Whatever the fine is, it will have to be paid.

Where the train can't deliver you to within walking distance of your favorite café, public transport is essential. Verona's main station is on the wrong side of two busy circular roads and a maze of interconnections for fast traffic leaving town. It's not a happy location. But buses leave every few minutes to take you straight to the grand Roman amphitheater in the central square. Ticket purchases are easy, and there is a strong and immediately perceptible flow between town and railway that suggests a healthy integration between individual needs and collective endeavor.

Not so Crotone.

"Do you know Crotone?" I asked the pretty girl sitting opposite. I had seen from Google that the station was quite a way out of town.

She did she said. She lived a few miles away.

"Do you know how I can get to the center from the station?"

She frowned and reflected. "I think there's a bus," she said. "I think you sort of walk for a while and then you find a place with buses."

It wasn't encouraging.

The older woman beside her leaned across.

"Sometimes there's a taxi."

Imagine!

But I had won my bet. As the wheels squealed to a stop, I texted, "Caro Giuseppe, the Englishman was right! In Crotone. Only twenty minutes late. *Evviva!*"

Ominously, he texted back, "Carissimo Tim, on arrival in Crotone any cause for celebration, however small, is welcome. *Buona fortuna!*"

So much for my triumph over the Sicilians.

The two-carriage train was onward bound to the small coastal resort of Sibari, some fifty miles north, along the Gulf of Taranto. On the platform a handful of people got off to be met by waiting relatives. The usual *extra-comunitari* occupied the platform benches. It wasn't clear what they could be waiting for, since this was the only train passing through here for quite a while. The station buildings are unexpectedly large, and there is an extended area of freight sidings cluttered with rusty wagons and green with weeds. This must have been a busy place when the chemical plant was still running on the coast nearby; it had been one of the largest in Italy. Now the rails were rusted against a backdrop of steep, red-brown hills with sparse gray vegetation. Inside the building, a modern ticket window carried the sign "This Desk Is Temporarily Closed." Anyone seeking a ticket refund was instructed to phone a call center, which would give them an address to which they could mail a written request with the original ticket attached. I suppose there are people who actually do this sort of thing, but the instructions read like an invitation to let the matter drop.

To describe the area outside the station as a piazza would be generous. It was a deserted car park of broken asphalt serving not so much the station itself as the low industrial buildings all around. A brown bus bearing the legend Ferrovie di Calabria had a very stationary if not abandoned look to it. There was no bus stop, no timetable, no explanation, no driver. I turned to take the one taxi parked at the station exit, only to see it accelerating away with a young black woman in the back, looking very smart in white and purple.

I began to walk toward town. To my left, against a cement wall topped with blue railings, a metal board had been mounted on an iron scaffolding, in the 1970s perhaps. The surface of the board was white and there was evidence that many years ago it might have carried useful information. At the top, what had once been a map was too drastically faded to make out anything at all, but beneath it—on the map's legend perhaps—I did manage to read the words MUSEO, CHIESA,

PALAZZO, CASTELLO, RESTI ARCHEOLOGICI. Appropriately, Crotone was referred to, in fancy letters at the top, by its ancient name, *KROTON.* Only one tiny square of the whole twelve square feet of surface area was still colored and vivid: the *AGIP* logo of Italian Petroleum, a black lion on a yellow background. Apparently, when the company had closed down its plant here, all useful relationship between town and station had been severed. I climbed a bridge over a stinking, stagnant creek on whose dark surface raw sewage was all too visible. Evening time and still ninety-three degrees. *Benvenuto a Crotone.* Maybe the Sicilians had been wrong about the trains, but I began to fear that they were right about Crotone.

YET AN HOUR LATER, I was a happy boy. After walking through some dispiriting outskirts, the old center of the town was immediately intriguing, a honeycomb of alleys climbing up and around a steep conical hill, each thread of street crisscrossed above with drying laundry and inhabited below by folks lounging on chairs outside the heavy bead curtains that kept flies from their front doors. People were eating, drinking, smoking, playing cards, reading newspapers, or simply checking things on their phones. Outside one door a TV had been brought down to the street. Elsewhere a man was sharpening knives on a grindstone he turned with pedals and a chain. At the top of the hill was a castle housing a museum of Greek and Roman artifacts, closed now but definitely something to look at in the morning. There was also a public library with the bizarre name of Biblioteca A. Lucifero. Most of all, on the far side of the hill, there was a warm sea to swim in. I hurried to my hotel to dump my bag.

I had booked into the Hotel Concordia, really the only hotel in the center. Outside, on the wall beside a busy café, a stone plaque told me others had gotten here before me: George Gissing in 1897, Norman Douglas ten years later. Even before I established exactly where the entrance was, a voice boomed *"Benvenuto Meester Parkus."*

"*Buona sera,*" I said.

"You have booked with Booking dot com."

"That's right."

Not only was I recognizable as English, but apparently the only Englishman around here must be Mr. Parkus.

Watching life go by on the sidewalk outside his hotel, the proprietor had a paunch to show off and the air of the man who knows everything anyone could know about the square mile he lives in.

"Where's your car?" he asked.

"I came by train."

That threw him.

"*I treni fanno schifo,*" he announced immediately—the trains stink—and as if fearing contamination he made a strange little gesture—a tic, perhaps—as though washing his hands.

I climbed a steep flight of stone steps, left my little backpack in the tiny room that the proprietor's languid daughter assigned me to, and hurried out to take a swim as the sun sank behind the hills west of the town. The waterfront was a pleasant hum of cafés where mostly local beachgoers were grabbing an *aperitivo* before dinner. A small band was grinding out old covers, cheerfully enough. I swam a little way out to get a good view of the esplanade and rolled over on my back. The water is so calm in this part of the world that you can just float and breathe. I must say I felt immensely pleased with myself, pleased to have made it here, pleased that my Sicilian friends were as wrong about Crotone as they had been about the trains, pleased that in general the southerners were turning out to be far less threatening than I had imagined. My adopted country was bigger than I had thought, I realized, bigger than Verona and Milan, bigger than Florence and Rome. It stretched this far. I had traveled a long way and still hadn't left home. Feet toward the open sea, I lay still, letting my head fall back and back onto its warm cushion of water. Behind me the hills rose on either side of the town in the dull yellows and greens of thirsty vegetation interrupted here and there by outcrops of reddish rock. To

the right was Cape Colonna, where the grand temple to Hera, Zeus's
wife, had been built. Perhaps my country stretched into the past, too,
I thought. In this bay, right where I was swimming, in the times of
Magna Grecia, there would have been scores of ships at anchor. That
was how the Greeks conquered and traded, exactly as the British
did two thousand and more years later, moving arms and resources
great distances by sea. Now there were just a few fishing boats and the
sound of the band grinding out "Fernando." I sat up, splashed, and
trod water for a while, taking it all in. A young woman in a white dress
was swaying along the promenade, two men in close attendance. Not
true the trains stink, I rebuked my host. Not true at all. They brought
me to a wonderful place safe and sound and bang on time.

THE TRAINS ALSO BROUGHT Gissing and Douglas, more than a hundred years ago. Having eaten miserably, in the restaurant below the
Concordia, I returned to my room, went online, and downloaded
Gissing's *By the Ionian Sea*. He had eaten miserably, too, he said. And
he, too, had found the river by the station an "all but stagnant and
wholly pestilential stream." I downloaded Douglas's *Old Calabria*
and found the same observation on the river, though Douglas felt the
food had much improved since Gissing's visit ten years before. Both
authors spent most of their time in Crotone considering how a place
that was once the capital of Magna Grecia and famed for its healthy
climate, a city boasting twelve square miles of walled habitations
and a huge temple to the goddess Hera, had become little more than
a squalid fishing village. Gissing rails against a certain Archbishop
Antonio Lucifero, yes, he who had given his name to the library I had
noticed, who apparently had started dismantling Hera's temple in the
fifteenth century to use its stones to build his ecclesiastical palazzo.
Douglas ironizes, thanking Lucifero for leaving two of the forty-eight
columns of the temple when he could have taken all of them.

Here and there both authors had intriguing train anecdotes.

This is Gissing's comment on departing from Taranto for Metaponto, the same journey I would be taking in the opposite direction
soon enough:

Official time-bills of the month marked a train for Metaponto
at 4:56 a.m., and this I decided to take, as it seemed probable
that I might find a stay of some hours sufficient, and so be able
to resume my journey before night. I asked the waiter to call me
at a quarter to four. In the middle of the night (as it seemed to
me) I was aroused by a knocking, and the waiter's voice called
to me that, if I wished to leave early for Metaponto, I had better
get up at once, as the departure of the train had been changed
to 4:15—it was now half-past three. There ensued an argument,
sustained, on my side, rather by the desire to stay in bed this
cold morning than by any faith in the reasonableness of the
railway company. There must be a mistake! The *orario* for the
month gave 4:56, and how could the time of a train be changed
without public notice? Changed it was, insisted the waiter; it
had happened a few days ago, and they had only heard of it at
the hotel this very morning. Angry and uncomfortable, I got my
clothes on, and drove to the station, where I found that a sudden change in the time-table, without any regard for persons
relying upon the official guide, was taken as a matter of course.

Here is Douglas similarly irritated by early rather than late trains,
returning to Taranto after a day trip to Grottaglie:

A characteristic episode. I had carefully timed myself to catch
the returning train to Taranto. Great was my surprise when,
half-way to the station, I perceived the train swiftly approaching. I raced it, and managed to jump into a carriage just as it
drew out of the station. The guard straightway demanded my
ticket and a fine for entering the train without one (return tickets,

for weighty reasons of "internal administration," are not sold). I looked at my watch, which showed that we had left six minutes before the scheduled hour. He produced his; it coincided with my own. "No matter," he said. "I am not responsible for the eccentricities of the driver, who probably had some urgent private affairs to settle at Taranto. The fine must be paid." A fellow passenger took a more charitable view of the case. He suggested that an inspector of the line had been traveling along with us, and that the driver, knowing this, was naturally ambitious to show how fast he could go.

With so much that is familiar here, the one surprise is that the inspector's watch "coincided" with Douglas's.

But the anecdote that had me laughing myself to sleep, a train story I know I shall never be able to match, was this gem that Gissing found in a religious pamphlet distributed by an itinerant preacher in Taranto.

A few days ago—thus, after a pious exordium, the relation began—in that part of Italy called Marca, there came into a railway station a Capuchin friar of grave, thoughtful, melancholy aspect, who besought the station-master to allow him to go without ticket by the train just starting, as he greatly desired to reach the Sanctuary of Loreto that day, and had no money to pay his fare. The official gave a contemptuous refusal, and paid no heed to the entreaties of the friar, who urged all manner of religious motives for the granting of his request. The two engines on the train (which was a very long one) seemed about to steam away—but, behold, *con grande stupore di tutti*, the waggons moved not at all! Presently a third engine was put on, but still all efforts to start the train proved useless. Alone of the people who viewed this inexplicable event, the friar showed no astonishment; he remarked calmly, that so long as he was refused permission to travel by it, the train would not stir. At length *un ricco signore* found a way out of the difficulty by purchasing the friar a third-class ticket; with a grave reproof to the station-master, the friar took his seat, and the train went its way.

But the matter, of course, did not end here. Indignant and amazed, and wishing to be revenged upon that *frataccio*, the station-master telegraphed to Loreto, that in a certain carriage of a certain train was traveling a friar, whom it behoved the authorities to arrest for having hindered the departure of the said train for fifteen minutes, and also for the offense of mendicancy within a railway station. Accordingly, the Loreto police sought the offender, but, in the compartment where he had traveled, found no person; there, however, lay a letter couched in these terms: "He who was in this waggon under the guise of a humble friar, has now ascended into the arms of his *Santissima Madre Maria*. He wished to make known to the world how easy it is for him to crush the pride of unbelievers, or to reward those who respect religion."

Nothing more was discoverable; wherefore the learned of the Church—*i dotti della chiesa*—came to the conclusion that under the guise of a friar there had actually appeared "*Nostro Signore Gesù Cristo*."

It occurs to me I might translate this little story back into the Italian Gissing found it in and hand it out to every ticket inspector who gives me grief.

MARK TWAIN MUST HAVE been lying, or at least tongue in cheek, when he claimed he admired the Italians more for their trains than their antiquities and art treasures; these last are so abundant and persuasive. Any visit to the archaeological museum in Crotone immediately makes nonsense of concepts of progress in human achievement, at least in the fields of art and craftsmanship. We may acquire more and more technology, but the ability to conjure ideas and visions of every kind from the most ordinary materials was as powerful thousands of years ago as it ever can be. And it's no good Twain pretending he can't understand it; one needs only to be human. Almost at once, as one turns the corner from entrance corridor to display rooms, there's a tall, two-handled vase, its elegant curves suggestively feminine, black at the slim top, and again at the narrow base, with a wide band of intense orange around the full swell of the belly. Across this field of light moves a band of graceful black warriors in battle, one falling back on his knee as another stands over him with his spear, others just behind waiting to join the fray; their helmet plumes have the nobility of horses' manes, combed up and braided; their belts and straps, of armor and shields; the pleats of their skirts, the details of their weapons, are shown with fine orange lines cutting through the solid figures, so you realize that the whole complex image has been created with an intricate, highly stylized pattern of glazed black shapes interlocking but not quite touching on this luminous background. The orange of the vase glows against the black, with the glow of the Mediterranean sun that the men fought under; they stand out stark against it, their moment of glory stamped on the undifferentiated light of eternity. But because of those bright lines crossing their bodies they also seem part of the light, or to partake of it, as if they'd materialized out of it and were ready to break up into it, as if the whole of life were an alternation of black and orange, vivid, brief appearance in a flaming circle of light. This is the realm of Apollo, at once an aesthetic and a philosophy. Of course we're talking violence here. We're talking weapons and pain and death under a hot sun. The art isn't attempting to hide that, but to transform it. Somebody might choose to deplore this glorification of struggle, but no one could deny its accomplishment and impact. You can't not understand.

What a rich museum they have in this provincial outpost. There are beautiful bas-relief faces, winged horses, a mermaid, a tiny rabbit, its head thrown right back so that the neck can form the spout for the cosmetic oil it held. Fine-tooth combs carved in ivory, brooches and buckles and mirrors of bronze. All of them found in the area immediately around the town, all of it fashioned by the artisans of Magna Grecia. A spearhead is engraved with the words "Acan-thropos son of Teognide"; there are decorated ax heads, armor, model chariots, a highly stylized bronze horse, at once animal and abstract, a model ship that is also a lamp. There are votive terra-cotta ornaments, objects placed in temples to give punch to prayers and supplications, forerunners of the same tradition in the Catholic Church. There are winged girls in bronze, too busty and cheerful to be angels, terracotta busts, perfectly harmonious and poised, their faces serene and solemn, monstrous animal heads, belts of braided chain, rings, brooches, earrings, bracelets. Brightest of all, there is a gold laminate diadem fashioned into a circle of leaves and berries, emblem of the goddess Hera, a most lavish gift for some Olympian winner maybe.

Yet all this wonderful art and craftsmanship is held in the most unprepossessing low building in an empty square at the top of the old town, where no one passes by. As I enter—and the entrance is rather incongruously graced with the Italian and EU flags—the two staff members seem surprised to be disturbed for a ticket; no other visitor came while I was there, nor did any guard follow me about to see if I might be tampering or taking photos. The exhibits are all housed in tall glass cases with heavy black bases—practical, no doubt, but of a rigidity and brutal angularity alien to the grace and fluid movement of the art displayed. The captions and supporting panels of infor-mation, explaining how the Achaeans founded the colony of Kroton after consulting Apollo's oracle at Delhi, how Pythagoras founded his school here in the fifth century BC, how Crotone was famous for its doctors, its artists, and above all its athletes, how the grand temple of Hera was excavated and its treasures unearthed, are diligent but a little dull, too long, too lame, too dusty and academic. It's Italy's eter-nal dilemma: how to be equal to such a rich tradition on a daily basis, how to preserve beauty without becoming prisoner to the past, how not to kill it with the dullness of a school-trip atmosphere. Yet when you bend down and look closely at these lavishly fashioned earrings, these tiny bronze animals and fish whose stoppered mouths held oils for a beautiful woman's skin, the humble cooking tripods and the glittering trophies, what strikes you is that these people really did live here all those years ago, on the southern Italian coast, and that they had style. In abundance. Then, in about 290 BC, the Romans arrived, and these indigenous people were no longer masters of their own destiny; they were drawn into something far bigger. Two large marble basins and the base of a statue announce the arrival from the north. It was hard not to think of it as a sad development. Coming out of the place, I felt an immense desire to rush down to the waterfront for another swim before my next appointment with Trenitalia. And I did.

LIKE A VAST BEACHED sea monster, the abandoned chemical plant north of Crotone disfigures the coastline: another failed attempt to do something with the South. Because the conundrum is always this: why is it that the South finds it so difficult to turn its very real assets into tangible success? Here we have smart people, extraordinary landscapes, a beautiful coastline, beaches, seas, art treasures. So why is there so little tourism? Where are the English swarms, the German hordes who invade the coast of Spain? Instead of building hotels, they had tried to introduce a massive chemicals industry. It failed. In Taranto, just across the gulf, they had introduced what is now Italy's largest steel plant; magistrates are trying to close it because the levels of pollution are scandalously high. In a newspaper this morning, just before boarding the train, I saw that Wind Jet, the Sicilian low-cost airline that one of my hosts was boasting about during our dinner in Modica, has stopped flying, leaving hundreds of passengers stranded. They have failed. They can't compete. They spent too much money on all the wrong things. The trains are still running but mainly empty, costing the passenger next to nothing, costing the state a fortune. A section of line between Metaponto and Taranto, my next destination, is out of action and has been for more than a year. Damaged by landslides, which will mean another bus ride.

Never mind, I told myself. Sit back, gaze through the smeared windows, enjoy it.

Beaches. Bleached-white riverbeds. Mile after mile of olive groves. The Gulf of Taranto, empty sand with clear blue seas. Kiwi plants, row after endless row of them. Field after field. Broken walls. *Stazione di Torre Melissa.* Vineyards. Promontories with gray rock against blue sea. *Stazione di Cirò.* The *capotreno*'s whistle. An ancient tower on a low hillside. Squat, square masonry. Abandoned factories. Cactuses and scorched grass. *Stazione di Crucoli.* Graffiti: *"Ti penso sempre, amore mio."* Immigrants with cheap merchandise climbing on and off, getting stuck between swing doors. A stocky Slav on the seat behind me organizing them. Get off here. Get off there. *Stazione di Cariati.* *"Anna e Giulia troie"* (scrubbers). No sign of railway personnel anywhere. In English: "Boys 1978. Wanderers Everywhere."

In the seats across the corridor four children are headed for the beach with bags and towels and snorkels. It seems that Calabrian railways is offering free travel to under eighteens heading for seaside destinations on certain regional trains. Fill in a form, show an ID, get a travel card; a lot of bureaucracy to save a couple of euros.

Stazione di Mandatoriccio Campana. An urgent bell announces the train coming the other way. Once it has gone by we can proceed on our single track. KM 173+863, says a sign. A one-carriage train, a tiny station building, a very long platform. *Stazione di Calopezzati.* As well as their big boards laden with trinkets, the immigrant vendors also carry backpacks with further supplies. One trusts they have some water with them. Their days must be intolerably hot. It is in the high nineties again. *Stazione di Mirto Crosia.* "Katerina ti *amo." "Piccola, perdonami."* Forgive me. *Stazione di Rossano.* Yellow plastic tables on the platform and men drinking wine. In this heat. *"Domani sarà tardi per rimpiangere."* Tomorrow it'll be too late for regrets.

A STOCKY MAN CLIMBS on board with his stocky wife; they are healthy and solid and sunburned. He asks why I'm taking pictures of the stations. The graffiti. I tell him. He's Albanian, he says. He's been in Italy fifteen years. Drives a truck, in Taranto. There is no work now with the economic crisis. In particular there is no work for an Albanian. After fifteen years here he's still not treated as an equal. It doesn't bother him now. He came illegally on a rubber dinghy but managed to get his papers in the end. It's harder these days. He was lucky. His wife nods and smiles at everything he says. They speak Italian to me and Albanian to each other. Now he wants to see my camera. It's a cheap digital Olympus. He turns it over in hairy hands, his forearm tattooed with a blurry Cupid. He asks me what the camera's memory is. I've no idea. I never inquire about such things. They have been holidaying with their son, he says. In Catanzaro. He has four sons. Ten grand-children. Three great-grandchildren. Ah. This is what he wanted to tell me. He's proud of his family.

"Guess how old I am," he challenges.

His wife is smiling complacently. I have no idea. I'm rather taken aback that he claims to have great-grandchildren. He doesn't look that old. What's the youngest you can be to have great-grandchildren?

"I'd say you're sixty-five."

"Fifty-seven," he says, grinning triumphantly.

He's my age! I calculate. Average childbearing age between eighteen and nineteen.

"My first at seventeen," the wife says.

"Can't stop it," he says with a laugh. "It's life!"

He seems blissfully happy with his lot.

"People try," I said. "To stop it, I mean."

"You can't." He shakes his head. "Fools. It's life."

AT SIBARI WE SWITCH trains for the section to Metaponto; that is, we exchange one heavily scrawled, poorly air-conditioned, single-carriage diesel for another heavily scrawled, poorly air-conditioned, single-carriage diesel. The train revs and the fumes intensify. The air-conditioning is just enough to stop us from losing our heads. Just. A whistle and a lurch. One is usually so worried on trains about time, or at least so conscious of it. Will we depart on time? Are we running on time? Will we arrive on time? Will I win my bet? "This Regionale is traveling with a delay of eleven minutes. Trenitalia apologizes for the inconvenience." "This Interregionale Veloce is now approaching Verona Porta Nuova. Terminus of our journey. On time! Thank you for traveling Trenitalia." Time time time. But today I've decided to pay no attention. I shan't think of time at all. I refuse. After all, there is only one train running north and east along the Gulf of Taranto, rattling and swaying and stinking of diesel. Our train. There are no branch lines. There are no choices among Regionale, Regionale Veloce, or Intercity, no Eurostar, no Frecciarossa. There is nowhere else to go but where we are going, along the timeless Mediterranean coast.

I have firmly decided I'm not going to look at my watch the whole four-hour journey. I'm on holiday, in a part of my country I have never visited. It's hard, though. Hard not to look at your watch, hard to be here now, on each stretch of the journey, without being anxious for the end, without wanting anything to happen on the trip that you can engage with and write about. Buy your ticket each day now, I tell myself, wait for the train, climb aboard. Don't expect company for the journey. Don't expect to understand when there is a delay. Or even if there is a delay. Don't ask whether the train is punctual. Don't worry what Taranto will be like, what Lecce will be like, or Brindisi, or Bari. Don't be concerned that you may have nothing to say about these places. Just be here, on the journey, at every moment of the journey; when the train is hurrying on and the landscape is whisked away—here and gone, here and gone—when the train stops and the same dull station name imposes itself for twenty minutes, Trebisacce, Trebisacce, Trebisacce. Learn to be happy with Trebisacce, and happy when the inspector blows his whistle; an electric warning sounds and the doors slide shut. Trebisacce slips behind at last. It's gone. I almost miss it. Now Roseto, now Monte Giordano. Accept the names that come and go, places that will never mean anything to you—Rocca Imperiale, Policoro. You are simply here, on a journey from Crotone to Taranto, from this moment to the next, transported by Le Ferrovie dello Stato.

I think I am learning to take the journeys less anxiously. The sun helps, and the general feeling that these railways are not part of an urgent business world, they can't be speeded up, they just are what they are. I'm learning to take them day by day and to accept that I really did move my life to Italy thirty years ago. I'm not sure why, but this trip to the South has made me think about that decision again. Thirty years ago I surrendered my identity, my Britishness. I became this strange hybrid, neither here nor there. Between places, between cultures. Recognized everywhere as English, but not really English now. Accept that. Now you are on a journey through tiny stations whose names are all new to you—Scanzano Jonico—but as real to those who live here as any other place. They are as much a part of your adoptive country as Verona, as Milan. Look at the bamboo growing in the gulley. Look at the dry gorse, look at the ruins and broken doors and the fat mother crouching on the platform to spray deodorant onto the armpits of her infant children. You are here now, arriving in the station of Metaponto, whether on time or not on time. It doesn't matter.

So for a few hours my mind lapsed into this strange mood, lulled perhaps by the rhythm of wheels on rails, stifled by the poor ventilation, mesmerized by the fierce sunlight on this arid landscape.

TARANTO, BRINDISI, LECCE, BARI. If the provincial rail lines here are little more than buses on rails, running half empty, nevertheless when a mainline Intercity arrives from the distant North, then the carriages are full, the stations are full. Summer is the time of return. Students studying in Milan, Bologna, Turin, young men and women who went north to get education and find work. Their families are waiting for them, right on the platform. Mothers and fathers are there when they tumble out of the carriage, brothers and sisters. A grandmother, a cousin. Perhaps a boyfriend or a girlfriend. The first embrace is always for Mother, smiles and joy, as the last embrace will again be for Mother when these same young people depart once more in a month's time.

The train station is the ideal scenario for greetings and farewells. The car is too banal. What does it mean to set off in a car? Nothing. The airport is too exhausting and impersonal, the plane itself remote, unseen, the barriers and security disturbing. Here the powerful beast of the locomotive thrusts its nose under the great arch of the station. The lines straighten from the last bend. Clanking and squealing, the train slows. The last moments of waiting begin. Eyes focus on the platform, keen to possess their loved ones; in the train corridor, meanwhile, the long-awaited beloved is jostling and jostled, luggage at his heels. The train slows, slows, slows, teasing everyone on both sides of the divide, making them wait, making them savor the tension between absence and presence. Text messages are flying back and forth: "The last carriage but one." "The first after the restaurant car." "You'll have to help with my bags." "Be nice to Zia Eleonora, her dog just died." "I look a state without my makeup."

It's simply agonizing how long a train can take to stop in a terminal station where the *macchinista* high up in his cabin must gauge the distance to the buffers. The beast is inching now, steel wheel on steel rail. If this were an old Regionale, people would hang out of the windows, but the Intercity carriages are sealed—bursting with life, but silent. Then with a wonderful sigh and a last jarring squeal it has stopped, it is still. And still, the doors can't open. Why is there such a long wait on trains, ten seconds, even twenty, almost a minute, between the locomotive stopping and the green light that tells you that you can push the button and open? All along the twelve packed carriages the buttons are pushed, and again with agonizing slowness—it must be done on purpose—the heavy doors begin to inch away from the carriagework. If the whole of railway technology, the whole cultural and architectural heritage that is the Italian rail station, had been designed on purpose to maximize the emotional drama of return from afar, it could not have been done better. Now, after trips of six or eight or even ten hours, the passengers are tumbling out. Some will have to wait in the corridor while others fuss with their clumsy bags on the steep steps. Some are already striding down the platform.

The family greeting their firstborn son, their beautiful daughter, sees a stream of strange faces flowing toward them, a dam release of insignificant others, people who mean nothing to them, pushing past, themselves irritated by these idiots blocking the way. When will the known face declare itself? When will Luca or Chiara appear and be mine? In the meantime, other trains are arriving and departing. *Coincidenza, coincidenza! Regionale per Metaponto in partenza dal binario 4, anziché binario 7.* Appearance, presence, is so mysterious. Not there, not there, not there, then suddenly, yes, yes, there, there she is. Stefania! *Finalmente!* That's her face, her walk, *her.* So different from anybody else on the planet. You have the crowd, and in the midst of it, infinitely more special, *her,* Lucia, my daughter, my girlfriend, my sister.

In a space of twenty or so square yards toward the end of the platform dozens of families, lovers, mothers are sighting their object of desire. Now they must just survive the last tumultuous but strangely embarrassing seconds when the beloved is seen, recognized, but not yet close enough to speak to and embrace; all you can do is observe, watch, as they approach, and you too are observed and watched by your darling child; all this emotion is ready to pour out of you and instead there you are observing your beloved and observed by them, judging and being judged: Mario definitely looks thinner than he should. Why does Mamma always get so stupidly excited? And what an old-fashioned blouse! Then the embrace, the contact, and the southern child is back, possessed, adored, perhaps already regretting the freedoms and anonymity of Milan.

It's so much more intense down here, the emotions on these platforms where Trenitalia hits its southernmost buffer and releases these Mediterranean children from the prison of the train into the loving clutches of *mamma e papà*. The sense that one *has* to go north for a serious career, or at least the start of that career, increases the South's perception of itself as forever the victim, abandoned, even punished by the callous and confident North. Poor us, poor us! And this winds up the emotions of greeting and parting; when perhaps the truth for many of these kids is that the South's asphyxiating family traditions, its asphyxiating adoration of its offspring, is as much the trigger for departure as anything else. True, the economic situation is dire. Youth unemployment is almost 50 percent in the South. But many of these young men and women, after being spoiled silly in the summer weeks ahead, eating heavily and scorching themselves on perfect beaches, will be only too glad to be on the train again in early September. Then the carriages will be already there, waiting on the platform, and Father will quietly carry the bags on board, find the *prenotazione obbligatoria*, hoist his daughter's heavy bags full of gifts onto the luggage rack, exchange a last embrace. The son will cross the corridor to wave to his mother standing on the platform and looking up at the window. She looks small and rather pathetic down there, her tired face upturned with a mole at the corner of her mouth; and he looks scandalously healthy after his days of seaside idleness, glowing with sunshine and sleek with pasta and pastries. It's embarrassing because no one can speak now. The windows are sealed. They can only look at each other through the greasy carriage glass. But you can't just turn away and sit down. You have to wait until the train moves. Papà has his arm around Mamma's shoulder and she is trying not to cry, or giving that impression. Really the boy is already gone, but, unfortunately, he isn't gone, the train should have left but it hasn't and Mamma is standing there on the platform and won't go away. He smiles wishing she would leave and, showing her the palm of his hand, waves it a little from side to side in stifled farewell. Then she really does begin to cry and his father exchanges a pained look of weary complicity until, at last, again with that heartrending slowness that only a long train weighing hundreds of tons is capable of, the carriage begins to move, Mamma is inching away. She's waving and trying to laugh through her tears now. The motion brings relief and he can wave back properly unembarrassed before the quiet passengers around him. Mamma is gone. Papà is gone. Taranto. Reggio Calabria, Bari, gone. It's back to reality, adulthood, the North, grayness, Milan.

Standing on platforms in Brindisi, Lecce, Taranto, observing a few of these scenes, I suddenly felt that it was a disgrace that in thirty years in Italy I had spent so little time in the South. And I felt it was a conspiracy of the North that had held me back. But also the testimony of those very children, so often my students, who when they arrive in Milan shrug their shoulders and tell you that you really don't need to make that journey, there is nothing there, in the South. This is my future, they tell you. The North. Yet of course many must go back. Or where would those mothers and fathers on the platforms come from? Perhaps they lose their enthusiasm for the North after they have graduated from my care. Perhaps Milan and Turin wear them down, or they find a state job in teaching and have themselves transferred to some school near home. They say you can live well on a state income in the South.

WHAT THEY DIDN'T TELL me in particular about the South was how remarkable these old city centers are. I don't mean architecturally, or not only. There are remarkable city centers architecturally all over Italy. But socially, anthropologically. In Taranto and Bari there are large medieval towns just a stone's throw from the train station, still mostly ungentrified, populated by a working class, almost an underclass, that speaks its own incomprehensible dialect and enjoys a sense of community and intense collective identity lost in most of Europe. Walk down a short road lined with palm trees from the station in Taranto, cross the swing bridge that divides the so-called Little Sea, to the left, from the Gulf of Taranto to the right, and you are already in an extraordinary world of suffocatingly narrow streets and people who don't seem to make much distinction between being inside or outside, sitting on kitchen chairs in alleys watching their own TVs through the window in rooms whose walls are rough, bare stones piled up centuries ago. Men and women call to each other along the streets with distinctive cries, coded whistles, a fluid repertoire of gestures. At once you are on the alert; you sense this is not your place; you really are a stranger here, a stranger under observation through the cracks between shutters. Taking a photo, you take care not to offend, not to intrude, hopefully not to be seen.

The proximity of the train hasn't changed this, or hasn't destroyed it. True, the train sucks away the sons of these families, too, not to my university classes in Milan maybe, but to the factories of Frankfurt, Cologne, and Dortmund. Instead of taking money from home to study, they send money back home. These are the kind of migrants who return on retirement; who in a sense never left and never wanted to leave.

Another kind of train that regularly leaves Taranto, though never announced in the station, is the freight train from ILVA, the huge steelworks on the coast of the Little Sea, a large internal lagoon in full view of the city. Built in 1961 when the steel industry was under state control, its location absolutely a matter of politics rather than any commercial logic, an attempt to bring work to the South and secure the votes of a grateful community, ILVA is now reputedly the largest steelworks in Europe and certainly by far the largest in Italy. I watched trains carrying huge black steel tubes, three to a wagon, bound who knows where. But only days after my visit, magistrates served an order to close the plant down, with a criminal charge of *disastro ecologico*. The pollution blowing across the Little Sea into Taranto is all too visible. A study claims that the steel industry here has been responsible over the past seven years for 11,550 deaths from respiratory conditions and heart disease. It's not clear yet whether the plant really will close. One suspects not. One might as well say good-bye to half the Italian steel industry. In any event, it's likely that in the near future the trains will be taking more and more men and less and less steel northward to Germany. There will be more tearful farewells on the platforms.

IN GENERAL BRINDISI WAS a wonderful surprise, a busy port town with ferries to Greece and Croatia, not otherwise on anyone's tourist itinerary, but undeservedly so; the center is elegant and well signposted, while my hotel actually honored me with a proper receipt. As so often an easy, well-signposted movement between station and town is an indication that the local authorities are paying attention. One thing they've chosen to overlook in Brindisi, though, is the kind of inscription that has been scrubbed away in most Italian towns; on a grandiose monumental fountain looking north across the water of the town's harbor you can read

ANNO DOMINI MCMXL/ XVIII AB ITALIA PER FASCES
RENOVATA/ VICTORIO EMMANUELE REGE ET
IMPERATORE/ BENITO MUSSOLINI DVCE/ PROVINCIA
F. F. (Feliciter Fecit)

In the year of our lord 1940, eighteen years after the revival of Italy by Fascism under Victor Emmanuel III, King and Emperor, and Benito Mussolini, Duce; gladly donated by the Province.

BUT NOTHING IN THE warm air of Brindisi felt dangerous that evening. Finding a table just off the sidewalk and with a small band tuning up, I sat and ordered a beer. It is always fascinating to watch a crowd gather. A couple in their twenties sits at the table to my left; they seem morose, not unhappy with each other, just bored. Then two others join them and the conversation raises smiles. Then four more. Another table has to be brought. Someone is taking photos. They order pizzas. Now the original two are chattering away, to each other, too, glowing with happiness. I've noticed again and again in Italy how often couples are dependent on groups, presumably the groups they met in. No doubt this is related to that strong Italian attachment to the hometown, an emotional dependency and richness that lies behind endless weekend train journeys. The couple find themselves among their old friends in the familiar piazza, and they are happy.

The band so far is just a couple of guys in their late forties, riffing jazz on keyboards and guitar, warming up, but then they're joined by a young woman, energetically overweight, who starts to make some serious soul sounds into the mic. Things are beginning to look promising. I order another beer.

I had begun to notice a typical face in the South, a woman's face, and sure enough, sitting at the table between me and the band, here was another example. The nose is the dominant feature, long, thrust forward, slim, very slightly hooked. The eyes are large and very carefully defined with makeup, the eyebrows plucked in high arches. The forehead slopes back at quite a marked angle, accentuating the nose, and the thick raven hair, which is firmly gathered and swept back, is held tense and tight by a headband and three long wooden skewers, poking up and out at spiky angles. The neck is tall, the lips shapely,

very slightly puckered, the teeth large, protruding a little, all adding
to that feeling of forward thrust and intensity. Slim, small-breasted,
these women are not beautiful. They are designs on terracotta. Or, no,
I'm wrong, they are fantastically beautiful. Are they? I'm not sure. It's
a type. They seem to have a wisdom about their bodies, their man-
ners, their sly, ancient smiles. That's what draws the eye. Anyway, the
band has begun to play, a soulful jazz in the summer twilight; between
the songs loud june bugs fill the silence; the drone of their noisy wings
swells and fades, swells and fades beneath the chatter of forty or fifty
local people enjoying an evening out in town. All this just five minutes'
walk from the station in the port of Brindisi, whence the following
morning the next and last stop would be Lecce, the so-called Florence
of the South.

Chapter 7

LECCE–OTRANTO

OUTSIDE THE STATION AT LECCE I SAW THESE WORDS PRINTED on a sheet of A4 and taped, together with a phone number, on a bin: *TAXI DA LECCE PER OTRANTO, 60 EUROS.* A shame, I thought, that there was no train to take me onward all the way to Otranto, or even Gallipoli, to the very end of the land, the tip of Italy's stiletto heel. I had checked the FS train map, but there was nothing on offer for the forty miles south of Lecce. It was sad—I would have liked to see Horace Walpole's Castle of Otranto; it had always seemed odd to me that the English gothic novel, which one always associates with decaying battlements deep in gloomy forests and ghosts that appear between sheets of rain, should have begun on the sunbaked shores of Puglia, where surely castles would not look anything like the places we visited as children. I also remembered, from my work on the Medicis in the fifteenth century, that Otranto had been the object of one of the most devastating Turkish incursions into Italian territory, one that threatened to be a bridgehead to an attack on the center of Christendom: in August 1480 the Turks took the town, killing twelve thousand people and shipping ten thousand more back to Turkey for a life of slavery.

It was one of those moments when the direction of history hangs in the balance. For Lorenzo de' Medici, however, the threat turned out to be a godsend; his Florentine armies were being hard pressed at the time by papal troops; but now the pope took fright, made his peace with Lorenzo, and drew Florence into a defensive pact with himself and the Kingdom of Naples. It was the kings of Naples, then in possession of Puglia, who would reinforce the castle over the coming centuries, transforming it into an impregnable bastion against the Turks. No sooner, then, did I see the name Otranto on the notice taped to the garbage bin soliciting taxi fares than I was yearning to go there. Except that Otranto was not on the train network. Let it go, I thought. If one wants to see everything historically important in Italy one will never get home at all.

And, of course, there was Lecce. My Regionale from Brindisi arrived in just thirty minutes, passing fields of solar panels on the way. Lecce is about seven miles from the Adriatic coast to the east and fifteen from the Ionian to the west, on the relatively flat, unspectacular plain of Italy's narrow heel. So there are none of the dramatic hills here that make Ragusa and Modica so picturesque, nor do you have the coastline that gives Taranto and Crotone their tang and visual sweep. To compensate, Lecce's historic center is spectacular almost beyond belief.

The effect is due to the fortuitous combination of a stone and a style. *Pietra leccese* is a calcareous rock, tough enough to build with, resistant to time and rain, but apparently very easy to sculpt and carve. The style, needless to say, is baroque, a style that thrives on an extravagance of sculpted ornamentation, a willful excess of fuss and flourish, as if no abundance could ever be enough for the act of worship involved in building a church, for, as always in Italy, it is the churches that make the city center what it is.

This rock, then, and this architectural style were made for each other. The sculptors could sculpt to their heart's delight. The facades of Lecce's churches simply froth with cherubs and roses, laurels and angels' wings, saints, columns, scrolls, gargoyles, the whole gamut of mythical animals. But there is something else, too. All these stony frills come not in the lava black of Catania's baroque, or the stuccoed facades of other southern churches, but in the most delicate yellowish white, for that is the color of *pietra leccese*, a color that takes on luminous depth from its surface roughness, soaking up the light, so that the lavishly fashioned stone assumes the glow and dapple of pale yellow roses in low sunshine.

A FEW MINUTES' WALK from the station, one leaves ordinary urban streets behind and enters a maze, not of narrow alleys, as in Crotone or Taranto, but stately piazzas, whose odd geometry combined with the hypnotic pulse of so many baroque facades can soon have you absolutely disorientated. You give up trying to figure out quite where you are and just wander into and out of one astonishing church after another, where it is never this or that single artwork that amazes, but the avalanche of it all, the candles and canvases, colored marbles and carved pulpits, tombs, Madonnas, organ pipes, banners, bas-relief, white and gold ceilings seething with saints and cherubs.

Small towns like this will have at most a couple of railway stations. How could they need more? But it seems there is simply no end to the number of churches, major churches, that an Italian town can accommodate. Who maintains them? Who can ever keep track of what's in them? The Duomo di Maria Santissima Assunta, the Chiesa di Sant'Irene dei Teatini, the Basilica di Santa Croce, the Chiesa del Gesù, the Basilica di San Giovanni Battista al Rosario (even their names are too much), the Chiesa di Santa Chiara, Chiesa del Carmine, Chiesa di San Matteo, Chiesa dei Santi Niccolò e Cataldo. All these major churches can be found in a restricted space of a few piazzas and sunstruck streets. There are many others. It seems that in the seventeenth century, with Lecce now part of the Kingdom of Naples, governed at the time by the Spanish Aragons, a determined attempt was made to transform the city into a center of pious splendor; the main piazzas were turned into building sites for many decades, feeding an extensive industry of ecclesiastical supplies. At the same time, with the Turks still threatening from across the water, stout city walls were built with splendid gates, which again had the shape and feel of baroque facades. Often what older churches there were in the town were revamped to fit the new style. The result is that Lecce has a homogeneous grace that is unusual even in Italy. Only the hundred-foot-high column topped with the statue of Sant'Oronzo, the city's patron saint who miraculously turned away the plague in 1656, jars a little, built as it was by putting two old Roman columns carved from white marble on top of each other. Somehow it just doesn't fit.

Alternating orange juice and espressos between the various monuments, I finally tackled the Duomo, which dominates a simply huge piazza, three of whose sides form a broad canyon of glowing yellow stone. Eager to escape the sun, I pushed through the heavy curtains at the door, wandered around the aisles a while and then, suddenly feeling I'd seen enough for one day, settled down on a hard seat to rest. I have always liked to sit and look and listen in Italian churches; they are so different from the churches my father preached in, where people came for the main services, matins, and evensong, and that was it. Here in Lecce, quite apart from the tourists, there was a constant trickle of the faithful, renewing their prayers and superstitions, a constant soft muttering and shuffling of respectful feet on marble paving, in the lush loftiness of ornamented altars and countless candelabra.

I closed my eyes. After a while, a rosary recital began. Apparently it was coming from a side chapel to my left; voices losing themselves in the hypnotic rhythms of the rosary. I listened, trying to share the experience the worshipers were presumably enjoying, until very gradually I became aware that the voice leading the prayers was . . . *recorded*.

No! It couldn't be. But yes, it was.

I sat up. There was definitely that metallic ring of a fairly amateur recording. Amazingly, in all this enormous and unsparingly lavish church, they didn't have a priest around to lead the ritual, just a flatly recorded chant:

Ave, Maria, piena di grazia,
il Signore è con te.
Tu sei benedetta fra le donne,
e benedetto è il frutto del tuo seno, Gesù.

The electronic voice droned on, with pauses, empty of all the pathos we normally feel when the individual will submits to the collective rote. And in fact no sooner had I realized it was recorded than I couldn't even pretend to succumb to it. Instead, I found myself comparing it with the electronic announcements in those stations whose *capistazione* have long been pensioned off together with all their underlings. Endlessly repeated, the voice comes from far away, or years before, made present only by wires and microchips. There is something arrogant and condescending about this: the organization providing the transport, whether of prayers or trains, has become so powerful and so torpid it feels no need to keep a real-life presence to guide its passengers and worshipers. So it becomes distant and absurd, at which point people feel absolutely at ease when they cheat; imagining they can gain absolution with perfunctory confessions, sitting in first class without a valid travel document, and in other areas of life, avoiding taxes, ignoring the building regulations.

Sitting on my chair, in the cool of the cathedral, following the unmanned stations of the cross, pursuing analogies between church and railway, with the column dedicated to Lecce's patron saint, Sant'Oronzo, fresh in my memory, I was reminded of an article I'd recently read that went something like this: "The Ferrovie dello Stato are in dire need of a patron saint in these hard times and hence will be happy to hear that the pope has canonized Paolo Pio Perazzo, a railway man who died in 1911 after a lifetime's abnegation; Paolo could have married and instead he dedicated his energies to the development of the railway workers' union, giving away his meager salary to the poor boys selling matches outside the train stations of the South."

I had thought until I read this article that St. Christopher would be the patron saint of railwaymen, though I had also discovered that in Catanzaro the local Trenitalia employees celebrate Sant'Antonio of Padova. On August 22, 1943, three years after the inauguration of that fountain in Brindisi celebrating Fascism's renewal of Italy, Allied bombers destroyed a complex of railway workshops and depots outside the station of Catanzaro Lido. With no time to take cover, the workers jumped over a low wall and dived into an orchard, but not before someone had cried for help to a small statue of Sant'Antonio standing in the yard of the depot. Up to that point, it seems, this statue had been a bone of contention between Christian workers and Communists, leading to all kinds of quarrels. However, the railway men survived, and when they got to their feet they found that the whole industrial complex behind them had been flattened but for that statue of Sant'Antonio. Seventy years on, the day is still celebrated, and the same statue, now housed in the railway men's social club, enjoys an annual tour of the station and even a ride in a locomotive. The miracle—for what else could it have been?—was instrumental, apparently, in the conversion of a number of Communists.

SMILING MY SKEPTICISM, I left the cathedral. The automatic rosary was getting on my nerves. But then on return to the station, again regretting that this was the end of the line and that after my walk round Lecce le Ferrovie dello Stato had nothing to offer me but the long ride home, I experienced a little miracle of my own. I looked up at the departures board and saw the word Otranto. How could that be? A vision? I hurried to consult the Trenitalia departures timetable, a printed yellow poster on the wall, but nothing. The departure wasn't there. Nothing went south of Lecce. I thought of going out to the platforms to see if the train was really there, but I didn't have a ticket, and it was late in the day to be traveling to Otranto, since I still had my hotel in Brindisi, an hour to the north. On the other hand, why not look at it at least, this ghost train that couldn't be? A mystery worthy of Walpole's gothic novel.

In the underpass beneath the platforms a large German shepherd dog was stretched out on the tiles, taking refuge from the sun. The stairs climbed to a last track; then you had to cross the rails to another, the very last, where a single ancient one-carriage train was pouring out diesel fumes. Was it the train to Otranto? I asked, mystified. Not exactly, I was told. First you changed at Zollino for Maglie, then at Maglie for Otranto.

"But one can get to Otranto?"

"Yes."

I hurried back to the ticket hall and waited my turn. The problem was that tomorrow I had planned to take fairly leisurely trains from Brindisi all the way back to Milan, since the morning after that, a Friday, I was due to preside, alas, over a thesis commission at 9:00 a.m. And thesis commissions, as I always have to remind myself, are appointments that cannot be missed, on pain of legal sanctions. On the other hand, if there was a train to the end of the land, I should take it.

Struck by a bright idea, I broke away from the ticket line, consulted the yellow timetable again, and saw that there was, as I suspected, a night train that ran up the Adriatic coast, then across to Bologna, arriving in Milan at 7:10. Assuming it arrived punctually, that would give me all the time in the world to make it to the university and be sitting up on the dais, albeit a little disheveled, when the students arrived for their great day.

It was a risk: over 600 miles by train and a margin for possible lateness of just one hour.

Do it.

"Can I have a ticket to Otranto, please, for tomorrow. Early in the morning, preferably."

The ride was about 30 miles.

A tired young man looked at me with a mixture of irritation and pity; apparently I had committed a grave faux pas.

"Trenitalia does not have a train to Otranto."

"But I saw Otranto on the departures board."

"That is not Trenitalia."

"So?"

He hesitated: "That service, *signore*, is run by"—he sighed deeply—"le Ferrovie del Sud Est."

"And how can I get a ticket?"

His expression suggested I was pushing my luck.

"Platform one," he muttered.

I WENT TO PLATFORM one, looked up and down, but saw nothing, no sign, no special timetable. As in most stations, platform one carried the main line, in this case bringing passengers from Bari and the North. It was busy. A Frecciabianca was *in arrivo*. Eventually, after a long walk, beyond all other services, machines, and gadgets, beyond even the shelter that kept sun and rain off the platform, poking from the wall just a few yards from the end of the station complex, half obscured by a couple of gray lampposts in front and with an overgrown siding behind, a discreet green sign appeared: beside the logo FSE was the word *biglietteria*.

It was a room eight by eight feet—no benches, no comfort, no design—with a single ticket window and a jolly man sitting behind giving information to four or five customers. Lots of information. Long explanations were necessary, I discovered, because FSE, which I had never previously heard of, ran a complex crisscross of ancient lines, most dating back to the nineteenth century and never relaid; to get to almost anywhere you had to change twice, and the timetables, posted oddly high above eye level on the wall, were set up in a rather novel way that allowed you, theoretically, to follow your connections by tracing your finger along the columns, then jumping from one to the next where appropriate; apparently the trains themselves were scheduled to meet at stations where the line doubled; here they could pass each other and take the opportunity to redistribute the travelers as they did so.

I couldn't follow it; it was too complicated. I realized that without Trenitalia's actually rather impressive information system, I was lost. Trains for me had become Trenitalia. My mind had integrated with Trenitalia logic, as my fingers on the keyboard had capitulated years ago to Microsoft. Italo had been simple enough: one fast train after another hammering down the same stretch of fast line, no changes, connections, or branches. This, on the contrary, was something old, provincial, almost botanical in its branching.

The *bigliettaio* laughed. He was in shirtsleeves, spared the Trenitalia uniform, spared that bureaucratic look. He seemed at ease with his exile out on the last gravelly yards of platform one.

"Don't worry," he told me. "It'll all be clear once you board."

The ticket cost not €60, but €3.20.

Then, handing me a small square of printed paper, he added, "Though we have problems with a driver off sick, I'm afraid."

He scratched his head.

"But . . ."

"I'm sure we'll work something out," he said with a smile. "We always do. Perhaps not quite on time, but you'll definitely get there."

"And back?" I didn't want to be marooned out in Otranto.

"Why not?" He smiled again. "Have faith!"

Once more the problem of baggage presented itself. If I was going to enjoy my trip to Otranto, but without having a hotel there, since I'd be spending the night on the train to Milan, I needed to find some place to leave my bag. Wikipedia had told me that the station in Lecce did have a Left Luggage Office, but I couldn't find it anywhere and in the end had to ask at the ticket window.

"Outside the station, turn right."

The station had a long, low facade featuring a series of arches in a creamily stuccoed wall, almost a Brighton Pavilion look. The left-luggage office was a good hundred yards beyond anything you would have thought of as part of the station, or even to do with the station. There was a door with an improvised sign. I knocked, then put my head in. The room was mainly empty. There was not a single bag in it, nor shelves on which bags might be set. But on either side of a wooden table in the far corner two men in orange jumpsuits were playing cards.

"*Chiedo scusa*, I need to leave my bag here tomorrow. That okay? Will you be open at eight?"

One of them looked up: "You'll need an ID."

Apparently it was an engrossing game they were playing.

OUT OF CURIOSITY THAT evening I typed *"Lecce deposito bagagli"* into Google and found a short chat:

"It's a shit hole that left-luggage place, they steal everything, forget it and go somewhere else."

But there was nowhere else.

I also did a little research on Ferrovie Sud Est. I had imagined a small provincial operation taking over disused FS lines in an attempt to breathe some life and sense back into local transport. Instead the FSE was constituted in 1933 and brought together a number of local lines that for some reason or other had never been nationalized. They were 100 percent publicly owned and always had been, but locally. In short, an anomaly. Why wouldn't the line have been nationalized and integrated with the Ferrovie dello Stato? Why wouldn't its services be at least evident and advertised in one of the main stations it ran from? Why was it possible to book a ticket connecting with French or German railways through Trenitalia's website—to go, say, to Paris or Munich—but not connecting with another state-run Italian line, to go to Otranto or Gallipoli?

———

THE FOLLOWING MORNING, HAVING taken a very early train from Brindisi, I again knocked on the door of the Lecce Left Luggage Office, which actually looked more like a door to a private home than anything else.

Inside, two men in orange jumpsuits were sitting at a table playing cards. But not the same two men. This time one seemed vaguely embarrassed to be seen playing cards at 8:15 and hurried out. The other, a surly young man, made a photocopy of my ID and told me I could leave my backpack on the floor, right there at my feet. In it were my computer, my Kindle, and an assortment of dirty laundry.

Not seeing any description of the service or price list, I asked if I had to pay now or later.

"On return. Five euros for the first five hours; seventy cents for every additional hour."

The young man spoke good Italian but with no frills, like politeness. I thanked him warmly.

At 8:53, then, on a remote platform, there were myself, two Japanese girls, and one returning student from the North with a huge bag. She had traveled all night from Milan and was exhausted; it was a scandal, she said, that there were no timed connections between Trenitalia and FSE.

"*Separati in casa.*" An estranged couple in the same house.

"*Già.*"

The sun was now in absolute command. We needed to find shade fast. Fortunately the FSE train was already on the platform. We had started to board when two men appeared and told us this was the wrong train.

So it began. There was chatter back and forth with these railway men, an easy, friendly exchange you rarely get on Trenitalia. It was attractive. No automated announcements here, no sense of a distant, monolithic organization. Actually, very little sense of any organization at all. These generous railway men explained so much that in the end you understood nothing at all. This train, they said, was going to Zollino and so was the train to Otranto, which should be leaving now, but wasn't here yet, though it would probably be along soon, but they weren't sure, because someone somewhere wasn't answering the phone and someone somewhere else had been ill but was feeling better now, and it would all work out. We should wait for the next train.

"It's very hot," I said.

"There is air-conditioning in the station building," they said, pointing back across eight platforms.

"The girls have heavy bags," I said. It had been a struggle getting them up and down the stairs of the underpass.

The man considered the bags. The Japanese girls looked bewildered.

"Okay, get on this train, then," one man decided. It wasn't clear whether these railway men were wearing uniforms. They had the same dark-colored pants and shirts, but, as it were, by chance.

The student now told me in an aside that these men were not giving us the whole truth. She had actually boarded the train, the *correct* train, to Otranto, shortly after seven when her night train arrived from Milan, and they had let her board, but then asked her to get off again because the train, they said, had to go somewhere to fill up with diesel fuel. She had imagined some ten or fifteen minutes, and now here she was ninety minutes later.

I sensed at once that FSE was, if not an organization, at least a "happening" that brought people together.

In any event, on the advice of our railway man, we boarded the wrong train, which had truly ancient brown seats bolted to the floor. The driver, a lean man in complacent middle age, came out of his cabin and assured us that it dated back to 1936. I almost believed him, and we set off.

Yet the stations could not be prettier. They are built in the same *pietra leccese* as the city's churches, recently cleaned and charmingly refurbished up front with bright green steel columns to support elegant platform shelters and nice new ticket machines (which I couldn't for the life of me figure out how to use) and all kinds of fresh, bright green, friendly signs, well designed and absolutely attractive. On almost every station there was a blue-and-white plaque thanking the European Community for its financial contribution and itemizing the many purchases made with these generous handouts. But one finds the same thankful acknowledgments on Trenitalia stations, too. I photographed one that thanks the European Community for underwriting a

> contract for the supply of services controlling infesting vegetation by mechanical means and chemical formulas along the railway lines and in open spaces falling under the jurisdiction of the regional infrastructure management of Bari, relative to the territorial infrastructure of Bari for financial years 2008, 2009, 2010, and 2011.

Along with the names of everyone involved (the list is long), the plaque also gives the cost of this service: €3,614,750.57. Three million, six hundred fourteen thousand, seven hundred fifty euros and fifty-seven cents. "To deal with weeds over a four-year period."

I always feel that every form of rhetoric and every detail must ultimately have its function and logic. Here, I can only assume that the fifty-seven cents are mentioned to give an impression of honesty and rigor worthy of the fiercest *pignolo*. It is common knowledge that, together with Sicily, Puglia is one of the two European regions most wasteful in its handling of Community subsidies.

When we got down at the darling little station of Zollino, a railway man asked us where we were going and I said Otranto.

"You were on the wrong train," he observed.

"But the train to Otranto is coming?"

"I hope so," he said. "I'd better phone."

Unable to understand why they were worried that we hadn't

arrived where we were on the other train, I went into the station to escape from the sun. Again everything was very small, very cute, very new, or at least freshly renovated. Out of curiosity I went to the glass door leading into the street and small village outside. It was locked. How bizarre. We couldn't get out of the station, and presumably no one could get in. I tried the door again. I must be mistaken. I was not. Outside there was a dead tree and a street of low white buildings with flat roofs. I went back to the platform and asked no questions.

The train to Otranto arrived. It was of a different vintage than the first—from the sixties, apparently, but similar. Ferrovie Sud Est use orange curtains, which look wonderful when the windows are open all along the carriage and they flap about in the hot, dry air. Actually this train was not going to Otranto either, but to Maglie, whence the third train, the one that really would at last have gone to Otranto, had been canceled because someone was ill, but not to worry, there would be a bus.

The railway man who gave us this news—I hesitate to call these men who spoke to us inspectors, because none of them looked at my ticket and it wasn't clear if they were attached to any train in particular, or simply using their own service to get to this or that place of work—had a told-you-so complacency about him. It evidently did not occur to him that if there were no passengers the service that gave him his livelihood might one day be discontinued. But perhaps he knows things I don't.

The bus took an age. The landscape was flat and dry and very, very stony. White stone walls and groves of dusty olive trees and small, hot, sprawling villages with flat Arab roofs. Every time two roads crossed, invariably there would be a sign to Otranto, and invariably our driver took the opposite direction. There seemed to be a sort of rule about this. I began to find it uncanny, and despite having promised myself a few days ago, on that Regionale from Crotone to Sibari, that never again would I worry about a train's punctuality, especially if I was on holiday, nevertheless I began to grow impatient. At a place called Bagnolo the driver did it again. And again at another place whose name I couldn't see. Otranto to the left, we turn to the right. The €60 for the taxi began to look like a deal. Eventually I realized that the bus was doing this so as to visit all the tiny stations the train would have gone through if its driver hadn't been ill. These stations were no doubt sensibly and very directly linked by rail but not by road. At none of these stations did we set anyone down or pick anyone up.

But when we did finally get there, the station at Otranto was definitely worth seeing. To be honest it looked more like a stately home than a station: three stories of white stucco with fine lines and good, solid, sober proportions. Tall palm trees rose above the roof behind it, a brand-new roundabout had been laid out in front, with attractive stone paving and a lawn and plenty of parking space. Absolutely no cars or buses or people or animals of any kind were anywhere in sight, but the june bugs were deafening. The air was electrically still. While my fellow passengers set off on foot toward the town and the beach, I went into the station. You had to climb a flight of stairs and go through to the other side of the building to reach the head of the platform, which was surrounded by a charming little garden that had a hothouse feel to it. Going back through the station I noticed a ticket window, which was actually occupied. Two men were talking. There was no one to interrupt them.

THE STREETS DOWN TO the sea offer the typical southern combination of the ramshackle and the haphazard. There seems no logic to their direction, or to the orientation of the buildings thrown up beside them. Scrub, cactuses, sheds, a small café, a pleasant bungalow. You cross a busy road, then move down more purposefully toward the sea, the waterfront, the place where all the action is.

It's dazzling, a well-rounded bay with perhaps half a mile of promenade, looking eastward across an absolutely transparent sea, a shimmer of pale turquoise and happy bathers. The road between town and beach is jammed with cars inching along looking for parking spots. The promenade is a line of cafés and restaurants, low prefab buildings mixing outside and inside, packed with vacationers drinking, eating, and smoking in various states of undress. Everywhere you are aware of commerce satisfying appetite in an atmosphere of easy hedonism. I turn right and walk along the waterfront to the castle that dominates the distant promontory.

It has nothing of the Gothic castle. It's just a zigzag of massive brick-built fortifications defending the southern approach to the bay, an absolutely impenetrable vantage point from which to bombard marauding Turks. Walpole's story of the place as home to an ancient family doomed to extinction by mysterious supernatural powers is sheer fantasy. Inside there is an Andy Warhol exhibition titled I WANT TO BE A MACHINE. There's the famous image of Marilyn Monroe in a garishly colored photographic negative. This is at once hilarious and too much; I can't bring myself to see it. To think that the railways brought me all the way to the foot of Italy to rediscover Andy Warhol throws me into a state of denial. I opt for a tour of the rest of the building. Windowless underground vaults have been transformed into conference venues. The bare brick of arched walls and ceilings where once prisoners or munitions were housed has been scrubbed clean and softened with discreet lighting. In another room a wedding has just ended. Guests in smart clothes are gathering outside ready to throw confetti over the happy couple. I make a rapid exit.

The truth is that you can't visit the past. Either you find a ruin, which is merely melancholy, or some new purpose has been found for the place. In Verona, too, Juliet's tomb (yes, she of *Romeo and Juliet* fame) has been transformed into a marriage registry office. Why anyone would want to marry in a place of such ill omen is beyond me, but my son did. His reasoning was that if one isn't going to marry in church, at least a fine medieval building adds a touch of solemnity. He wasn't marrying in church because his beautiful bride was Muslim; not a marauding Turk, but of the same religion. I took comfort from the fact that it isn't really Juliet's tomb, of course; the designation is merest legend with crass commercial intent.

But the Castle of Otranto really is the Castle of Otranto; a once-serious military structure is now important only insofar as it completes a picturesque seaside panorama and has space to accommodate a variety of public services. Modern Italian genius is largely about inhabiting the past in a way that makes sense and money. Whole university degrees are dedicated to the subject. On the website of Ferrovie Sud Est I had noticed that they offered day trips from Bari to visit historical sites in the countryside, traveling in historical rail carriages—the present packaging itself as the past to survive in the future.

But now to find a place to swim where I wouldn't be anxious that someone would grab my wallet and camera. It wasn't easy, because most of the waterfront was just sand, sunshades, and sea. However, at the other end of the bay the road climbs onto a low hill, then drops down again to a rocky coast of rugged black volcanic stone arranged in flat slabs with deep crevasses. I climbed down to where rocks met the sea in convenient little outcrops and lazy pools of clear water. The crevasses seemed made for hiding things. I stripped off and dived in. Swimming out beyond the rocks, it felt good to be in a place that was neither past nor future, nor commerce nor image but just me, now, in the salty water under the hot sun.

DRYING OFF ON MY towel, I tried to get my mind around Ferrovie Sud Est. It was a railway of some one thousand miles, so its website claimed, serving the heel of Italy. There was a station as far south as Santa Maria di Leuca, on the very tip of the land. All around, the coastline was marvelous and the villages of the interior picturesque, a tourist's dream, for the most part undeveloped, used almost exclusively in July and August, when the Italians themselves holiday, but empty for the rest of the year. Foreigners were rare. And even where there was a steady flow of people between towns or from town to coast, the rail service was underused. The European Union, it seems, had thrown money at it. It was politically correct to throw money at railways since they were understood to be an environmentally sustainable form of transport. But the money they had thrown was wasted because there hadn't been enough of it to create a service that people would actually use. People preferred their cars, which gave them speed and freedom, even though it's generally agreed that cars are one of the major factors behind global warming and we would all be better off if they were used a great deal less.

What would it take to get people to use these railways, or indeed any local railways?

The service would have to be such that you arrived at an easily accessible station and found regular and punctual trains heading straight for your destination at reasonable prices, with easy onward transport from that destination.

This was a lot to ask. It was an investment far beyond the funding for quaint stations and weed killing.

Then even if by some miracle this service were provided, would people use it? Some would. But not enough. To have a significant number of people use it, other forms of transport would have to be made decidedly unattractive. Cars would have to be too expensive, too hard to drive and park and keep. Of course, this is already happening. In the very week I write, gasoline has just passed the €2 a liter ($10 a gallon) threshold. Highways are expensive. Parking can be difficult. In fact, car sales are falling sharply (20 percent last year). But it's still not enough, such is the desire for personal freedom, the desire to travel alone, to start and stop whenever and wherever you like, moving at exhilarating speed, hitting brake and accelerator, controlling every aspect of one's journey, with an on-board navigator to eliminate anxieties about routing, your air-conditioning set at exactly the temperature you desire, and your own music system playing the songs you like, not to mention the space in the trunk for all the luggage you want to carry. People find this an attractive package.

So what would it take to make this railway, any local railway, viable?

An effort of collective will. A decision, a draconian decision, made together, as a society, that rail travel was the thing, that car travel must be penalized. This is the only way that an efficient, perhaps even solvent rail service could be introduced.

But would such a decision be right?

I had been following the debate on rail travel in England, where prices are so high that those who have to commute by rail find themselves paying season tickets costing thousands of pounds. On the radio I had heard the antirail lobby questioning whether those who don't use the railways should be asked to subsidize them, as if it were a matter of paying for someone else's cinema tickets; and the prorailway lobby saying in timid response that road users should be happy because the railways kept further car users off the road, making road travel easier for them.

What pious nonsense. As if there was ever a question of a level playing field in the competition among modern transportation systems. As if the roads hadn't received vast amounts of state subsidy. As if the principle that one should only pay for what one uses could ever make sense in a society, or indeed allow for the existence of a society at all; one's reminded of those Americans who object to paying a school tax because they don't have children, as if we didn't all have an interest in an educated younger generation. Could the users of a subway system pay for it before it was there? They could not.

So, I concluded, the underlying issue is this: do we make decisions about transportation on the basis of what is most comfortable for each individual now, or can we plan for what is collectively most efficient and sustainable, even if not always and in each moment the most desirable? Clearly a train line whisking everyone from Lecce to all points along the coast is a much more efficient use of resources than the present reliance on cars. It would mean less pollution in the air, and less in the mind, too, since I'm sure the mind is dangerously polluted and agitated by the driving experience.

But again, to get to that situation where people used trains, one would have to penalize cars. Seriously. And if they seriously penalized cars in this area, people would go elsewhere—to Calabria, say, or Sicily. And the trains would remain empty.

So any measures must be national, not local.

But if they penalized cars all over Italy (this is unimaginable)—and not internal domestic flights, too, since planes pollute three times as much as trains—then non-Italians would go elsewhere, perhaps to France or Spain. The government that introduced the measures would lose the next elections.

So any measures must be international, not national. A change like this would have to be Europe-wide, perhaps worldwide.

So, I reflected—and it was definitely time to put my T-shirt back on, because the sun was blistering—to get people to use Ferrovie Sud Est from Lecce to Otranto there would have to be a massive swing in *world* opinion away from the present individualism that prefers cars and in general favors individual destiny over the fate of the collective and our contemporary life now over the inheritance of future generations.

And even if there were that swing in opinion across the world, there would remain the thorny question of governance. How could massive decisions penalizing car travel be made worldwide when the world is composed of hundreds of separate and competing nations, some democracies and some not, all at different stages of development?

So, I realized, stepping into a bar to order a lemon granita before the return trip, the problem of how to make Ferrovie Sud Est viable was exactly the same increasingly urgent problem that now faces the whole damn human race: how to govern the planet when there are unpleasant decisions that sooner or later will have to be made and that no one nation wants to make or has the power to make alone. Until that problem is solved, we will never have a transportation system, or much else, that makes sense. There'll just be this pious half-assed funding that keeps alive the *idea* of a train service and that makes sure there are well-designed logos and stair elevators for the handicapped, but in a general context that feels unviable and with levels of efficiency and hygiene that only second-class citizens can accept.

The granita was good. I was sitting outside a small kiosk on a low hill looking down over the beach and the Bay of Otranto, with the castle looking squat and forbidding in the distance, but, as I had already observed, very far from the Gothic pile evoked in Horace Walpole's celebrated novel. They say that Gothic novels came into being because science and eighteenth-century rationalism were threatening to empty the world of any romance, spirituality, or caprice. Two hundred years later the planet is full of technology but utterly irrational. And I don't feel any need for Gothic excitement.

NOR, FORTUNATELY, WOULD I be getting any during the night to come. In Lecce I retrieved my bag from two men in orange jumpsuits playing cards. They showed only mild irritation at the interruption. Everything was intact. Ninety euros purchased me an upper berth in a so-called Cabina Comfort on the 19:10 night train to Milano. No lower berths were available.

"Let me apologize in advance," I tell the couple already under the sheets below me as I climb the ladder to my bunk, "if I wake you during the night to head for the bathroom."

"Oh, please, that's no problem."

This is an old Intercity carriage, beautifully refurbished and impeccably clean. There are freshly laundered sheets and blankets in polyethylene bags. I spread them out, remove my pants in the half light, and get under the covers in my underwear. I lie there, listening. The couple below me are speaking in soft whispers. Outside, the familiar station noises are muffled and pleasant: a bustle of passengers in the corridor, an urgent *coincidenza* ringing around the platforms. I'm in the midst of life here, but protected, too. It feels good. Then, with a lurch, the train begins to move, the station lights flash across the cabin walls, the rails begin to tick as the train gathers speed, and I know that despite the early hour, sleep will soon be irresistible.

Sometime later the train has stopped and I'm aware of a young man climbing up to the bunk opposite mine. Is this Bari? Foggia? He's wearing shorts and a T-shirt but carries a smart office worker's briefcase. He knows how things work, has his ladder up quietly enough, and is soon in bed. *"Buona notte,"* he murmurs. *"Buona notte,"* the couple reply. *"Buona notte,"* I say, so softly I'm not sure if they heard.

Then at 3:00 a.m., there I am of course having to creep down the ladder to go to the bathroom. Can I go in my underwear? No. I wriggle into my pants on the bed. The first step on the ladder makes it creak. Damn. Have I woken them? I don't think so. There's a night-light that gives just the visibility you need to move while allowing people to sleep. There's air-conditioning at exactly the right temperature. The knob turns and the door opens without a sound. Thank you, Trenitalia. It seems they've gotten this one just right.

We're racing up the Adriatic. On my way back from the bathroom I stand in the corridor, holding the bar across the windows, looking out. The rails are running right by the sea, on a raised dike. On the beach you can see the dark spears of rows upon rows of closed sunshades, then the luminous surf beyond. I watch it for a while, the mystery of the sea at night and the throb of the train under my feet, then hurry back to bed. When I wake again, it's to hear an announcement warning me that we will shortly be arriving in Milano Centrale. I can't believe it. It's only 6:50. Twenty minutes early. Faith rewarded. Opposite me, the young man from Foggia is pulling smart office clothes from his briefcase. He is turning into a businessman. Likewise the couple beneath me. They are already dressed for work. I wait discreetly until they've finished, then get going myself.

Why is it so exciting to pull into Milan this morning, a city I've arrived in literally thousands of times before? The slow leftward bend of the rails as the train rumbles through Lambrate, turning south toward Centrale, the streets already busy below us, a woman on an upper floor opening a shutter to greet the morning, then the great glass arch of the station itself. Stepping down from the carriage, I have a feeling I have returned from farthest margins to the throbbing heart, the center whose commercial energy keeps the whole body alive and breathing. On the platform people are streaming toward the ticket hall.

Then I realize that I have two problems. I'm too early, and I don't have a clean shirt. I keep a decent jacket in my cupboard at the faculty, but not a shirt. Taking time for a cappuccino, I see the obvious. The moment has come, the moment when I shall have to confess that the shopping center in Milano Centrale does have its uses. Instead of the stairs, I head for the *tapis roulant*. I stand patiently behind the others as it slides slowly downward. And, yes, the shops are already open at 7:00 a.m. I gaze at their glossy windows. Books, sports gear, menswear. Professor Parks may not have showered, but he will have a fresh white shirt when he passes judgment from the dais.

EPILOGUE

"WHERE ARE YOU," A VOICE ASKED. "WHY AREN'T YOU HERE?" This was a Thursday evening in Verona; the car had just emerged from a tunnel, in heavy traffic, when the phone rang. Or rather when I noticed that the phone was ringing, perhaps had been for some time. One shouldn't answer the phone when driving, of course, but of course I did. And why is it so hard to get the phone from one's pocket while at the wheel? I wriggled and pulled and tried to be careful not to push the button that would cancel the call and give the wrong impression to whomever it was, all the while hanging on to my place in a double line of cars now pushing toward an intersection. It's the low position of the seat, I suppose, or the cut of the trousers. I had the impression that my caller must be about to hang up, so I didn't take the time to look at the display before pressing the green button. I was expecting a call from my daughter.

"Tim. Where are you? You weren't on the train."

Train? Who was this? What train? I had no idea. Now there was a traffic light.

"Who is this?" These days I reckon I'm old enough for people to forgive me a lapse of memory.

"Edoardo. We're all waiting."

Damn. Edoardo who? I would have to ask.

"Edoardo who?"

Now the voice hesitated—irritated, perhaps, perhaps concerned for my health.

"I know a lot of Edoardos," I said. Which wasn't true.

"Edoardo Parisi."

It dawned.

"Edoardo! But it's tomorrow!"

"Today," he said. "Don't you remember I sent you the e-mail with the change of date? You even acknowledged it."

I was due to spend five days on a meditation retreat in the mountain home of Edoardo Parisi, a Vipassana teacher, in Maroggia high in the mountains of the Valtellina, northeast of Lake Como. The hope, of course, is always that one might calm oneself at some very deep level, become a paragon of serenity. And here I was so wired up I'd gotten the dates wrong and would lose a day. It was too late to make it out there this evening unless I used the car, and using the car for all that autostrada and then mountain road that I didn't know, late in the evening, seemed unwise. It would have to be the train, tomorrow, as early as possible.

My plan had been first to return to Milan for a few duties at the university, then take the small train that runs up Lake Como in time for what I had thought would be an evening start. Instead, I now decided to go via Brescia, then north to Bergamo, then through the foothills of the Alps to Lecco, then up Lake Como to the station of Morbegno, where Edoardo's wife would pick me up while the meditators were eating lunch. That way I hoped to gain a couple of hours.

I left Verona at 6:40 a.m. and arrived at Morbegno at 12:01 p.m. Five hours and three changes to go 120 miles. Seedy, run-down stations, miserable, poky trains where your knees all touched, rather worse actually than anything I had encountered in the South. Evidently there had been no European money here to brighten things up. The cash goes to the poorer regions. And whereas the coastal trains in the South had been mostly empty, these were packed.

At Calolziocorte, between Bergamo and Lecco, an ancient man climbed on in peasant work clothes and sat opposite me, his watery eyes at once anxious and vacant, his skin hanging loosely from his skull. Some ten minutes later it became evident that he had had some kind of accident. The carriage began to stink. We were all packed in, with people standing. There was nowhere to move. The man frowned and closed his eyes. In his early seventies, I reckoned. Probably he figured there was nothing he could do but wait for his stop and get off. So for about twenty minutes we all savored together, in mute general awareness, the ordinary human smell of shit.

There is no first class on this line. There is no way of isolating yourself from unpleasantness. To take a train like this is to open yourself to humanity *as it is*. I was reminded of a British minister for transport under the Thatcher government who confessed that he never took public transport because he never knew what riffraff you might meet there. I was also reminded of all the people who tell me they would never go to a meditation retreat where you have to share your room with whoever happens to turn up, where you sit quite close to other people, sometimes scores of them, who may have irritating tics, or sneeze and cough constantly, or even, yes, it does happen, fart. They would rather pay for a single room, they tell me, and a private guru. They could not concentrate on their meditation in a crowd. But for me the first lesson of Vipassana, as I have always experienced it, is just that: you accept whatever comes your way, good or bad, you don't attach to it, in pleasure or in aversion. "Just observe," the teacher tells you, "just observe life *as it is*, not as you would wish it to be, *as it is*."

Edoardo's house in Maroggia is high up the mountainside, looking across the great valley that sweeps down from the Alpine peaks to Como. No train will ever reach up here, but in the long hours of silence, beginning at 4:00 a.m. and through until 8:30 in the evening, you occasionally hear the distant whistle of a locomotive as it strains up the valley to Sondrio or rushes down to Morbegno and Bellano. Why do trains whistle these days? To warn people? At a road crossing? Or approaching a country platform? Hearing that whistle, my mind would stray. It is always such a struggle when meditating to keep the mind focused on the present moment, on the breath and the flesh, as it is. The whistle should have warned me that my attention was slipping; instead it drew me into another world.

Cross-legged, at the back of the room, behind a dozen others, I began to follow the train down the valley toward Morbegno and beyond, trying to remember the names of the stations, Colico, Varenna, Lecco. These trains are driven, I thought, like the mind, by electric current, and at once I was imagining all the pylons and the wires running down the valley, creating a path, a network, that was separate from the landscape so that we could pass through it at great speed, as thoughts also hurtle by so fast but are rarely in contact with reality. The mind likes to move on rails, I decided after a couple of days in Maroggia, always the same old reflections and anxieties and obsessions, one leading to the other with great predictability. The same switches, the same buffers and terminuses that you never get beyond. Gallipolis of the mind.

The hours passed. The train whistled. How many times a day. Five? I thought of the earth under the sleepers and the flesh beneath these thoughts; I tried to conceive of the meeting point where the steel weighs down on the soil, and the idea meshes with a tangle of nerves and veins and in your head the train of thought rattles by with a shrill whistle. Was there a man on board that early morning train, I wondered, who had shat in his pants, or a woman snoring garlic breath over her neighbors, or a student reading St. Augustine? No doubt people were speaking on their phones so that radio waves flew back and forth from the train as it clattered down the valley, messages reaching out all over Lombardy, Italy, all over the world, perhaps. Why not? How hard it is when you really try to imagine everything that might be going on on a single train. Everything is constantly in motion, the wheels on the rails, the curtains flapping beside an open window, the *capotreno* moving down the carriage, the Gypsy boy one step ahead of him, getting out of one door and climbing in another when the official's back is turned, the businessman's fingers on his keyboard, the actors in a film that a student is watching on her iPad as the train goes into and out of tunnels beside Lake Como, where the sun sparkles on the water in dazzling and perpetual motion. The stiller you sit as a meditator the more you are aware of the infinite movement inside mind and body—the waves and tingles and currents and pulses. There is nothing that does not move inside this flesh and bone—or out there in the valley, for that matter—nothing that is not as lively as light on water or a ball thrown back and forth across second-class seats by kids on their way to school.

A man climbs down on the platform at Lecco and puffs hard on a cigarette before the *capotreno*'s whistle blows and he must toss it away and climb on board again. Are there passengers needing to make connections, I wondered, on this train? People anxious about time, about the onward journey from Milan? Where to? To Venice? To Rome? Naples? Palermo, even? It wasn't impossible.

I began to think of the many train journeys I had taken in these thirty years in Italy, my mind reaching out across the Trenitalia map that isn't Italy itself, but as it were a cobweb woven across it, with thousands and thousands of steel spiders speeding back and forth along its silvery threads. I heard a station bell tinkling through drumming rain, a strong smell of cow dung and pine trees. That must be Fortezza, just below the Brenner Pass, where the hero of my novel *Cleaver* changed trains on the way to his penitential retreat high up by the Austrian border. I heard a door slam in the balmy twilight as an old Rapido shuddered into motion on the platform at Peschiera; a young man with a shock of blond hair jumped down with a Gucci bag in his hand, and that was my villain Morris Duckworth committing his first crime, on Italian railways, of all places. And now flags are fluttering from the open windows of a filthy Regionale, a storm of blue-and-yellow flags.

It's the Brigate Gialloblù, the Hellas boys, chanting insults as the train squeals into neighboring Vicenza for the annual derby. And I'm in that crowd, too, waving my flag. My soccer days.

These trains have eaten into my mind and my writing, I realized, sitting in this quiet room in Maroggia with twenty or so other meditators. I hadn't realized how many train scenes I'd put in my books. And now they are preventing me from observing my breath, from concentrating on the sensations in skin and bone and belly. Now I remember a man in pain, physical and mental pain, obliged to move from the plush green seat of a first-class compartment on the Torino–Roma night train. He doesn't have a reservation. He doesn't even have a ticket. He finds a place in second class where two women are discussing the supposed superiority of Swiss railway carriages. It is Christopher Burton in *Destiny* on his way to bury his son. Anything can happen on an Italian train, he tells himself when he is moved again. Later he passes out when two prostitutes put the make on him and the *capotreno* has to call an ambulance to pick him up at the station in Genoa.

How I have cursed, I remembered then in the meditation room, the times a train of mine was delayed because a passenger was ill—once a wait of half an hour in Milano Centrale while they tried to get an ambulance up the platform—or again because someone had committed suicide on the line. How I fumed for the lost time. What an ungenerous fellow I am. Traveling by train means sharing a common fate; we are on this journey together, as the meditators at the retreat share their silent journey together through the long hours of the day; a journey to no particular destination. We know we will not reach enlightenment.

The train whistled again at the beginning of the *metta bhavana* on the last day, the meditation of loving kindness. "Let your mind go out to all those who are close to you and wish them well," Edoardo instructed us. "Then to all those you are acquainted with. Finally, to all people and creatures everywhere. If you have offended anyone, perhaps, in your thoughts, you could seek pardon from them; and if anyone has offended you, you could try to grant them your sincere pardon."

I began my *metta* and the train whistled. Have I offended people on trains, or in this book? I'm sure I have. I can be very rude on trains and in print. I seek pardon. Have I been offended on trains? Oh, infinite, infinite times! Offended by noises, offended by smells, offended by delays, offended by ticket inspectors, offended by loud conversations, offended by filthy bathrooms, offended just a week or so ago by a young man who sat opposite me and picked his nose quite grossly all the way from Verona to Milan. I'd never realized how offensive that can be. I grant pardon. I grant my sincere pardon to the nose picker, and the ticket inspectors, the stinkers, and the loudmouths. I wish them well, all the men and women traveling on Trenitalia this morning, all the inspectors and the drivers, the ticket sellers and the minibar men, I wish them well. And especially I wish well to any passenger with a book in his hand, any man or woman following the lines on the page, perhaps these very lines, as the wheels follow the rails across the landscape, hurrying forward through the world yet not quite part of it. What a beautiful respite a train journey is and a good book, too, and best of all the book on the train, in life and out of it at the same time, before we arrive at Termini and disembark and the book is put down and we must all part and go our separate ways, forever.

Acknowledgments

FOR SOME OF THE HISTORICAL BACKGROUND HERE I AM INDEBTED to Stefano Maggi and his excellent book *Le ferrovie*. I would also like to thank the Failla family and Angela Pia Salamina for their hospitality during my travels down South. The book would not have been written without much prodding from Matt Weiland whose editorial assistance proved invaluable when it came to giving shape to my endless backs and forths; many thanks to him, then, and likewise, finally, to all those thousands of Trenitalia employees, ticket collectors included, who have taken me safely around my adopted patria for more than thirty years.